CYCLING IN ONTARIO

John Lynes

Author John Lynes	**Production Director** Pascale Couture	**Series Director** Claude Morneau
Project Supervisor Claude Morneau	**Layout** Stephanie Heidenreich Tara Salman	**Cover Photograph** SuperStock
Editing Tara Salman Stephanie Heidenreich	**Cartography** André Duchesne *Assistants* Patrick Thivierge Alain Legault	**Illustrations** Lorette Pierson **Design** Patrick Farei (Atoll Direction)

Thanks to my wife Roxanne, my sister Katherine; cycling partners Kirk Morrell, Walter Campney, my father John Lynes Sr., my son Brad and cyclist Joe Cote.

Ulysses Travel Publications acknowledges the financial support of the Government of Canada through the Book Publishing Industry Development Program (BPIDP) for its publishing activities. We would also like to thank SODEC for their financial support.

DISTRIBUTORS

AUSTRALIA: Little Hills Press, 11/37-43 Alexander St., Crows Nest NSW 2065, ☎ (612) 437-6995, Fax: (612) 438-5762

BELGIUM AND LUXEMBOURG: Vander, Vrijwilligerlaan 321, B-1150 Brussel, ☎ (02) 762 98 04, Fax: (02) 762 06 62

CANADA: Ulysses Books & Maps, 4176 Saint-Denis, Montréal, Québec, H2W 2M5, ☎ (514) 843-9882, ext.2232, 800-748-9171, Fax: 514-843-9448, www.ulysses.ca

GERMANY AND AUSTRIA: Brettschneider, Fernreisebedarf, Feldfirchner Strasse 2, D-85551 Heimstetten, München, ☎ 89-99 02 03 30, Fax: 89-99 02 03 31, Brettschneider_Fernreisebedarf@t-online.de

GREAT BRITAIN AND IRELAND: World Leisure Marketing, Unit 11, Newmarket Court, Newmarket Drive, Derby DE24 8NW, ☎ 1 332 57 37 37, Fax: 1 332 57 33 99

ITALY: Centro Cartografico del Riccio, Via di Soffiano 164/A, 50143 Firenze, ☎ (055) 71 33 33, Fax: (055) 71 63 50

NETHERLANDS: Nilsson & Lamm, Pampuslaan 212-214, 1380 AD Weesp (NL), ☎ 0294-494949, Fax: 0294-494455, E-mail: nilam@euronet.nl

PORTUGAL: Dinapress, Lg. Dr. Antonio de Sousa de Macedo, 2, Lisboa 1200, ☎ (1) 395 52 70, Fax: (1) 395 03 90

SCANDINAVIA: Scanvik, Esplanaden 8B, 1263 Copenhagen K, DK, ☎ (45) 33.12.77.66, Fax: (45) 33.91.28.82

SPAIN: Altaïr, Balmes 69, E-08007 Barcelona, ☎ 454 29 66, Fax: 451 25 59, altair@globalcom.es

SWITZERLAND: OLF, P.O. Box 1061, CH-1701 Fribourg, ☎ (026) 467.51.11, Fax: (026) 467.54.66

U.S.A.: The Globe Pequot Press, 6 Business Park Road, P.O. Box 833, Old Saybrook, CT 06475, ☎ 1-800-243-0495, Fax: 800-820-2329, sales@globe-pequot.com

Other countries, contact Ulysses Books & Maps (Montréal), Fax: (514) 843-9448

ISBN 2-89464-191-5
© March 1999, Ulysses Travel Publications.

TABLE OF CONTENTS

FOREWORD 11

CYCLING IN ONTARIO 15
    Ontario: an overview 16
        Geography 16
        Flora and fauna 17
        Tourist information 17
        The regions 18
        Climate 18
    Money 19
    Holidays 20
    Emergencies 21
    Travelling to Ontario 21
    Road signs 26
    Ontario cycling laws 27
    Canadian cycling attitudes 29
    Equipment 29
    Types of cycling tours 31
    Rail trails and off-road cycling 34
    Accommodations 35
    Tour preparation and training 38
    Cycling with children 42
    The tours 43
    How this guide works 44
    On the road 45
    Additional reference materials 47

SOUTHWESTERN ONTARIO 51
    THE TOURS 51
    1. Magical Pelee Island 51
    2. Sarnia Circle Tour: Bluewater Discovery 57
    3. Lake Erie's North Shore:
        Woodstock, Port Dover and Tillsonburg . . 64
    4. Shakespeare's Stonetown:
        Stratford and St. Marys 74
    5. Two Sunsets, a River and a Trail:
        Goderich and Scenic Huron County 80
    6. Down by the Old Mill Stream:
        London and Dorchester 86
    OFF-ROAD CYCLING 9

FESTIVAL COUNTRY 97
    THE TOURS 97
    7. Quarries and Cataracts:
        Elora to Cataract Rail Trail Adventure 97
    8. Dundas Valley and the Niagara Escarpment
        (including Webster and Tew's Falls) 105
    9. Elmira and St. Jacob's Countryside Tour 111
    10. Elora Gorge Adventure (Guelph to Elora) ... 118
    11. Paris to Cambridge Rail Trail 123
    12. Welland Canal Explorer:
        Port Dalhousie, St. Catharines
        and Welland 127
    13. Myths, Miracles and Pathways 136
    14. Wineries and Vineyards 142
    OFF-ROAD CYCLING 148

THE GEORGIAN LAKELANDS 153
    THE TOURS 153
    15. Breweries, Sulfur Springs and Boxing:
        Cycling in the Queen's Bush 153
    16. Cycling the Bruce Peninsula:
        Owen Sound, Tobermory and
        Sauble Falls 159
    17. Beaver Valley Explorer: Thornbury, Meaford
        and Markdale (including Eugenia Falls) .. 171
    18. Cycling to the Big Chute and Back:
        Midland, Port Severn and Severn Falls .. 179
    19. Lake of the Bays and Muskoka Hills 184
    OFF-ROAD CYCLING 190

THE GREATER TORONTO AREA 193
    THE TOURS 193
    20. Toronto Islands, Lakeshore and Beaches ... 193
    21. Olde Town Toronto 201
    OFF-ROAD CYCLING 207

CENTRAL ONTARIO 209
   THE TOURS 209
   22. Peterborough: The Heart of the Kawarthas . 209
   23. Victoria County Adventure 217
   24. Kawartha Cycling and Spelunking Adventure:
       Peterborough, Lakefield and the
       Otonabee River 224
   25. Port Hope to Cobourg and Back (including
       Portions of the Waterfront Trail) 229
   26. Kent Portage: The Oldest Road in Ontario . . 236
   27. Lake on the Mountain Adventure: Picton
       and Prince Edward County 240
   28. Lighthouse and Lookouts 246
   29. Athol Bay, Sandbanks and Sand Dunes 250
   OFF-ROAD CYCLING 254

EASTERN ONTARIO 257
   THE TOURS 257
   30. Limestone and Black Powder:
       Discovering Kingston 257
   31. The Rideau Canal and the 1000 Islands
       Parkway: Kingston, Ottawa
       and Brockville 267
   32. Ottawa Explorer: A Full Day
       in Under Two Hours 279
   33. Gatineau Hills Legwarmer 286
   34. To Hog's Back Falls and Back:
       Ottawa's Rideau Canal
       Recreational Trail 290
   OFF-ROAD CYCLING 294

RAINBOW COUNTRY 297
   THE TOURS 297
   35. Sudbury: Nickel Capital of the World 297
   36. Riding for Gold at Wavy Lake 303
   37. Manitoulin Day Tripping: Lake Mindemoya,
       the Bridal Veil Falls and the Cup and
       Saucer Lookout 305
   OFF-ROAD CYCLING 312

INDEX 314

LIST OF MAPS

WHERE IS ONTARIO? .... p 9
ONTARIO .... p 10
SOUTHWESTERN ONTARIO .... p 52
  1. Magical Pelee Island .... p 53
  2. Sarnia Circle Tour: Bluewater Discovery .... p 59
  3. Lake Erie's North Shore .... p 65
  4. Shakespeare's Stonetown .... p 75
  5. Two Sunsets, a River and a Trail .... p 81
  6. Down by the Old Mill Stream .... p 87
FESTIVAL COUNTRY .... p 98
  7. Quarries and Cataracts .... p 99
  8. Dundas Valley and the Niagara Escarpment .... p 107
  9. Elmira and St. Jacobs Countryside Tour .... p 113
  10. Elora Gorge Adventure .... p 119
  11. Paris to Cambridge Rail Trail .... p 124
  12. Welland Canal Explorer .... p 129
  13. Myths, Miracles and Pathways .... p 137
  14. Wineries and Vineyards .... p 143
THE GEORGIAN LAKELANDS .... p 152
  15. Breweries, Natural Springs and Boxing .... p 155
  16. Cycling the Bruce Peninsula .... p 161
  17. Beaver Valley Explorer including Eugenia Falls .... p 173
  18. Cycling to the Big Chute and Back .... p 181
  19. Lake of the Bays and Muskoka Hills .... p 185
THE GREATER TORONTO AREA .... p 194
  20. Toronto islands, Lakeshore and Beaches .... p 195
  21. Olde Town Toronto .... p 203
CENTRAL ONTARIO .... p 210
  22. Peterborough: The Heart of the Kawarthas ...... p 211
  23. Victoria County Adventure .... p 219
  24. Kawartha Cycling and Spelunking Adventure ..... p 225
  25. Port Hope to Cobourg and Back .... p 231
  26. Kente Portage: The Oldest Road in Ontario ..... p 237
  27. Lake on the Mountain Adventure .... p 241
  28. Lighthouse and Lookouts .... p 247
  29. Athol Bay, Sandbanks and Sand Dunes .... p 251
EASTERN ONTARIO .... p 258
  30. Limestone and Black Powder .... p 259
  31. The Rideau Canal and the 1000 Islands Parkway .. p 269
  32. Ottawa Explorer .... p 281
  33. Gatineau Hills Leg Warmer .... p 287
  34. To Hog's Back Falls and Back .... p 291
RAINBOW COUNTRY .... p 296
  35. Sudbury: Nickel Capital of the World .... p 299
  36. Riding for Gold at Wavy Lake .... p 305
  37. Manitoulin Day Tripping .... p 307

WRITE TO US

CANADIAN CATALOGUING

Lynes, John Allan, 1956-
        Cycling in Ontario
        (Ulysses green escapes)
        Includes index.

ISBN 2-89464-191-5

1. Bicycle touring - Ontario - Guidebooks.   2. Ontario - Guidebooks
I. Title   II. Series.

GV1046.C32057 1999   796.6'4'09713   C98-941548-1

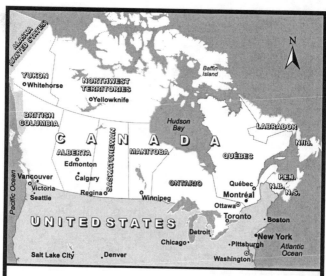

Where is Ontario ?

CANADA
Capital: Ottawa
Population: 30,300,000 inhab.
Currency: Canadian dollar
Area: 9,970,610 km²

ONTARIO
Capital: Toronto
Population: 10,753,573 inhab.
Area: 1,068,630 km²

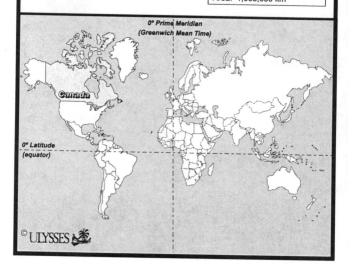

© ULYSSES

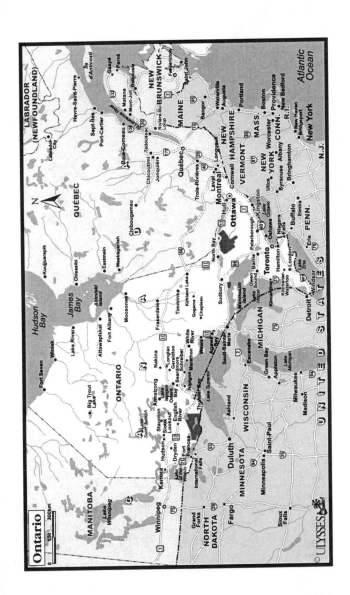

FOREWORD

For my 50th birthday my wife treated me to a bike trip. You see, I'm fairly athletic, at least in my mind. I once had a share in some Blue Jays season tickets, I've subscribed to Sports Illustrated for a decade and I even know two people who are serious marathoners. So my wife and I treated ourselves to a countryside cycling trip.

Now, we've watched a lot of television coverage of cycling events, and noticed the kind of backup support racing teams have. Our idea was to take it easy, keep it to 50 kilometres a day, and while we're at it, pick a route through wine country.

Okay, so we're athletic wine lovers.

The planning began in a bicycle shop where I bought a pair of padded gloves. I then read several cycling magazines, and picked up maps of the province's wine-growing districts. Every day I devoted at least ten minutes to the task of planning a route.

Training? Well, that summer I that up and down on the lad muscles.

We decided not to take our own push bikes, preferring to drive to the vineyards and rent locally. I should have checked my rental more closely. Its chain tended to derail a lot, but by then we were already climbing along the escarpment, looking down on sunny vineyards and orchards.

Inspired by the view I tucked my head in, and tried a sprint to the crest of one hill, then took a long break in the shade of one lonely tree. Stretching away into the haze, row upon row of grapes ripened in the late summer sun. Which is just about when we remembered that we'd forgotten to carry water.

I was almost delirious when we found a little bar full of fellows quietly drinking and eating lunch. I recall there were a lot of flies buzzing about, but I was so exhausted from the heat and the hill, that it tasted just fine.

All my planning with the road maps were for nought, since just after lunch I made the wrong turn and glided serenely down a long hill, not into the winery we were headed for, but straight onto a busy provincial highway. No sense reclimbing the hill we reasoned, so we gritted our teeth and headed for an early stop at the nearest B&B.

That night we were sore, but not too sore to sit down to dinner, somewhat anaesthetized by a bottle of the local merlot. Three days later blisters were popping like corn, and the soft life back home was taking its toll.

I started walking up some of the steeper hills.

By week's end it had been a cheap and glorious way to see the countryside and sample a lot of the season's vintage. We even made some friends, chatting with field workers and comparing notes with other cyclists along the way, people who always seemed to have better gear than us.

The only common denominator was the guide book. We were all working from assorted pamphlets and photocopies. This is where John Lynes enters the story.

I wandered into John's travel agency one day in Embro, just outside of Woodstock, in the heart of dairy country. I was looking for directions and ended up recording a radio interview about John's new quest to design bicycle tours of the province.

At that stage fresh from my celebrated birthday jaunt, I was mostly talking rather than performing a good line about cycling. My daily show on CBC Radio had already got into the biking craze. Our columnist Susan Wallis of London usually arrives, helmet in hand, to regale me with stories of long distance treks through autumn leaves and the need for activism to push for road design and laws that are friendly to bicycles.

Over the years this "Bike Beat" feature has introduced CBC listeners to the growing network of trails on abandoned railway lines, the routes that follow the rugged Niagara Escarpment, across enchanting Prince Edward County, along the historic Ottawa Valley, and through scores of other scenic and challenging corners of Ontario.

What John Lynes has produced is a guide not only to many splendid rides but the kind of advice I so desperately needed before my 50th birthday jaunt. What to wear, how to prepare and what to expect along the way, from repair facilities to interesting detours, from places to eat and stay, to titbits of local lore and history.

Someday with the support of the growing army of cyclists, along with sympathetic politicians and planners we will indeed have a provincial network of bike trails, as well as safe and protected bike lanes through our communities. In the meantime, I plan to work my way through John Lynes' book, rediscovering the treasure of Ontario, of course at a nice easy bicycle pace. It's a big place so last year we bought a carry rack in order to ferry our own bicycles on vacations.

This is progress.

JOE COTE
Host of "Ontario Morning" on CBC Radio

CYCLING IN ONTARIO

Ontario's immense size and geological variety offers cyclists a lifetime of adventure. Whether you cycle along Highway 141, one of the provinces most scenic roads, down an abandon jeep trail to a long-forgotten gold mine, or along a stretch of world class single-track, you are in for a powerful experience. Like a good wine, Ontario offers the cyclist a different experience each time it is explored.

In addition to the scenic hills and dales, you can be assured of a friendly smile, lots of questions and a helping hand at each stop along the way. Whether cycling by yourself, as a group or as a family, this guide will lead you along some of Ontario's most fascinating paths. Paths to unique communities, intriguing individuals and lifelong friendships.

It is my hope that you will be able to experience the pleasure, satisfaction and sense of accomplishment that can only come from taking your favourite two-wheeled vehicle to the roads, greenways and trails of one of Canada's most interesting provinces – Ontario.

ONTARIO: AN OVERVIEW

Ontario is as rich in human resources as it is in natural ones. As Canada's melting pot, Ontario continues to develop a healthy society by successfully mixing many unique peoples, cultures and traditions, past and present, with an exciting countryside. There are festivals throughout the year that celebrate the province's ancestry, its love for music and dancing and its appreciation of the skilful talents of local artists and people.

Ontario is a province with one hand steadily holding onto the traditions, architecture and community values of the past, while the other hand stretches forward in anticipation and hope for what the future holds.

Geography

ONTARIO is derived from a native word meaning "beautiful waters." It is appropriately named since over 20% of the province's area is taken up by nearly 250,000 lakes and rivers that sparkle brightly and blend harmoniously with a landscape of extensive forests, rocky outcrops, rolling hills and lush farmlands. Miles of shoreline are found within Ontario's borders, which encompass four of the five Great Lakes – Superior, Huron, Erie and Ontario – as well as the St. Lawrence Seaway and the connecting waterways of the Trent-Severn and Rideau canal systems. Home to the largest provincial population (10,746,300) in Canada, it is second only to Quebec in geographical size, covering an area of 1.6 million square kilometres (412,582 square miles). Ontario stretches 1680 kilometres from its most southernly point, which lies on the same latitude as northern California, to the cool arctic waters of Hudson Bay in the north where the land is almost at sea level. In breadth, the province just falls short of its height, covering some 1,600 kilometres from east to west.

Flora and Fauna

Ontario's provincial flower and tree grow profusely in wooded lots and forests throughout the province. Delicate, white and three-petalled, the Trillium is easily recognizable and is a welcome sight in May and early June. The provincial tree, the Eastern White Pine, can be identified by its long slender needles and continues to be a valuable resource in the lumber and tourist industries. Ontario's abundance of water has also bestowed on it the enormous responsibility of caring for its many natural wetland areas. These areas provide habitat for many forms of wildlife, and opportunities to investigate, study and promote the management of the land, birds, reptiles and other aspects of nature.

Tourist Information

Tourism Ontario: ☎(800) 668-2746, http://ontario-canada.com/.

Ontario Travel Associations

Southwestern Ontario	☎(800) 661-6804
Festival Country	☎(800) 267-3399
Lakelands	☎(800) 487-6642
Toronto	☎(800) 363-1990
Getaway Country	☎(800) 461-1912
Ontario East	☎(800) 567-3278
Ontario Near North	☎(800) 387-0516
Rainbow Country	☎(800) 465-6655
Algoma Country	☎(705) 254-4293
James Bay Frontier	☎(800) 461-3766
North of Superior	☎(807) 626-9420
Sunset Country	☎(800) 665-0730

The Regions

Travelling from west to east, the province of Ontario can be divided into seven different areas. This book concentrates on the six southern and most populated areas, which offer cyclists a host of touring opportunities.

Area 1	Southwestern Ontario
Area 2	Festival Country
Area 3	Georgian Lakelands
Area 4	Toronto Area
Area 5	Central Ontario
Area 6	Eastern Ontario
Area 7	Ontario's North

For descriptions of the regions, see the first page of the corresponding chapter.

Climate

Ontario's climate is moderate and consistent. From the middle of May until the last week in October, temperatures are generally pleasant, the average provincial temperature is 20 degrees Celsius. Clothing should be of light to medium weight. During July and the first part of August, the roads are much busier, as this is peak vacation time. However, this should not deter you from your travels. In September and October, there is considerably less daylight available, most attractions are only open on the weekends and the temperatures are much cooler. Waterproof clothing is advisable throughout the year.

Weather Information on the Internet

Weather Channel: www.weather.com
Environment Canada: www.tor.ec.gc.ca/forecasts/indexe.html
Weather Network: www.theweathernetwork.com

Weather Information by Telephone

Road Conditions: ☎(800) 268-1376
Weather Network: ☎(900) 565-9328

Canadian Broadcasting Corporation

Web address: www.cbc.ca

CBC Radio Frequencies:

Atikokan	90.1 FM	Nipigon	89.9 FM
Bancroft	600 AM	North Bay/Timmins	96.1 FM
Chatham	88.1 FM	Orillia	91.5 FM
Cornwall	95.5 FM	Ottawa	1.5 FM
Dryden	100.9 FM	Owen Sound	98.7 FM
Elliot Lake	90.3 FM	Parry Sound	89.9 FM
Fort Hope	101.5 FM	Pembroke	92.5 FM
Fort Frances	90.5 FM	Penetanguishene	107.5 FM
Haliburton	92.3 FM	Peterborough	93.5 FM
Hearst	91.9 FM	Sioux Lookout	1240 AM
Huntsville	94.3 FM	Sturgeon Falls	96.1 FM
Kapuskasing	105.1 FM	Sudbury	99.9 FM
Kenora	98.7 FM	Temagami	1340 AM
Kingston	107.5 FM	Thunder Bay	88.3 FM
Kirkland Lake	90.3 FM	Toronto	99.1 FM
Little Current	97.5 FM	The Tri-Towns	102.3 FM
London	93.5 FM	Wawa	88.3 FM
Mindemoya	97.5 FM	White River	1010 AM
Moosonee	1340 AM	Windsor	1550 AM

MONEY

Currency

One Canadian dollar equals 100 cents. Bank notes come in
denominations of $1000, 100, 500, 50, 20, 10 and 5. Coins

come in denominations of 1 and 2 dollars and 50, 25, 10, 5, 1 cents.

Banking

All international credit cards are accepted. Travellers cheques are best purchased in Canadian dollars. All Ontario financial institutions, banks, credit unions, and trust companies have automatic teller machines (ATMs); you will also find ATMs located in large and small shopping centres, airports, train stations, and even many gas stations and corner stores. There are two international networks operating in Canada: the Plus Network (affiliated with the Visa credit card) and Cirrus (affiliated with MasterCard). All Canadian financial institutions are members of one or the other; the Bank of Montreal and Royal Bank are members of both.

Taxes

Ontario has two taxes on goods purchased within the province. A 8% Provincial Sales Tax (PST) and the 7% Federal Goods and Services Tax (GST) are charged on most products and services sold or provided in the province. Foreign visitors to Canada can apply for a rebate on GST paid for accommodations (up to 30 nights per visit) and on goods purchased in Canada that are subsequently exported.

HOLIDAYS

New Year's Day:	January 1
Good Friday:	date varies, late March to late April
Easter Monday:	the Monday after Good Friday; most shops open
Victoria Day:	the Monday on May 19 or closest prior Monday
Canada Day:	July 1; formerly called Dominion Day
Civic Holiday:	the 1st Monday in August
Labour Day:	the 1st Monday in September

Thanksgiving:	the 2nd Monday in October
Remembrance Day:	November 11
Christmas:	December 25
Boxing Day:	December 26

EMERGENCIES

In case of an accident, fire or other emergency dial ☎**911** or **0**.

Police

Ontario is policed by three levels of government: federally, by the Royal Canadian Mounted Police; provincially by the Ontario Provincial Police and municipally, most often by local law enforcement officers.

TRAVELLING TO ONTARIO

Travel Documents

From the United States: American visitors crossing the Canadian border (either way) may be asked to verify their citizenship with a document such as a passport or a birth or baptismal certificate. Naturalized US citizens should carry a naturalization certificate. Permanent US residents who are not citizens are advised to bring their Alien Registration Receipt Card.

From all other countries: Citizens of all other countries, except Greenland and residents of St. Pierre et Miquelon, must have a valid passport. Travellers from some countries may be required to obtain a visitor's visa: for details, consult the nearest Canadian embassy or consulate serving your home country.

Transporting Your Bicycle

Each form of transportation has its own idiosyncrasies when you are travelling with a bicycle. It is recommended that you contact your choice of transport several weeks ahead of departure to verify fares and special requirements (by booking in advance you will also generally enjoy a reduced fare). If shipping containers are required, they can be ordered and made available to you several days before departure. Always pack your own bike. Tightly secure (use extra padding) everything inside the shipping container. Make sure no parts are rattling around as they could easily get lost or damage your bicycle. Wrap duct tape around the box to prevent the case from being split open. One of the best ways to ship your bicycle is to purchase or rent a commercial bicycle case. It will provide additional protection and you can rest assured that your bicycle will arrive at its destination safely. If your arrival and departure gateways are different, or if you have no place to leave the container (most hotel/motels will gladly store your bicycle box if you are staying there on the first and last night), the commercial bicycle case will most likely be out of the question and you will have to use one of the boxes available from your chosen carrier. Finally, if you do not want to travel with your bicycle, it is possible to ship it by a commercial parcel carrier. The disadvantages are that you need a final shipping address and some flexibility on delivery time, but if you can allow three to four days for delivery, the savings on transporting your bicycle by parcel carrier can be quite dramatic.

Courier Companies

Federal Express	☎(800) 238-5355
United Parcel Service	☎(800) 742-5877
DHL Worldwide	☎(800) 225-5345
Airbourne Express	☎(800) 247-2676

By Train

Amtrak	☎(800) 872-7245
GO Transit	☎(888) 438-6646
	☎(416) 869-3600
VIA Rail Canada Inc.	☎(416) 686-7277
	☎(416) 868-7277 (information)

By Car

There are bridges connecting Canada to the United States at Baudette International Falls, Point Edward and Niagara Falls. Two tunnel connections are located in the Windsor-Detroit and Sarnia-Point Huron. Ontario can also be accessed from northern Michigan at Sault Ste. Marie, from Minnesota at Grand Portage and Fort Frances, from Manitoba at Granite Lake, and from Quebec at Hull and Montreal.

By Plane

Ontario has a network of 13 regional and national airlines transporting travellers to and within the province. Over 50 international airlines land at Ontario's main international airport, Toronto's Lester B. Pearson International Airport. Ottawa, Windsor, Hamilton and London (Ontario) also have international airports. In addition, there are local airports in over 50 of Ontario's smaller communities. Most airlines have a policy for transporting bicycles. All require your bicycle to be partially disassembled and placed in a cardboard box or similar container. It is strongly suggested that you check with the airline before departure to find out what is required, what they supply and what their rates are, as they vary dramatically.

Airlines

Air Canada: ☎(800) 361-7585 or (514) 393-6831, http://www.aircanada.ca/home.html

Canadian Airlines: ☎(800) 665-5554 Canada, ☎(800) 426-7000 US, http://www.cdnair.ca/
Air Ontario: ☎(416) 203-3887
Canada 3000: ☎(888) 226-3000

By Train

VIA Rail

It is still possible to go all the way from Vancouver to Halifax with Canada's national passenger rail service. VIA Rail links most of Ontario's major cities, and in southern Ontario trains between major centres run several times a day between major centres. The train service connects with rail lines from the United States (Amtrak) at various border crossings. Its schedules include express, frequent-stop and (on some lines) request-stop services. VIA is flexible when it comes to transporting your bicycle. One condition set by VIA is that the train must have a baggage car. If you have a direct connection (no transfers), you do not have to box your bike (but you are responsible for damage); if there is a transfer, you must box the bicycle (provided free) as per standard packing instructions; turn the handlebars and remove the pedals, and remember that tools are not provided. Rates for transporting bicycles by rail are quite reasonable, making it one of the most economical ways for you and your bicycle to reach your destination.

Toronto & Area Rail Service
(Subway and Commuter Trains)

Toronto and its immediate surroundings are served by a complex network of subways, streetcars, light rail transit (LRT) lines, and suburban (GO) trains. GO Transit operates trains over six routes. The Lakeshore line has all-day service, between Pickering and Oakville, seven days a week. This service is extended to Oshawa and Hamilton on weekdays at rush hours. The other five lines are named for their suburban terminal points: Milton, Georgetown, Bradford, Richmond Hill, and Stouffville. Bicycles are allowed on non rush-hour GO Trains.

Cyclists may take bikes on board all trains on Saturdays, Sundays and statutory holidays, and on weekday trains except those arriving at Union Station, Toronto's main station, between 6:30am and 9:30am, or departing from Union Station between 3:30pm and 6:30pm. Bicycles will be carried only in the two vestibules just inside the doors of each train car – two bicycles are allowed per vestibule. Stow your bicycle on either end of the handrail posts. Bicycles exceeding 68" (173 cm) in length or 16" (41 cm) in width will not be carried. Bicycles are prohibited in all handicapped-equipped coaches (the 5th car from the east end of the train). Rates for transporting bicycles by Go-Transit are quite reasonable, offering a viable and economical way to get to your destination around the Toronto area.

By Bus

Greyhound is the nation's largest intercity bus company and the only nationwide provider of intercity bus service. It is the most economical way to travel across the country. Greyhounds will transport bicycles as freight. Requirements for shipping are that the bicycle be partially disassembled and placed in a cardboard box or similar container. Greyhound offers shipping cartons for reasonable rates, but the depots in smaller communities generally do not carry them in stock, so they must be ordered ahead. Another alternative is to get a box at your local bike shop. However, it will be smaller and you will have to remove your handlebars, seat, front wheel and pedals. Since the bicycle is considered freight, it will also be your responsibility to move it from bus to bus if you are travelling with it and transfers are required.

Bus Companies

Greyhound Canada: Passenger Sales Centre (fares and schedules) ☎(800) 661-TRIP (8747); GCX (Courier Express) Customer Service (rates and services) ☎(800) 661-1145; Customer Service ☎(800) 268-9000, http://www.greyhound.ca/.

ROAD SIGNS

Distance/Direction Signs
Ontario Road signs come in all shapes, sizes and colours.

Information/Direction Signs: green background/white letters, rectangular shape indicate distance and destination.

Regulatory Signs: White or black background, vertical/rectangle or square shape. These signs must be obeyed. They indicate highway numbers, speed limit and local traffic directions. When these signs are used in a permissive situation and have a green ring-shaped band displayed, they indicate that whatever is depicted within the ring-shaped symbol is mandatory or permitted. When the sign displays a red ring-shaped circle and a diagonal red stroke, this indicates whatever is depicted within the symbol is prohibited.

Warning Signs: Yellow with black lettering, diamond shape warn of dangerous or unusual conditions ahead, such as a curve, turn, dip or side road.

Temporary Conditions: Orange/black letters warn and provide directions on road conditions ahead.

School Crossing: Blue, rectangular or pentagon in shape indicate crossing for children going to school.

Facilities: Brown or blue with white lettering, square or rectangular indicate facilities where fuel, food, accommodations or camping is available.

No Bicycles

Bicycles are not allowed on Ontario highways in the 400 series, the Queen Elizabeth Way and other multi-lane, divided routes with controlled access.

Bicycles Allowed

All roads numbered from 2 up are conventional highways of two or more lanes (some also include a cycling lane). Highways in the 500-600 series (pavement and loose surface) are Secondary Highways and roads in the 800 series are Tertiary Roads located in Northern Ontario. County and regional roads have local number and name designations. Recently the Ontario Government has undertaken a project to rename many of the roads to facilitate the province-wide 911 EMERGENCY Action Plan. Many of the roads have been renamed, but some of them still retain their old designations. Be aware that some road names may have changed since the printing of this guide.

ONTARIO CYCLING LAWS

1. Your bicycle must have a warning device such as a bell or horn that sounds loud and clear.

2. When riding half an hour before sunrise and half an hour following sunset or when the light is poor, your bicycle must have a white or amber light on the front and a red light on the rear. Also, reflective material at least 25 cm (10 inches) long and 2 cm (1 inch) wide should be visible (white in the front, and red in the back).

Cycling Associations

Ontario Cycling Association: 1185 Eglinton Ave. E., North York, Ontario M3C 3C6, ☎(416) 426-7242, www.ontariocycling.org, Email: info@ontariocycling.org.

Canadian Cycling Association: 1600 James Naismith Drive, Gloucester, Ontario K1B 5N4, ☎(613) 748-5629, www.canadiancycling.com, general@canadiancycling.com.

3. All riders under the age of 18 must wear a government-approved cycling helmet.

4. Bicycles are prohibited on expressways and freeway-type highways such as the 400 series, the Queen Elizabeth Way and on roads where "NO BICYCLE" signs have been posted.

5. Cyclists are required to obey all traffic laws under the Highway Traffic Act.

General Information

Road Conditions: ☎(800) 268-1376

Telephone Number Information: Canada and USA ☎(800) 555-1212

Signals and Other Peculiar Traffic Rules

Right Turns: In Ontario a right turn may be made on at a traffic light when it is "Red." The turn can be completed if there is no oncoming traffic and it is safe to make the turn.

Single File Only: Toronto currently is the only city in Ontario that has a bylaw that prohibits riding two abreast.

CANADIAN CYCLING ATTITUDES

Although cycling is an internationally recognized form of transportation, Canada is still a relatively young country where cycling is concerned. Over the last number of years, the province has made great strides in public education and people who share the roads with bicycles are gradually becoming more aware and considerate towards cyclists. On the less travelled backroads where traffic is light it is legal to ride two abreast, but it's common courtesy to get into single file when traffic approaches from the front or rear. Use your hand signals to let others know your intentions and keep at least one bicycle length between you and the rider in front of you. This is especially true when travelling with children who constantly wander off and on the road. If you do go off the road, ride on the shoulder for a bit until you have regained control, then return to the pavement once the way is clear. Be aware of what is going on in front and behind at all times. If you find yourself in an uncomfortable situation always yield the right of way, take to the shoulder, walk your bike, or stop until the situation has changed and you are again comfortable riding your bicycle.

EQUIPMENT

The Bicycle

Racing bicycles are lightweight, quick-handling (road or track) with high quality components: narrow lightweight wheel rims and tires, a short wheelbase, and either close-ratio gearing or a fixed gear.

Road bicycles/Randonneuse Bicycles are lightweight and designed to carry at least 20 pounds of supplies in cargo packs. They have a long wheelbase for stability (42 inches or more), long chain stays, generous fork rake, heavy-duty but narrow wheels, and cantilever brakes. Head tube and seat tube angles are shallow, usually 72 to 73 degrees. The bottom bracket is set low for stability.

Touring bicycles are more robust versions of road bicycles. They have heavy duty components and construction. They offer a wide range of gears, and often have triple chain rings for hill climbing. A touring bicycle is designed to carry 40 to 50 pounds of cargo.

Hybrid bicycles are often referred to as all-purpose adventure bikes. These bicycles are essentially a cross between a mountain bike and a road bicycle. They have cantilever-style brakes, triple chain rings, wide-range gearing, and flat handlebars similar to mountain bikes. On the other hand, they have somewhat larger diameter wheels (700 cc instead of 26 inch) and narrower tires (1.5 inches instead of 2). The frames are more like those of road bikes. 72 degree head tube angles and 73 degree seat angles are common as are 17 inch or shorter chain stays.

The Mountain bike is a sturdily built bicycle specially designed for off-road, or rough terrain riding. Mountain bikes have flat handlebars, cantilever-style brakes, triple chain rings, wide-range gearing, and knobby tires, approximately two inches wide. Most mountain bikes now have a 70- to 72-degree head angle, 1.5 to 2 inches of fork rake, and a 68- to 74-degree seat tube angle. On a good road, a mountain bike is about 10% slower than a road bike. When used for touring, they offer the rider stability, load carrying ability and long-distance comfort. They have a long wheelbase with a generous fork rake and long chain stays. The handlebars are wider than on other bikes, and there are rack mounting bosses near the front and rear wheels.

Bicycle Panniers and Loading

As the majority of the tours in this guide are planned as day trips or weekend getaways, a medium-sized, rear top rack bag and two rear side panniers (1500-1800cc), with enough room for both the essentials and food, are adequate. For the best handling, a bicycle should carry 60% of its load in the rear, 35% in the front panniers, and 5% in the handlebar bag. The front panniers should be mounted low and be centred fore and aft on the axle. Great care should be taken to keep this load balanced, or the bike will become unsafe. One new idea that offers cyclists a better way to transport gear is the new single-wheel tag-a-long trailer that easily attaches to the rear wheel quick release mechanism. These trailers give you an increased luggage capacity and more control over the bicycle handling when fully loaded.

TYPES OF CYCLING TOURS

Independent Cycling

Independent cycling in this manner means that you plan and create your own cycling tour. Generally, this allows your dollar to stretch a little further. Often you will determine your own route, use a route travelled by others or rely on written instructions and mapping from books such as this. You can travel in the lap of luxury by staying in deluxe accommodations or camp along the road. This type of cycling lets you travel at your own pace, allowing time to enjoy the countryside and interact with the locals and your chosen travelling companions.

In a Group

Travelling with a group of cyclists can be a rewarding experience. It's a fun and easy way to learn the ropes and it offers an excellent venue for the exchange of information and ideas. Travelling on group tours also provides companionship and moral support along the way. Some discussion with travelling companions at the beginning of a tour is important. There is nothing wrong with a bit of friendly competition throughout the day, but you don't want the tour to turn into an endurance race.

Organized Group Tours

If you are a single rider or are concerned about doing your first bicycle tour, one option is to join an organized group outing. Ontario has a number of reputable Bicycle Tour Operators who are registered with the Ontario Government providing quality tour packages.

Tour Companies:

Bloomfield Bicycle Company: 225 Main Street, P.O. Box 78 Bloomfield, Ontario K0K 1G0, ☎(613) 393-1060

Bicycle Ontario Tours: P.O. Box 20044, North Bay, Ontario, P1B 9N1, ☎(705) 752-5693, home.on.rogers.wave.ca/bikeon.

Butterfield & Robinson Inc.: 70 Bond Street, Toronto, Ontario, Canada M5B 1X3, ☎(416) 864-1354, 1-800-678-1147, www.butterfield.com.

Camp-on-Two Wheels: ☎(Bicycle tours for teens), R.R. 4, Bracebridge, Ontario P1L 1X2.

Canadian Trails Bicycle Tours: Suite 153, 162-2025 Corydon Ave., Winnipeg, Manitoba, R3P 0N5 ☎(800) 668-2453, www.canadiantrails.com.

Countryroads Bike Tours: P.O. Box 992, Kingston, Ontario, K7L 4X8, ☎(613) 542-4169.

Cycle Canada: 145 King Street West, Suite 1000, Toronto, Ontario M5H 1J8, ☎(416) 484-8339, www.CycleCanada.com.

Cyclone: Cycle Ontario Experience, PO Box 25054, 1375 Weber Street East, Kitchener, Ontario, N2A 4A5, ☎(519) 650-1709, www.kwic.com/~biketour.

Georgian Shores Cycle Tours: 688 8th Street A East, Owen Sound, Ontario, Canada N4K 1N2, ☎(519) 371-7889, www.bmts.com/~gsct.

Grand Bicycle Tours: Box 37, Site 2, RR 1, Elora, Ontario N0B 1S0, ☎(519) 846-8455.

Great Canadian Bicycle Tours: PO Box 5, St. George, Ontario N0E 1N0, ☎(519) 622-0894, www.freenet.hamilton/on/ca/~ah782/Profile.html, icycle@golden.net.

Ontario Cycling Association: 1185 Eglinton Ave. E., Suite 408, North York, Ontario, M3C 3C6, ☎(416) 426-7349, www.ontariocycling.org.

Ottawa Bicycle Club: PO Box 4298, Station E., Ottawa, Ontario, K1S 5B3, ☎(613) 230-1064.

Spinning Wheel Bicycle Tours: Box 51A, Jordan Station, Ontario, L0R 1S0, ☎(905) 562-7169

Steve Bauer Bike Tours Inc.: PO Box 428, Vineland, Ontario, L0R 2C0, ☎(905) 562-0674, www.stevebauer.com.

The Adventure Mountain Bike School: RR 3, Collingwood, Ontario L9Y 3Z2, ☎(705) 455-0231 ext. 6125.

Venture Travel Club: Suite 101, 24-94 Bridgeport Road. E., Waterloo, Ontario, N2J 2J9, ☎(519) 746-5715.

W.O.W.: 1506 Oran Court, Mississauga Ontario L5N 1L3, ☎(905) 567-7593, www.wowmtb.com.

RAIL TRAILS AND OFF-ROAD CYCLING

Multi-Use Trails

Multi-Use Trails are the most popular trail used by cyclists today. Their surfaces vary from asphalt paths to the unsurfaced, man-made nature trails and reconditioned railbeds. These trails are shared by hikers, cyclists, horseback riders and in winter by snowmobiles; in some cases the trail will share a roadway with automobiles.

Trans Canada Trail

The Trans Canada Trail is a lasting legacy from the Canada 125 Celebration in 1992. A promise was made, giving meaning to Canada's 125th birthday, that connecting greenways would be built across Canada in an effort to unify the country. The Trans Canada Trail will be a shared-use recreational trail stretching over 15,000 km from the Atlantic to the Pacific, and north to the Arctic Ocean. When fully completed, it will accommodate hikers, walkers, horseback riders, cyclists, cross-country skiers and, where appropriate, snowmobiles.

Trans Canada Trail (Ontario)
Box 462, Station D
Etobicoke, Ontario M9A 4X4
☎(416) 234-5057

"Rails to Trails" in Ontario

Ontario's abandoned rail lines are increasingly being turned into scenic cycling paths. The surface of redeveloped railbeds varies depending on the character and needs of the communities through which it passes. Local terrain, the frequency of use, the type of use and the amount of funds, manpower and local governmental support all dictate what the trail will look like.

Currently there are a little over 241 km of designated rail trails in southern Ontario.

Ontario Trails
First Floor
90 Sheppard Ave East,
North York, Ontario M2N 3A1
☎(416) 314-1092

Single and Double Track Trails

Single Track Trails are hard-packed routes that are found in natural areas. Generally, bicycles can only travel in single file, the terrain is more technical and demands a higher skill level from the cyclist.

Double Track Trails are unsurfaced, hard-packed routes wide enough to accommodate two riders abreast, and are generally preferred by less experienced cyclists.

Resort and Conservation Trails

These trails are well maintained and thoughtfully designed, and in most cases are privately owned or operated by a local conservation authority. There may be a user fee at some of these locations.

ACCOMMODATIONS

Once your route and travel dates are set, you need to arrange your accommodations. Always book your accommodations before you depart. Never assume that there will be a vacancy when you arrive in the evening.

Hotels and Motels

Generally, these are the most expensive types of accommodations and are not found in all areas. If you decide to stay in these places, try to get a room on the ground floor so that you will be able to put your bicycle in your hotel room more easily.

Bed & Breakfasts

A unique way to enjoy Ontario hospitality, Bed & Breakfasts are family homes that rent out rooms to visitors. They can be a relaxing experience that give you a glimpse into the local community. When booking, remember to ask if they have a garage to store your bicycle. Also upon request, some B&Bs will even allow you to camp in the backyard and provide breakfast in the morning.

Ontario Bed & Breakfast:
☎(416) 515-1293, www.bbcanada.com/obba/html

Camping

The most economical form of accommodation, camping also brings you closest to nature. One drawback, however, is that it always takes longer to dismantle a tent in the morning than to walk out of a hotel room. Generally, the flexibility and the fresh air afforded by this type of accommodation outweigh any drawbacks encountered.

Camping Organizations

Provincial Park Vacancies:
☎(800) 668-2746
Ontario Parks:
☎(800) 668-2246, www.mnr.gov.on.ca/MNR/parks/index.html

Ontario Private Campgrounds:
☎(519) 371-3393, www.campgrounds.org

Showers

Often, showers or a place to wash up are hard to locate when camping. Most towns usually have a public pool (some have showers) offering cyclists an economical way to clean up and relax after a long day's ride.

Bicycle Camping Equipment

Tent

Your tent should be a lightweight (one or two person) backpacking tent with a fly, and not more than 24 inches wide when rolled up. Make sure that the tent has an extendable foyer or enough room inside for your panniers. Tip: get some plastic, cut a ground sheet (the same size) as the bottom of your tent and put it under the tent as it will allow the tent floor to last longer.

Gas Camping Stoves

There are a number of excellent products on the market that are reasonably priced. An important consideration is size and weight. A stove (single burner) designed for white gas naphtha and backpacking will do. WARNING: NEVER START A STOVE OR ANY OTHER FLAMMABLE PRODUCT IN A TENT OR ENCLOSED AREA.

Cooking & Other Equipment

Travel as light as possible. Lightweight cookware (stainless steel is recommended) is available in the camping department of most major retail outlets. A Swiss Army Knife can always come in handy, especially for camping and emergencies. Lastly, take some grey duct tape. If all else fails, this stuff won't let you down – it repairs everything! Step on the roll and flatten it out so that it does not take up too much room.

Food

Plan your daily menu before you go on tour. This will also help you budget for your trip. Most groceries should be picked up along the way, but some items will have to be purchased before departure. Fresh fruit is a must and can be complimented by cereal or granola bars as these items will help to keep your energy level up throughout the day. Your menus should also include food high in carbohydrates; a combination of milk and pasta will satisfy this daily requirement. Try to include easy-to-carry, lightweight instant food, which can be purchased at your local grocery store before departure. You'll be surprised at the variety and quality (excellent taste and very nutritious) of instant foods available today. Most important is WATER! Keep your body constantly hydrated and you will be fine.

Food and Wildlife

Wildlife is also a concern. Racoons, skunks and black bears are attracted to food and garbage. When camping, always place food away from your tent, use bear-resistant food storage containers or suspend food four metres off the ground and one metre away from any nearby tree trunks. Keep all garbage until it can be disposed of in the proper manner – don't bury it!

TOUR PREPARATION AND TRAINING

Although the tours in this book can be cycled by almost everyone, it is suggested before embarking on a tour that some physical and mental preparation be undertaken. The most important consideration of any trip is to know your equipment, meaning your bicycle and your body.

You must make sure you are comfortable on your bicycle. After all, you will be spending many hours in the saddle each day. Your bicycle seat and handlebar position affect your knees, back, neck and wrists. If they are not in the correct position, your trip will be more difficult and uncomfortable. Try adjusting your riding position so that you are as upright as possible, so that about 75% of your weight is on the seat and you grip the handlebars from the top. Take some time to determine your correct riding position. If unsure, consult your local bicycle shop. As well, become familiar with how to complete some simple mechanical repairs. Don't rely on someone in your group to fix everything because most problems seem to occur when you become separated for one reason or another. Again, if you are unsure, turn to your local bicycle shop for advice or refer to one of the many repair manuals available.

Physical training is recommended before embarking on any bicycle trip, but don't go to extremes. The more consistent you are in the training program you follow (consult your physician), the more comfortable the cycling experience will be. Included in your exercise program should be daily time on an exercise bicycle and, in good weather, your own bicycle. This will not only help you become more familiar with your bicycle; it will also help you build some rear-end stamina! As departure day nears, increase your weekend riding, making sure to include some topography that will challenge you physically and mentally. Allow one day a week in your physical training schedule to rest: this will give your body a chance to recuperate.

You should do several weekend training rides with your bike and panniers fully loaded. This will show you the best way to pack, distribute the weight on your bicycle, and make you conscious of the changes in your bike's handling when packed for the tour.

A Cyclist's Motto

Packing for any kind of tour can be tedious. As you read the list on the next page, keep in mind the Touring Cyclist's Motto: "Take half as much clothing and twice as much money and you'll have a perfect holiday."

Equipment Checklist

Clothing

[ ]   3 pairs of cotton socks
[ ]   3 pairs of cotton underwear
[ ]   1 pair of pyjamas
[ ]   2 pairs of padded lycra shorts (wash well throughout trip)
[ ]   3 to 4 shirts (brightly coloured for better visibility)
[ ]   1 warm long-sleeve shirt
[ ]   1 pair sweat pants or tights
[ ]   2 pairs cycling shoes (1 pair can be a ridged sole running shoe)
[ ]   Rain gear/windbreaker
[ ]   Toiletries (towels etc.)
[ ]   bathing suit
[ ]   1 pair cycling gloves

Hardware

[ ]   Bicycle (I know; this goes without saying)
[ ]   Helmet
[ ]   Water bottles (2 minimum)
[ ]   Front/Back Panniers (as required)
[ ]   Rear rack top bag (handlebar bags not recommended as they impair steering and balance of your bicycle)
[ ]   Rear view mirror
[ ]   Compass
[ ]   Mini repair tool kit
[ ]   Tire repair kit
[ ]   Extra tire tube
[ ]   Bicycle pump
[ ]   Battery equipped front and rear lights
[ ]   Extra brake cable & brake pads
[ ]   Light lubricant
[ ]   Swiss Army knife
[ ]   Duct tape/electrician tape

[ ]   Bungie cords or small nylon tie-down straps (bring extras, they always seem to disappear)
[ ]   Small First Aid kit
[ ]   Pain reliever (Aspirin or Tylenol)
[ ]   Wallet (personal identification and currency)
[ ] $5 loose change (in case of emergency)
[ ]   Plastic sheet (painters drop sheet to cover bike, keep panniers dry)
[ ]   Small binoculars
[ ]   Hat
[ ]   Camera & extra film
[ ]   Bicycle lock & locks for panniers
[ ]   Sun screen
[ ]   Sunglasses
[ ]   Small flashlight
[ ]   Small sewing kit
[ ]   Large garbage bags (for clean up, in a pinch can be converted to a raincoat)
[ ]   Additional road maps as required
[ ]   Durable plastic bags & tie tags (to protect your gear on rainy days)
[ ]   This book and your daily journal

Camping Equipment

The following suggestions are the minimum required equipment for any cycling camping trip:

[ ]   Lightweight tent & fly
[ ]   Lightweight sleeping bag (mummy style preferred)
[ ]   Sleeping pad
[ ]   Lightweight stove
[ ]   Extra fuel tank and fuel for camp stove
[ ]   Lightweight cookware & eating utensils
[ ]   Matches
[ ]   Toilet Paper
[ ]   Fold up pillow (optional)
[ ]   Dehydrated food packages (as per your menu)
[ ]   Spices and condiments (as required)
[ ]   lightweight 9 X 12 plastic tarp
[ ]   Small whisk

CYCLING WITH CHILDREN

Cycling with children of any age can be a very rewarding experience. Listed below are some suggestions that will help make it even more fun.

1. Make sure they know the rules of the road and traffic signs.

2. Make sure they are familiar with their bicycle.

3. Make sure the bike is equipped with a working front light, back light and bell. (odometer is optional – but can be helpful when setting targets).

4. Make sure they keep a least one bicycle length between them and the rider in front – young eyes tend to wander when experiencing new sights and sounds.

5. Set time goals for stops – this will keep them pedalling in anticipation of an upcoming stop.

6. Provide them with a set of panniers (large or small, no matter) so that they will feel that they are contributing to the cycling adventure by carrying their own gear.

7. Provide a disposable camera so they can create their own memories of the cycling trip.

8. Allow them time to play; after all, they are only children. Pack a card game, a frisbee and a small toy.

9. Involve them in pre-trip preparations and map reading. Ask them from time to time what direction they are travelling when on route.

10. Relay the local information found in this book – it will help entertain them, keep their minds off the chore at hand and may lead to questions that together you can find the answers to.

Lastly, when choosing a tour for children, take into consideration that they will require more breaks and a lower average speed. When doing your pre-tour calculations on the length of your day, remember to add at least one to two hours.

THE TOURS

As you leaf through this book deciding which area of Ontario is of interest to you, notice that most regions have a tour of five or more days, a number of single day outings and several two- and three- day looped itineraries.

Generally, the tours begin in fairly large cities and each tour provides the necessary information for you to arrange your own cycling excursion. Suggested touring days accommodate all levels of riding ability, from ages eight to 80, from the skilled to the occasional cyclist. Most of the overnight tours can be completed as day outings, or expanded or combined with other tours in this guide by making a few simple changes, so you can design a tour that accommodates your available time and preferred destinations. Tours have been carefully planned so you have enough time to get off your bike to explore and experience the province's many attractions and unique features.

In an effort to accommodate the needs of all cyclists, maximum daily cycling distances of 70 kms, or 45 miles, a day are suggested. The roads chosen are primarily paved secondary roads. Wherever possible, the use of abandoned rail lines and off-road trails are incorporated into the itinerary. Routing has been designed to accommodate all cyclists and bicycle types. Alternative routing suggestions are included in most itineraries for those who prefer to remain on familiar roadways.

HOW THIS GUIDE WORKS

Bicycle Types

Listed in order of preference; when in (brackets), some sections of the route may require more physical effort for this type of bicycle

Difficulty

Each tour in this guide can be completed by all cyclists no matter what their riding ability, by simply extending daily riding time.

🚲	Easy, flat terrain
🚲 🚲	Easy/medium flat and slightly rolling
🚲 🚲 🚲	Medium, rolling terrain
🚲 🚲 🚲 🚲	Medium/hard, rolling terrain including 2 or 3 good climbs
🚲 🚲 🚲 🚲 🚲	Difficult, rolling terrain, numerous long 6 degree plus climbs

Abbreviations

Intersection	[T]
Junction	[Y]
Right	[R]
Left	[L]
Railbed	[RB]
Side Roads, gravel or Lose Surface Roads	[SR]
Asphalt Roads	[Apht]
County Road	[CTY]
Highway	[HWY]

Township Road	[TWP]
Road	Rd
Street	St
Drive	Dr
Avenue	Ave
Boulevard	Blvd
Crescent	Cresc
Highway	Hwy
Parkway	Pkwy
County	Cty
Route Road One	RR 1
North	N
South	S
East	E
West	W
Ontario	Ont

ON THE ROAD

Directions

To help you decide on which area of Ontario to visit, a brief description and indication of difficulty precede each tour itinerary. The guide has been designed to meet the needs of the independent cyclist. Detailed written directions including distance and local tidbits of information compliment the maps, making the guide easy to use. This book also includes contact information for local tourist centres, unique attractions, bicycle shops and interesting local events. This guide has tried to keep that sense of adventure alive in each tour while providing you with all the essential information.

Dehydration is a cyclist's greatest concern. Drink plenty of water throughout the day. A good way to make sure that you stay hydrated (even if you are not thirsty) is to follow this simple rule: every five kilometres drink at least one quarter of your water bottle, and more on hot days.

Do a **circle check** of your bicycle and equipment each morning beginning with a quick look at your tires, spokes, rack bolts

Some Advice

The old saying "the faster I go... the farther behind I get" is applicable to cycling as well. It is important that you set and stick to a comfortable cycling speed to make your touring experience a pleasant one.

and brakes. An early morning start is always recommended when the sun is low in the sky and since the temperatures are cooler and more comfortable. An early morning departure is even more important if you are camping, as it always seems to takes more time to repack your gear and get going. Review the day's itinerary and maps before setting out; never try to read a map while riding.

Theft

Whenever you leave your bicycle unattended LOCK IT UP! It is a good idea to lock your panniers as well. Never leave your wallet or expensive camera equipment in your bicycle unattended. They, like your bike, are just too tempting to curious eyes.

The Environment

It is important to remember when on tour that you are only an observer and should therefore respect all that Mother Nature has provided for us. The old Boy Scout adage of "leaving a place visited in a better condition than one found it in" is an excellent way to treat this world and more particularly, the communities that you are cycling through. After all, the impression you leave will affect others that follow.

Each tour provides ample time to stretch and explore. Don't be afraid to stop. Take some time to visit and enjoy the natural beauty of your surroundings and the area's many amenities. By doing so, you will find that your trip will be a relaxing and rewarding experience.

ADDITIONAL REFERENCE MATERIALS

Internet Sites

Here are a few of the many cycling sites available on the net:

Bicycling Magazine: www.bicyclingmagazine.com
Canadian Cycling Association: www.canadian-cycling.com
Cyber Cycling: www.blueridge.databolts.ibm.com/bikes
Manuels Cycling Page: www.eskimo.com/~manuel/home.htm
Ontario Cycling Association: www.ontariocycling.org
Ottawa Cycling Club: www.sce.carleton.ca/rads/greg/obc/
Rail Trails: www.railtrails.org
Trans Canada Trail: www.tctrail.ca
UCI- Union Cycliste Internationale: www.uci.ch.
VeloNews: www.greatoutdoors.com/velonews
Woodstock Cycling Club:
www.oxford.net/~lynebike/WCCA.html

Ontario Cycling Publications

Backroads & Railbeds, A Grand Adventure
Lynes Bicycle Adventures, ISBN 0-9683000-0-6

Backroads & Railbeds - North Shore Lake Erie Book
Lynes Bicycle Adventures, ISBN 0-9683000-1-4

Backroads & Railbeds - North Shore Lake Erie Book 2
Lynes Bicycle Adventures, ISBN0-9683000-2-2

Backroads and Railbeds - Pelee Island & Marsh Trails
Lynes Bicycle Adventures, ISBN 0-9683000-3-0

Bicycle Day Trips In And Around London
Wallis and Gordon, ISBN 0-9699594-0-0

Bicycle Guide to Eastern Ontario
Gary Horner, ISBN 1-895591-00-7

Bicycling the Bruce
Tom Hakala, ISBN 0-921773-22-6

Cycling Around the Sound
Tom Hakala, Owen Sound Area, ISBN 0-921773-32-3

The Canadian Cycling Association Complete Guide to Bicycle Touring in Canada
Elliot Katz ISBN 0-385025415-6

The Bicycle Guide to Southwestern Ontario
Gary Horner, ISBN 0-9698297-0-1

Day Trips on Bike Trails
by the Valley Girls, ☎(519) 599-6290

Lakeshore Cycle Guide - Toronto to Belleville
Donna McNeil, ISBN 0-9681255-0-6

Pioneer Cycle Guide - Haliburton to Lake Ontario
Donna McNeil, ISBN 0-9681255-1-4

The Waterfront Trail
Waterfront Regeneration Trust, ISBN 0-7778-4082-0

Cycling Magazines

Here are some interesting cycling magazines:

Bicycling Magazine	Bike
Mountain Bike	Pedal
Off Camber	Velo News

Maps of Ontario

Surveys and Plans Office
Ministry of Transportation
1201 Wilson Avenue
Downsview, Ontario M3J 1J8
☎(416) 235-4686

Other Publications

Baden-Powell, Lord of Gilwell *Scouting for Boys*. National Council Boy Scouts of Canada.

Beck, David. *Discover Southern Ontario*. Learnxs Press, 1978.

Berton, Pierre. *My Country - The Remarkable Past*. McClelland & Stewart, 1976.

Brown, Ron. *Ghost Town's of Ontario Vol. 1*. Cannon Books, 1987.

-----. *Ghost Railways of Ontario*. Broadview Press, 1995.

-----. *Ghost Towns of Ontario Vol. 3*. Cannon Books, 1983

-----. *Ghost Towns of Ontario Vol. 2*. Cannon Books, 1983.

Byers, Mary and Margaret McBurney. *The Governor's Road*. University of Toronto Press, 1982.

Canadian Automobile Association. *Tourist Guide Book of Ontario*.

Couture, Pascale. *Ontario*. Ulysses Travel Publications, 1998.

-----. *Ottawa*. Ulysses Travel Publications, 1998.

Dawe, Brian. *Old Oxford is Wide Awake*. William Brian Dawe, 1980.

Hakala, Tom. *Bicycling the Bruce*. The Ginger Press, 1994.

McMorran, Jennifer and Alain Rondeau. *Toronto*. Ulysses Travel Publications, 1998.

Ontario Ministry of Industry and Tourism. *Circle Tours of Festival Country*.

Pearen, Shelley J. *Exploring Manitoulin*. Revised ed. University of Toronto Press, 1996.

Readers Digest. *Canadian Book of the Road*. 1979.

Scott, David E. *Ontario Place Names*. Vancouver, Toronto: Whitecap Books, 1993.

Seca, Ron. *Ontario Mountain Bike Guide*. Stoddart Press, 1994.

Statistics Canada. *Canada Handbook*. Canadian Government Publishing Centre.

Tiessen, Ronald. *A Bicycle Guide to Pelee Island*. Ronald Tiessen, Pelee Island Heritage Centre, 1994.

Wallis, Susan and Mindy Gordon. *Bicycle Day Trips in and around London*. Forward Publications, 1996.

Waterfront Regeneration Trust. *The Waterfront Trail*. 1995.

SOUTHWESTERN ONTARIO

Southwestern Ontario stretches eastward from Windsor to Woodstock, the Dairy Capital of Canada and from the shipping port of Goderich in the north to the city of Leamington, in the South.

THE TOURS

---

1. Magical Pelee Island

This island glistens like an emerald amid the blue waters of Lake Erie. Upon disembarking at the west dock, you immediately get the feeling that time has stood still on this resort island. Much of the island's history is intact, waiting to be discovered as you begin to explore every nook and cranny. The romance of the wine industry wafts through the air, beckoning you to sample its wares. And, you can enjoy all this simply by taking a bicycle ride.

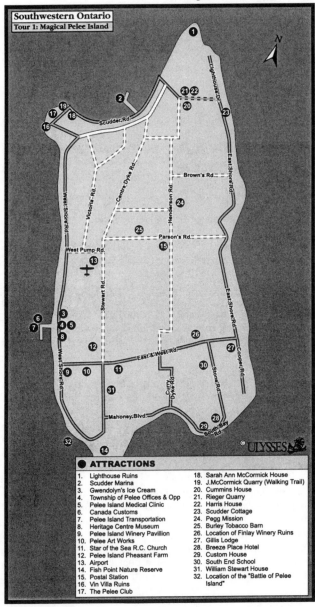

Southwestern Ontario
Tour 1: Magical Pelee Island

● ATTRACTIONS

1. Lighthouse Ruins
2. Scudder Marina
3. Gwendolyn's Ice Cream
4. Township of Pelee Offices & Opp
5. Pelee Island Medical Clinic
6. Canada Customs
7. Pelee Island Transportation
8. Heritage Centre Museum
9. Pelee Island Winery Pavillion
10. Pelee Art Works
11. Star of the Sea R.C. Church
12. Pelee Island Pheasant Farm
13. Airport
14. Fish Point Nature Reserve
15. Postal Station
16. Vin Villa Ruins
17. The Pelee Club
18. Sarah Ann McCormick House
19. J.McCormick Quarry (Walking Trail)
20. Cummins House
21. Rieger Quarry
22. Harris House
23. Scudder Cottage
24. Pegg Mission
25. Burley Tobacco Barn
26. Location of Finlay Winery Ruins
27. Gillis Lodge
28. Breeze Place Hotel
29. Custom House
30. South End School
31. William Stewart House
32. Location of the "Battle of Pelee Island"

Return Distance: 89 km of road on the island
No. of recommended legs: 1
Level of Difficulty: 🚲🚲
Surface: Asphalt and some gravel

Villages/Towns/Cities: Leamington, Pelee Island

Local Highlights: Point Pelee National Park, Jack Miner Bird Sanctuary, Colasanti's Tropical Gardens, Wheatley Provincial Park, Rondeau Provincial Park, John. R. Park Homestead, Pelee Island Museum, Pelee Island Winery, Fish Point Nature Reserve, Glacial Groves, Indian Grinding Stone, Pelee Lighthouse Ruins, Huldah's Rock, Vin Villa Ruins

Recommended Bicycles: Touring/Hybrid/Mountain

Tour Suggestions: To make the trip more enjoyable, try to spend at least one night on the island. Take the early morning ferry (1.5 hour one way) across, spend the day exploring, and then return to the mainland the next day to visit Point Pelee National Park. The island's roads are narrow and must be shared with motorized vehicles. Watch out for the tour tractor whose passenger cars have a tendency to swing wildly! Also, book your accommodations well ahead of time as the island's many Bed & Breakfasts are in popular demand.

How To Get There: From May to the end of August, the ferry departs from the city of **Leamington**. To get there from the north, take Hwy 401 to Hwy 77 S. From the east, follow Hwy 18 or Hwy 3, and from the west, take Hwy 3. From the south, the island may be reached by taking a ferry across the lake from neighbouring Sandusky, Ohio. A good way to ensure a spot on the ferry is to call ahead to make reservations.

From the earliest times, the French referred to the islands of Lake Erie collectively as the "Isles des Serpens Sonnettes," which meant Rattlesnake Islands. The name may have been a contributing factor in delaying exploration of **Pelee Island** which, despite its natural amenities has only a few truly historical treasures. It is perhaps best known for its famous wine which has been produced on the island since 1866.

Practical Information

Population: 200 permanent, 1000 in the summer months

 Tourist Information

Township of Pelee, 1045 West Shore Rd, Pelee Island, Ontario, N0R 1M0, (519) 724-2931, www.peleeisland.com
Ferry Information: Owen Sound Transportation Co. (Ontario Northland) Pelee Island Transportation Co., 1060 West Shore Rd, Pelee Island, Ontario N0R 1M0, (519) 724-2115 or (800) 661-2220

 Bicycle Shops

Dixie Lawn & Cycle, 27 Erie St North, Leamington, Ontario, N8H 2Z2 (519) 326-4572; Gt's Bike Shop, 76 Erie St North, Leamington, Ontario, N8H 2Z6, (519) 322-4711

 Special Sights and Events

Birders Haven, Victoria Day Celebration, Island Country Hoedown, Pelee Island Cyclist Tour, Great Pelee Island Bike, Run & Canoe, Canada Day, Summer Celebration, Vineyard Trolley Rides, Wine Down Party, Grape Harvest Moon, Louie's Birthday Bash, Relight the Lighthouse

 Accommodations

Cottages/Inns/B&B

Itinerary: The Ontario Northland ferry, M.V. Jilmann, is the largest on the lake. It is 80 metres long, weighs over 6,350 kilograms and generally docks at the island's West Dock. Once you put your wheels on dry land, locate the tourist information booth just south of the ferry entrance and stock up on information. Then stop in at the Pelee Island Heritage Centre, which is operated by historian Ron Tiessen, and found right in front of the booth. If you are looking for a more formal island bicycle tour, it can be booked here. For more detailed historical information while cycling on the island, pick up a copy of *A Bicycle Guide to Pelee Island*.

By cycling the island in a clockwise direction, you will finish the day at the Pelee Island Winery Pavilion and Vineyards. The winery is one of only three "Designated Viticultural Areas" in Ontario, and it boasts over 500 acres of vines.

Several of the island's sights are difficult to get to and not so easy to find. One which is not to be missed are the ruins of Vin Villa. These can be found through a grove of trees to the left of where Sheridan Point Rd swings right and turns into North Shore Dr. Cycle through the natural gateway of overgrown trees, ride a few metres down the little-used jeep trail and look to the left. Vin Villa was the home of the McCormick family and had a wine cellar built 3.5 metres into solid rock. Today, not much is left of the estate. Most of the walls have collapsed and those that are still standing are held together by creeping vines. Be careful as you explore, as there is an open hole in the middle of the ruins that drops down into the old wine cellar. At the end of the jeep road, Huldah's Rock rises out of the water.

As you continue your ride around the island on West Shore Rd, you'll see an empty field just opposite the Calvary Anglican Church. On the other side of the field is the lake, with a very secluded beach that has some of the best skipping stones on the island. It's also a pretty good place to go for a swim.

The second sight on the island that is not to be missed is a short distance down the road from Scudder Dock. While at the dock, take the time to ride your bicycle out onto the pier. Take a look around the old grain elevator, but be careful to avoid stepping on the remains of fileted fish. From the marina, follow the gravel Harris Garno Rd over to Lighthouse Dr. Turn [R] and cycle north along the road, which starts off in fairly good condition but quickly changes into a path as it travels through Lake Henry Marsh. The wetlands are filled with many wonderful sights, including hundreds of turtles sunning themselves on logs and numerous water snakes. When the water is high, the trail to the lighthouse may be covered in water which makes for an interesting, but feasible portage.

Riding south along the island's East Shore Rd, notice that all of the homes have been built on pillars that protect them from Lake Erie's horrendous winter storms. Also along the east side of the island, near the Glacial Grooves, are the warm sands of the island's public beach.

The day will pass quickly as you zig zag across Pelee Island. Remember to pack extra water as the East Shore Rd is long and water is scarce. If you happen to run out, the locals will be glad to help out. Make sure to leave yourself enough time to hike some of the trials in the Fish Point Nature Reserve before finishing off the day over a glass of fine wine and a self-cooked meal at the Pelee Island Winery.

---

2. Sarnia Circle Tour: Bluewater Discovery

A wonderful ride that combines Sarnia's city streets, industry and extensive park system with the back roads and villages of the Oil Heritage District. It was here that North America's first commercial oil well was discovered and the world's first oil company, the International Mining and Manufacturing Company, had its beginnings.

Return Distance: 115 km
No. of recommend legs: 2
Level of Difficulty: 🚲 🚲
Surface: City streets, paved greenways,
highways, paved country back roads

Villages/Town/Cities: Reece's Corners, Wyoming, Petrolia, Oil Springs, Mooretown, Corunna

Local Highlights: St. Clair River Waterfront and Park System, Walpole Island, Baker Environmental Science Centre, Dow Great Lake Models, Lawrence House, The Petrolia Discovery Oil Museum of Canada, Oil Springs Oil Fields, Victoria Playhouse,

Uncle Tom's Cabin, Rock Glen Falls, Rotary Nature Trail-Grand Bend

Recommend Bicycles: Touring/Hybrid/Mountain

Tour Suggestions: Strong cyclists can complete in one day. For a shorter excursion, cycle to Petrolia, returning to Sarnia via Cty Rd 4 & 20. Overnight in the Petrolia area where B&Bs and Camping are available.

How to get there: Take Hwy 402, which leads to exit 40B, to Point Edward and downtown Sarnia. A short drive eventually merges onto Front St. Turn right onto Front St, cross Exmouth and continue along Front St to Centennial Park; a parking area is located on your right. The parking lot can be used for day parking, but other arrangements should be made if the trip is going to be completed in two days.

What is now the city of **Sarnia** was referred to by the Chippewa Indians as "The Rapids" in 1831. The extensive hardwood forests and proximity to the St. Clair River helped create an international trade in lumber which led to the building of sawmills and secondary industries like shipbuilding, fishing and agriculture. In 1836, the settlers voted in a referendum to change the village's name to "Port Sarnia", shortened to the Celtic name of "Sarnia" in 1855. The town continued to grow with the arrival of the Great Western Railway, the nearby commercial oil fields at Oils Springs and the completion of the St. Clair River Railway tunnel in 1891. Today, Sarnia is home to Canada's largest complex of petrochemical plants and oil refineries and is connected to the United States by the dual span Blue Water Bridge at Port Huron, Michigan.

Itinerary: Before setting out, take some time to explore the immediate area. Look for a picturesque little marina hugging the St. Clair River and Sarnia's chemical valley in the distance. Extending south from the city for approximately 32 km, the chemical valley has an impressive fairyland appearance at night with its thousands of twinkling lights. Exit the parking lot by turning [R] onto Front St. Watch for the railway tracks. At London Rd turn [L] at the lights, then climb the slight incline to the traffic lights at Christina St N. Continue along London Rd

past the impressive steeple of Our Lady of Mercy Catholic Church. Further along on your right is the St. Joseph Health Centre. London Rd has four lanes and can be quite busy during rush hour until you pass the Murphy Rd Shopping District.

At Lambton College the road curves to the left. Turn [R] at the lights onto old Hwy 27, now Lambton Rd 22/London Rd. Cycle under Hwy 40, cross Wawanosh Creek and ride past Bethel Pentecostal Church. London Rd again becomes two lanes and has an excellent cycling lane once past the creative display of man and his buggy, at Blackwell Side Rd.

The route becomes easy as you go past the wind mill at Mandaumin Rd and the old Head Stones of the Oban Church Memorial Cemetery. Look for the old rusty steam engine at the Jackson Farm. There is a flashing light at **Reece's Corners** and a floating air plane at the Skyview Restaurant and Airport. At Reece's Corners, to the left, is a very unique tourist information office, which is a scale reproduction of an 1870 "Canadian

Drilling Rig." These rigs were used by local drillers in over 87 countries to discover many prosperous oil fields. At the stop-light turn [R] onto Oil Heritage Rd/Lambton Rd 21 and continue towards Wyoming.

Wyoming, whose name means "great plain" was founded around 1856 by a group of Pennsylvania settlers. Although oil was never found here, the village acted as a railway shipping centre for oil from Petrolia and Oil Springs in boom times. Notice the wooden church spire of Holy Rosary Catholic church on your right. At 528 Broadway/Lambton 21, a local bicycle enthusiast has his rebuilt bikes for sale, and may be of help if you have a mechanical problem. Turn [L] at Erie St, following it to a nice little park, which is a good spot for a morning break. In the downtown area, you will find all the amenities of home, including a restaurant and variety store.

Leaving Wyoming behind, cross two sets of railway tracks and Bear Creek No.3, then climb a long grade to arrive at Petrolia. At the flashing light, turn [R] onto Lambton Rd. 4/Petrolia St and cycle towards "Petrolia Discovery" and downtown Petrolia. Bridgeview Park is located on both sides of the road after Bear Creek. The park is an excellent lunch stop. Turn [R] following the entrance road to the Petrolia Discovery grounds. There is a small admission charge to enjoy this tribute to early oil pioneers but it is well worth the visit. Take some time to explore the village of **Petrolia**, ride around its streets, which feature some fascinating architecture, and learn some interesting tidbits of information about the town's incredibly prosperous era.

Resume your journey by retracing your steps to the flashing light at Lambton Rd 21. Turn [R] towards **Oil Springs**. After crossing Bear Creek No. 2, keep your eyes open as you ride pass Rockabye Line. Though its name is impressive, Oil City, played a less than impressive role in the development of the region's petroleum industry. This area was continuously bought and sold by speculators in hopes that they could capitalize on the anticipated boom in nearby Oil Springs.

Crossing Lambton Rd 80/Courtright Rd, turn [L] onto Oil Springs "Main St" and cycle past a number of commercial buildings including the Van Tuyl Fairbank Oil Supply Shop built in 1880, the Masonic Temple and a white frame building which was formally the home of the *Oil Springs Chronicle*, Lambton County's first daily newspaper on the north-east corner of Main & Kelly. Turn [R], heading south onto Kelly Rd, past Watson's Machine Shop, which was built in 1880 by the Oil Spring Supply Company and used by the company founders to repair and build tools and machinery for the local oilmen. One of Anderson and Murray's significant contributions to the oil industry was the development of a gas-powered engine for oil pumps that made oil production very efficient. The engines ran on natural gas, a by-product of the oil wells. The countryside around the Oil Museum of Canada is littered with abandoned shacks and the rusting steel of discarded oil rigs.

The Oil Museum of Canada, a national historic site is located where James Miller Williams dug the first commercial oil well in 1858. The museum preserves and glamourizes a past that must have been very exciting; there are many outside exhibits, which include a few of the original oilfield drilling rigs and buildings. Continue south and turn [L] onto Blind Line, where you will see the last remaining oil receiving station in Ontario on your right. As you cycle along, notice the in-ground holding tanks cribbed with logs, and a short distance ahead wooden jerker rods that creak as they sway back and forth pumping oil.

Turn [L] at the 18th Side Rd where you cycle back in time to the nineteenth century. Jerker lines, pump jacks and frame buildings appear much as they did over a hundred years ago. To your left, there are the salt flats and the Hugh Nixon Shaw "gusher." Just past the bridge on your right is the "Oil Tank Mural" painted in 1983 to commemorate the 125th anniversary of James Miller Williams' commercial oil discovery. Turn [L] onto Main St at the next stop sign. At Duryee St, look for the "Barn Mural" painted on the Fairbank barn to your left. As you continue along Main St towards Lambton Rd 21, the remaining historic buildings are fortunate to be around since a fire levelled most of the town after the oil boom.

Cross Lambton Rd 21, then turn [R] onto the hard-packed gravel surface of South Plank Rd. At Lambton Rd 80 (asphalt) turn [L]; when you pass the Valmack Farm's windmill, the village of Brigden and its bustling downtown core are only 1 km

Practical Information

Population:
Sarnia: 70,000
Petrolia: 4,200
Oil Springs: 645
Mooretown: 410

 Tourist Information

✦ **Sarnia:** Sarnia/Lambton Convention & Visitors Bureau, 224 N. Vidal St, N7T 5Y3, (519) 336-3232 or (800) 265-0316
✦ **Petrolia:** Town of Petrolia, Box 1270, N0N 1R0 (519) 882-1770

 Bicycle Shops

✦ **Sarnia:** The Bicycle Shop, 410 Front St N., N7T 5S9, (519) 344-0515; Blairs Source for Sports, 200 Vidal St N, N7T 2T5, (519) 336-3122; Centre Ice Sports & Cycle, 1030 Confederation St, N7S 6H1, (519) 337-4545

 Special Sights and Events

✦ **Sarnia:** Imperial Oil Centre for the Performing Arts, Discovery House Museum, Uncle Tom's Cabin Historic Site, Duc d'Orleans Cruise Ship, Return of the Swans, Arkona Blossom Festival, Envirofest, Corunna Firemen's Field Day, Chippewas of Sarnia Pow Wow, Canada Day Celebrations, Mackinac Festival & Boat Race, Boom Days, Walpole Island Pow Wow, Highland Games, Saturday & Sunday Farmers Market
✦ **Petrolia:** The Petrolia Discovery, The Oil Museum of Canada, Victoria Playhouse Theatre, Petrolia Discovery Auto Show, Canada Day Celebrations, Petrolia Boom Days, Petrolia & Enniskillen Fall Fair, Pumpkin Fest

> ✦ **Oil Springs:** Oil Museum of Canada, Spring Kite Fly, Oil Patch Quilt Show, Canada Day Celebrations, All Aboard-Railway Days
>
> ✦ **Mooretown**: Mooretown Strawberry Social, Moore Museum
>
> **Accommodations**
>
> ✦ **Sarnia:** Hotels/Motels/B&B/Camping
> ✦ **Petrolia:** Motel/B&B/Camping

away. Once you arrive at the flashing light on Lambton 31/Kimble Rd ahead in the distance, you can see the refinery smoke stacks of chemical valley.

Turning [R] onto Hwy 40, proceed to lights and turn [L] onto the Moore Line. The road is lined with lilac bushes and is a pure joy to ride in the early summer. Pass the Moore Union Cemetery and the local golf course, then keep the **Mooretown** Museum complex on your right as you turn [R] onto Emily St and [R] again onto the St. Clair Pkwy. When passing through **Corunna** take some time to walk around the inspiring St. Joseph's Church, built in 1862. There are a lot of good places to take a break along the parkway. Just north of town, the towers at the Shell Oil refinery climb skyward. Past the Shell Oil buildings, look for the Froome and Field Talford historic plaque and the "Welcome to Amjiwnaang" Chippewas of Sarnia First Nation sign.

Follow the parkway into the old chemical valley as it leaves the St. Clair River behind. On both sides of the road are Dow Chemical facilities, and on your right the familiar sign of the Bayer Cross. At this point the parkway turns into Vidal St. Upon crossing the second bridge move to the left preparing to make a [L] at the lights onto Confederation St. Proceed to the [T] intersection at Christina, cross the street and join the bike path to the right of Imperial Oil. The path exits onto Johnson St; turn [L] here and follow the road as it changes to Front St South. At the Ferry Dock Hill Rd street lights turn [L], proceed down a steep hill, cross the tracks and turn [R] onto the St Clair Riverbank trail.

The St. Clair River continues to play a vital role in the development of the petroleum and chemical industries. At one time oil was barrelled in Oil Springs and floated down Bear Creek and the Sydenham River to ensure quick delivery, avoiding the difficult land routing. Ships would pick up the barrels and disperse them to ports on the Great Lakes and England. By 1899, barges began to transport crude oil to Ohio following the construction of the Imperial Oil Refinery.

As you leave the oil refineries and the chemical valley behind, Sarnia's downtown is on your right. You are in for a refreshing ride along the waterfront before the pathway winds its way through numerous small parks that offer a historic perspective on the city through information and memorial plaques.

---

3. Lake Erie's North Shore:
Woodstock, Port Dover and Tillsonburg

Beginning in Woodstock, this tour follows the historic Stage Rd into Ontario's tobacco country and completes the first leg in the rural community of Simcoe. Leg two joins the Lynn Valley Greenway and follows it into the fishing village of Port Dover. As the day progresses, the back roads and villages visited along the shores of Lake Erie will be an adventure you'll never forget. The final leg starts off in the marshes of the Long Point Spit and heads north towards Tillsonburg. The highlight of the ride will be cycling on a long forgotten railbed into the village of Springford.

Return Distance: 210 km (64 km, 56 km, 89 km)
No. of recommended legs: 3
Level of Difficulty: 🚲
Surface: Asphalt, hard-packed gravel,
crushed gravel rail-bed

Villages/Towns/Cities: Woodstock, Oxford Centre, Vanessa, Simcoe, Port Dover, Port Ryerse, Turkey Point, Long Point,

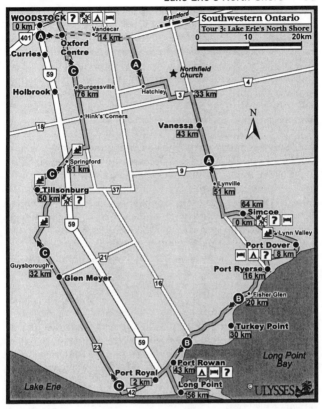

Port Rowan, Port Royal, Glen Meyer, Tillsonburg, Springford, Holbrook, Curries

Local Highlights: Woodstock Little Theatre, Beachville Museum, Woodstock Museum, Ross Butler Studio, Woodstock Art Gallery, Jakeman's Sugar Bush, Dairy Capital Princess, Woodstock Cycling Trails, Simcoe Fall Fair, Port Dover Harbour Museum, Lighthouse Theatre, Nanticoke Thermal Electric Generating Station, Port Ryerse Bakery, Hay Creek Conservation Area, St. Williams Forestry Station, Backus Heritage Conservation Area and cycling trails, Bluevale Witches Gate, Long Point Marsh, Long Point Bird Observatory,

Long Point Provincial Park, Big Creek Wildlife Area, Turkey Point Beach, Coyle's Factory, Annandale House, Tillsonburg's Farmer Market, Great Western Railway Station, Turkey Point Provincial Park and cycling trails, Normandale Fish Hatchery, McMillen's Iris Gardens, Norwich Historical Archives, Harvard Airplane Association

Recommended Bicycles: Hybrid/Mountain/Touring

Tour Suggestions: A nice three day outing for beginners, as the rides are leisurely. Meals can be obtained as you go since the tour passes through a number of larger centres.

How To Get There: Woodstock has three exits off Hwy 401. It can be reached from the north and south by following Hwy 59 and from the east and west by following Hwy 401. The tour begins at the lower parking lot of the Woodstock Quality Inn, which is found at the junction of Hwy 401 and Hwy 59. Parking arrangements can be made with the hotel's management.

Nicknamed the "City Beautiful," **Woodstock** is a unique blend of green areas, traditional buildings and modern facilities. In every corner of the city, there are private and public buildings that have been preserved. Founded by Admiral Henry Vansittart and developed by Captain Andrew Drew, Woodstock was known by many different names, like most cities in the province. The first was "Town Plot," which was quickly followed by "Oxford" and "Brighton." In 1852, the city was named Woodstock after a village in Oxfordshire, England. The first church, St. Paul's Anglican Church, was built in 1838, and still stands at the corner of Dundas and Huron Sts. One of the city's more memorable characters was Thomas "Carbide" Wilson, who in 1892 discovered a commercial process for producing calcium carbide, a chemical compound used in the manufacture of acetylene gas. This invention was used for many different purposes. In fact, it was used to produce a bicycle light that allowed riders of the big-wheeled penny farthings to travel at night. The area around Woodstock, Oxford County, is largely agricultural, and Woodstock has been considered the Dairy Capital of Canada for the last fifty years.

Practical Information

Population:
Woodstock: 32,000
Simcoe: 15,500
Port Dover: 5,000
Port Rowan (Long Point area): 800
Tillsonburg: 12,700

 Tourist Information

✦ **Woodstock:** Oxford County Tourist Association, 78 Light St, Woodstock, Ont, N4S 6H1 www.city.woodstock.on.ca
✦ **Simcoe:** Simcoe Chamber of Commerce, 76 Kent St S, Simcoe, Ont, N3Y 2Y1, (519) 426-5867, www.kwic.com/~chamber/simcoe.html
✦ **Port Dover:** Port Dover Chamber of Commerce, Box 239, 19 Market St W, Port Dover, Ont, N0A 1N0, (519) 583-1314
✦ **Port Rowan:** Backus Heritage Conservation Area, RR 1, Port Rowan, Ont, N0E 1M0, (519) 586-2201, www.lprca.on.ca
✦ **Tillsonburg:** Tillsonburg Chamber of Commerce, 2 Library Lane, Tillsonburg, Ont, N4G 4S7, (519) 842-5571, www.town.tillsonburg.on.ca

Bicycle Shops

✦ **Woodstock:** Pedal Power Bikes and Boards, 590 Dundas St, Woodstock, Ontario N4S 1C8, (519) 539-3847; FTC Bikes and Boards, 385 Springbank Ave N (Sobey's Plaza), Woodstock, Ont, N4T 1R3, (519) 533-0505; Oxford & Sports, 11 Riddell St, Woodstock, Ont, N4S 6L9, (519) 537-7801
✦ **Simcoe:** McArthur Source for Sports, 25 Sydenham St, Simcoe, Ont, N3Y 1R6, (519) 426-5190
✦ **Tillsonburg:** Oxford Cycle & Sports, 102-B Tillson Ave, Tillsonburg, Ont, N4G 3A4, (519) 688-3224.

Special Sights and Events

✦ **Woodstock:** Ontario Toy Show, Woodstock Wood Show, Ice Cream Festival, Canada Day, Gerard Streef Memorial Classic Rd Race, Dairy Capital Mountain Bike Race, Embro Highland Games
✦ **Simcoe:** Norfolk County Fair, Re-enactment of Governor Simcoe visiting Lynnwood Park, Christmas Panorama
✦ **Port Dover:** Human Polar Bear Swim, Spring Fling, Fish Fest, Blessing of the Fleet, Summer Theatre, Friday the Thirteenth, Daffodils in Dover
✦ **Port Rowan:** Call of Spring Amphibians, Tomato Fest, Wildlife Events
✦ **Tillsonburg:** Canada Day, Tillsonburg Air Show, Fathers Day Social, Lions Club Car Show

 Accommodations

✦ **Woodstock:** Hotel/Motel/ B&B/Camping
✦ **Simcoe:** Hotel/Motel/B&B
✦ **Port Dover:** Inns/Cottages/B&B/Camping
✦ **Port Rowan:** Motel/Cottages/B&B/Catholic Retreat & B&B/Camping

 Off-Road Cycling

✦ **Woodstock and Port Rowan:** Yes, refer to "Off-Road Cycling" at the end of this chapter.

 Market Days

✦ **Woodstock:** Saturdays, year round
✦ **Tillsonburg:** Farmer's market held Saturdays, early spring to late fall.

Itinerary: Leg 1 (Woodstock to Simcoe, 64 km). Starting at the corner of Hwy 59 and Juliana Dr in Woodstock, turn [R] onto Hwy 59 and follow it south to Old Stage Rd. At the Hillview Farms composting station, turn [L] onto Old Stage Rd. Sometimes known as the Thames River Rd, it was first used by native people who called it the Detroit Path. During the War of 1812, the road was used by both the British and the American armies. There's even a chest of stolen payroll gold still hidden somewhere along this section of the road!

Cycling east on this gravel road, formerly used by stagecoaches, you come to the village of **Oxford Centre**. Past the village to the south, look at the rough ground to the right. This area has been identified as the site of a native encampment. One kilometre further down the road, you will find the place where several British Army troops set up camp during the War of 1812. Just before reaching Cty Rd 14 you will come across a historic plaque in front of the school on your left. The infamous Elizabeth Bigley, or "Gold Brick Cassie" as she was better known, lived near here. She had the distinction of obtaining more money (about 1.5 million) by fraud and deceit then anyone else in the world up to the time of the Great Train Robbery in England.

Continue riding and cross Cty Rd 14. At Brant Rd 129, turn [L] getting back onto an asphalt surface. Cycle to a [L] turn onto another gravel road, the Sixth Concession Rd. Riding past the large Shur-Gain Research Complex at the West 1/4 Town Line, turn [R] and head to the Harley Rd/Brant Cty Rd 2. At the [T] intersection, turn [L] and pedal a short distance, then make a [R] turn onto Quarter Town Line and enjoy an easy ride to Hatchley Rd. Turn [L] and cycle through a small wetland area before stopping at the white-steepled Northfield Church for a midday break.

At Brant Cty Rd 24, turn [R] and ride south to Norwich Rd/Brant Cty Rd 3. Turn [L] and at the East Quarter Town Line make another [R] turn. The landscape here is very flat and the soil is quite sandy. At one time, thousands of acres in Ontario's "Golden Garden" were devoted to producing half of Canada's flue-cured tobacco crop. Today, with the continuing decline in tobacco, farmers have been turning to alternatives like ginseng and peanuts.

If you need to refill a water bottle, stop at the General Store in **Vanessa**; the proprietor will be more than happy to help you. Back in the late 1800's, a Methodist Church called Bethany stood at Vanessa's present location. Mills were built nearby, and soon the town grew large enough to have a post office. Unable to choose a name, the residents left the decision to Henry Bartholomew, the local post master.

In 1876, Bartholomew made his choice and Vanessa came into being. Bartholomew stayed in Vanessa for 57 years, becoming one of Canada's oldest post masters. The East Quarter Town Line meets Cty Rd 4 in the middle of a bend; turn [R] and then [L] onto W-East Quarter Town Line. Enjoy this flat stretch of blacktop as you ride further into the heart of tobacco country and Norfolk County. Along this section of road, ginseng farms have become quite common and today almost outnumber the tobacco farms. They can be identified by thousands of posts set six feet apart, and covered by a roof of slats. Ginseng is a much-sought-after commodity, in East Asia and in North American health food outlets. It is used as a tonic and cure-all.

Riding past 14th St West and over the Canadian National Railway tracks, signal and make a [L] turn when you reach Hwy 3/Queensway St. Simcoe is only a short distance away. At Hwy 24/Norfolk St turn [R] and ride along the maple-lined streets of downtown Simcoe.

Located at the headwaters of the Lynn River, **Simcoe** was originally known as Bird Town, and celebrated its 100th anniversary in 1978. The town quickly became a focal point for railway development in the late 1800s because of its abundance of agricultural products. Called the "People Place," Simcoe is best known for its annual Christmas "Festival of Lights," which features more than 60 colourful displays.

Itinerary: Leg 2 (Simcoe to Long Point, 56 km). Ride south towards Lake Erie on Hwy 24 past South St (hospital on corner), and turn [L] onto Woodhouse St. At Owen St, turn [R] and follow it to the Lynn Valley Trail in Memorial Park. Turn [L] onto this former rail-line, which was constructed along a pioneer river trail in 1873, and follows the twisting right of ways along the banks of the Lynn River to Port Dover.

Abandoned in 1988, the rail-corridor was purchased as a possible route for future water and sewer lines. In that same year, the Lynn Valley Trail Association was formed, and soon the greenway was developed into a recreational corridor. The rail-line was originally the Port Dover and Lake Huron Railway. It began in Stratford and ran through Tavistock, Hickson, Woodstock, Burgessville, Norwich, Simcoe, Lynn Valley and finally completed its run in Port Dover. Originally a main line, it ultimately became a feeder line to the Wellington, Grey and Bruce, as well as the Grand Trunk lines.

The rail-trail exits into **Port Dover** at the Ivey Flowers Mill, which was founded in 1908 and is one of Canada's oldest and largest growers of roses. Take some time to explore this historic fishing port, which at one time was the largest freshwater fishery in the world. Today more than 30 tugs still continue to ply their trade from here. Before leaving Port Dover, cycle out onto the pier and then browse the many nearby lakefront boutiques. To continue along the lakeshore, head north cycling back through town on Hwy 24. Turn [L] onto Nelson St, which eventually turns into Radical Rd.

Lake Erie will now be on your left. At Port Ryerse Rd turn [L], and ride past the Hay Creek Conservation area. Continue following the road as it heads for the blue waters of Lake Erie. The road descends into Port Ryerse. To continue along the lake, then turn [R] onto Front Rd.

As this leg is not very long, take the time to stop and sample the fresh baked goods at the Port Ryerse General Store. The store is also famous for an event that occurred many years ago, and is explained by the interesting post card article tacked up inside the store. **Port Ryerse** was discoverd by Colonel Samuel Ryerse in the fall of 1795. As he was exploring Lake Erie, he came to a place where a beautiful stream flowed into the lake, in front of a steep hill. Upon landing, he climbed the hill and declared; "Here is where I will settle and on this place where I stand, I will be buried." In 1812 he died and was buried on the spot he had designated. Before leaving Port Ryerse, visit the Anglican Memorial Church and cemetery, found on top of the hill, to the left of the General Store. Built in 1870, the church is an excellent example of board and batten architecture.

Follow Front Rd as it passes the Norfolk Conservation Park (historic plaque) and a Christian retreat. At the Fisher Glen Rd [T] intersection, signal and make a [L] turn, and enjoy the first of two great downhill rides on this leg. At the bottom of the hill, Fisher Glen Rd swings sharply to the right and then climbs to the Normandale Rd. Turn [L] and ride towards **Normandale**. Be sure to stop in at the old cemetery where many Lake Erie ship captains have been buried. The road descends as it arrives in Normandale. At the bottom of the hill, turn [R] onto Mill St (Lakeshore Rd) and ride uphill to the Turkey Point Golf Club. Turn [L] at the top of the hill onto Concession Rd A/Main St and follow it past the golf course and the commemorative stone cairn. This area was originally known as the town of Charlotteville; Fort Norfolk was located here. This former capital of the Western District of Upper Canada is now a ghost town. The thrilling downhill to the lake will leave your brakes smoking at the bottom of the hill!

At the lake, turn [R] onto Cedar St and ride past the sandy public beaches of **Turkey Point**. Thousands of people flock here during the summer months, as this beach has one of the safest swimming areas on the shores of Lake Erie. Cycling to Cty Rd 10, turn [R], and ride uphill. At the top of the hill, turn [L] onto Lakeshore Rd/Front Rd/the Talbot Trail. The view from the bluffs is simply stunning. Cycle past the fish hatchery; then upon reaching Cty Rd 16, turn [L] and then [R] and continue riding Lakeshore Rd/Front Rd towards Port Rowan. While in St. Williams, take a few minutes to ride a short distance north on Cty Rd 16 to see the Octagonal Bell Tower at the United Church. A little further north is the St. Williams Forestry Station.

As Front Rd/Haldimand-Norfolk Rd 42 winds its way through the countryside and eventually straightens out before passing through the village of **Port Rowan** (formally Dutcher's Corners).

At Hwy 59, turn [L] and ride out onto the spit of **Long Point**. (Or turn right and cycle out to the Backus Mills Conservation Area and cycling trails.) Known as "the ship killer," the spit has claimed more than 200 vessels over the years. You could spend days exploring this wetland. When walking in the marsh, wear a long-sleeved shirt and full-legged pants as the area deer carry a tick that may cause Lyme Disease. Three lighthouses have had to be built over the years because the sand spit is constantly shifting. Today, the area has developed into one of the country's best-run nature preserves thanks to the Long Point Company, which is held in high regard for its conservation practices.

Itinerary: Leg 3 (Long Point to Woodstock, 89 km). Starting at the flashing light at the junction of Hwy 59 and Haldimand-Norfolk Rd 42, cycle west along the lake through the village of **Port Royal**, which was named after its sister village in Nova Scotia. Cross Big Creek, turn [R] onto Haldimand-Norfolk Rd. 23, and ride for one kilometre on hard-packed gravel. Almost 14 km later, after cycling through the village of **Glen Meyer**, ride across Regional Rd 38 onto Regional Rd 28. This road is gravel, and the next section is a fun ride. At the [T] intersection at the bottom of the hill, turn [R] and pedal across Otter Creek. Turn [L] at the next [T] intersection and follow the gravel road as it joins the black-top once again at the top of the hill. Continue straight and swing right onto the [RB] a short distance ahead.

Be careful as you ride the railbed, as there will be a number of road crossings before you reach Tillsonburg. Turn [R] at Rokeby Sideroad, (the railbed ahead still has the ties in) and then turn [L] onto Bell Mill Sideroad and ride to Simcoe St. Turn [L] and follow Simcoe St to the stop lights at Tillson Ave. Make a [R] turn and cycle uphill, going past Annandale House to North St, several kilometres ahead. Cross North St and follow Cranberry Rd for a short distance. At the wishing well, turn [R] onto the abandoned Brantford-Norfolk & Port Burwell Railway line.

Main street **Tillsonburg** has an interesting characteristic. Riding straight through the lights at Tillson Ave to join the very wide Broadway St. It was designed to accommodate a team of oxen when they made a U-turn.

Continue along the railbed; as you pass a tract of recently planted pine trees, look for a number of beehives hidden among the trees on the right. Just after riding by Camp Twomoondy, the rail-trail exits into the Springford Ball Park. Cross Cty Rd 19 and Cty Rd 13, and continue riding past some silos to Conc Rd 7. Turn [R] and pedal this gravel road to Middletown Line. Make a [L] turn onto Middletown Line and enjoy a leisurely ride through the town of **Burgessville** and back through the village of Oxford Centre. At the first [T] intersection in Oxford Centre, turn [R] and then bear [L] at the next road. Riding uphill to Patullo Ridge, turn [L] and enjoy the ride past the local fish and game club, to Hwy 59. Turn [R] onto Norwich Ave/Hwy 59, and ride across the Hwy 401 bridge, finishing Leg 3 where you began the first leg 1 of the trip.

4. Shakespeare's Stonetown:
Stratford and St. Marys

This ride is an excellent afternoon excursion that leaves you plenty of time to enjoy an evening show at the Stratford Festival. Beginning along the banks of the Avon River, the tour quickly leaves Stratford behind and follows the Harmony Rd through the lush rolling farmlands of Perth County. It passes through the town of St. Marys with its many architecturally superb stone buildings before heading out of town on the former Grand Trunk Railway. The return route follows another peaceful country road through the hamlet of Avondale before joining the Stratford riverbank trail on its loop around Lake Victoria.

Return Distance: 65 km
No. of recommended legs: 1
Level of Difficulty: 🚲🚲
Surface: Asphalt, some gravel and
several kilometres of hard-packed railbed

Villages/Towns/Cities: Stratford, Harmony, St. Marys, Avonton

Local Highlights: Stratford Festival Theatre, Gallery Stratford, Stratford Perth Museum, St. Marys Museum, Canadian Baseball

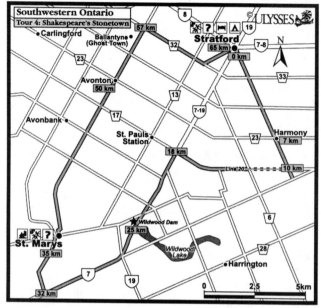

Hall of Fame, St. Marys Quarry, Historic Shakespeare, The Grand Trunk Railway Trail

Bicycle Type: Touring/Hybrid/Mountain

Tour Suggestion: Before setting out, ride the older residential streets near the river and in the downtown core. It's a great way to quickly become familiar with Stratford and its heritage homes. Also, pack a picnic lunch and enjoy it along the banks of the Thames River when visiting St. Marys.

How to get there: Stratford can be reached from the west by following Hwys 402, 81, 19 and 7. From the south, take Hwy 401 to Cty Rd 6, and from the east follow the Queen Elizabeth Way to Hwys 403, 6, 401 and 8. From the north, follow Hwy 19. This tour starts at the William Allman Arena located on Lakeside Dr at Nile St, two blocks north of Ontario St.

Practical Information

Population:
Stratford: 28,000
St. Marys: 5,500

 Tourist Information

✦   **Stratford:** Tourism Stratford, PO Box 818,
88 Wellington St, Stratford, Ont, N5A 6W1,
(519) 271-5140, www.city.stratford.on.ca
✦   **St. Marys:** Town of St. Marys Tourist Bureau,
PO Box 998, St. Marys, Ontario, N4X 1A9,
(519) 284-3500, stonetown.com/stmarys/index.asp

 Bicycle Shops

✦ **Sratford:** Wheel Goods, 29 Ontario St, Stratford, Ont,
N5A 3G7, (519) 273-2001
✦ **St. Marys:** Source For Sports, 154 Queen St E, St. Marys,
Ont, N4X 1B3, (519) 284-1446; Stonetown Cycle Shop,
211 James St, St. Marys, Ont, (519) 284-3095

 Special Sights and Events

✦ **Stratford:** Annual Swan Release and Festival, Kirkin' O'
the Tartan, Heartburn Day, Stratford & Area Collectors
Exhibit, Stratford Fall Fair, Canada Day, Stratford Guild of
Artist StudioTour, Stratford Festival Action, Summer
Psychic Fair, Dragon Boat Festival and Races, Harvest Day
Tours, Monday Night Alternative Film Series, Stratford
Festival Table Talk, HMS Razzmajazz, Concerts in the Park,
Jazz at the Cenotaph, Festival Costume Warehouse Tours;
✦ **St. Marys:** Victoria Day Open House, Fun Fest, Canada
Day, Stonetown Festival, Heritage & Antique Show,
St. Marys Fair, Train Market & Open House.

Accommodations

✦ **Stratford:** Hotel/ Motel/B&B/Camping
✦ **St. Marys:** Inn/B&B/Camping

Off-Road Cycling

✦ **Stratford** and **St. Marys:** Yes, refer to "Off-Road Cycling" at the end of this chapter.

Stratford was originally known as Little Thames, named after the nearby Thames River. The first hotel was built in 1832 and called the Shakespeare Inn, for the large painting of William Shakespeare that hung inside. In late 1832, the town was renamed Stratford after Shakespeare's birthplace because of the Shakespeare Inn's location close to the Avon River. It wasn't until 1953 that the townspeople decided to capitalize on the Shakespearian connection. The first Shakespeare festival was held in a tent along the Avon River; Sir Alec Guinness played Richard III, helping to make the event a huge success. Today, the city's theatre draws well over 500,000 patrons to Stratford on the Avon each year.

Itinerary: Turn [L] out of the parking lot onto Lakeside Dr and ride to the stop lights at Waterloo St. Turn [L] and cycle past Ontario St, which is Stratford's main thorougfare. Coast downhill and ride by the Church Restaurant and several other historic buildings. Veer [L] onto Downie St and pedal past the round church, built that way so the devil can't catch you in the corner! Cross Lorne Ave and begin the ride south, ending up in the village of **Harmony**.

After crossing the Perth Rd 26 the road dips and then climbs a short hill before gradually descending to the next turn. At Line 20, one road north of the [T] intersection, turn [R]. Riding a short distance on gravel, cross Perth Rd. 6/113 (the Embro Rd). Cycling on asphalt once more, Line 20 remains fairly level as it travels past Downie School House No. 10 to a stop sign at Hwy 7.

Turn [L] onto Hwy 7 and begin riding towards St. Marys. The cycling lane is fairly wide as you continue past the St. Pauls Station turnoff and over Wildwood Lake via the Wildwood Dam and past the junction of Hwy 19. A couple of kilometres past Hwy 19, look for the remains of the old Embro to St. Marys railbed. For the more adventurous, the railbed makes an interesting ride that eventually ends in downtown St. Marys.

Riding in a westerly direction, follow Hwy 7 over a set of railway tracks. At Perth Rd 123, turn [R] and follow Water St as it descends into St. Marys. Turn [L] at the sports complex just before the quarries swimming hole, Canada's largest, natural, spring-fed swimming pool, and join the Riverview Walkway. The walkway makes for a nice ride along the river into downtown St. Marys.

Before leaving the trail, stop to admire the view of the Thames River as it flows under one of the town's stone bridges. This is a good place to stop for a rest and a picnic lunch. The trail exits into a parking lot which joins Queen St East; take note of the Mill Wheel by the bridge on the left just before turning [R] onto Queen St.

Laura Secord's brother, Thomas Ingersoll, founded **St. Marys** in 1841. The town was initially called Little Falls for the falls that ran over the rocky ledges in the river. It was named St. Marys in accordance with the wishes of Mrs. Thomas Mercer Jones, who donated funds to pay for the new stone school house. Its nickname, "Stonetown," comes from the many limestone buildings built here between 1850 and the early 1900s. Another feature unique to the city are the two stone viaducts built in the late 1880s to accommodate the railways. It took 20 double teams of horses and 170 both skilled and unskilled men to build the 11 stone pillars that stand more than 213 metres above the river. Some of Canada's more interesting personalities grew up in or around St. Marys, including Sir Arthur Meighen, one of Canada's prime ministers, retailer Timothy Eaton and inventor Thomas Edison, who worked at the local railway station nearby. During Edison's time in St. Marys, he invented an automatic device that transmitted code by the simple turn of a crank. He pawned off his job turning the crank onto a friendly watchman so that he could get some sleep. Everything went well until a message came to hold the train: of course, Edison failed to relay the message. Fortunately for him, the trains saw each other and stopped. He slipped away silently during the investigation and became famous for inventing the phonograph and electric light bulb along with 1,029 other inventions.

The return route follows Queen St East to the lights at Church St S. At the top of the hill in front of you is the old water tower. Built in 1899, it served the town until 1987. Turn [L] and ride past the enormous town hall. In 1891, it was considered the most impressive municipal building in all of Canada. After crossing the bridge, make a [R] turn onto Station St and follow it to the left as it becomes James St N.

An alternative routing would be to turn [L] off the Riverwalk trail and cross over the Thames River. Ride to Ingersoll St, and turn [R] and cycle to the end of the street. Turn [R] again to join the recently completed St. Marys Grand Trunk Recreational Trail. Follow the [RB] over the new Sarnia walkway, go past the Optimist Park, and turn [L] on James St N.

As the James St hill crests, notice all the old Cadillacs on the right side of the road. The name of this county road was recently changed from Cty Rd 19 to Perth Rd 130. The landscape is predominantly flat until it descends into **Avonton**. Just before turning [R] onto Perth Rd. 32, look for the stone cairn on the left side of the road. Erected in 1929, it marks the settlement of Ballantyne which is now a ghost town.

Just before passing O'Loane Ave, the road dips and then climbs to Queensland Rd. If you're interested, you can ride the single track trails of the T.J. Dolan Natural Area, which are a short distance down O'Loane Ave on the right, and eventually exit onto John St.

Turn [L] onto Queensland Rd, follow it as it swings right past Hamlet Estates and becomes John St. Just a short distance past the hospital, the street descends to the entrance of the T.J. Dolan Park, which is where you find the O'Loane Ave single track. Turn [R] onto T. J. Dolan Dr, just before the road crosses the Avon River. Cycling along the river bank, ride across St. Vincent St and join the paved pathway. When the pathway ends, continue along the river and walk through a wooden turn-stile into the Shakespearean Gardens. Directly opposite the woolen mill's tall chimney is a magnificent old maple which is now beginning to lean out over the Avon River. The garden pathway exits onto Huron St via a few stairs. Turn [L] onto Huron St and cross over the Avon River. Make a [R] turn onto William St. At Waterloo St, turn [R] and, just before crossing back over the river, join the Lake Victoria recreational trail on the left side of the road. The river trail is a perfect finish to a day in Perth County. It eventually exits onto Lakeside Dr, where you swing [R] and follow the road back along Lake Victoria to the Stratford Arena.

---

5. Two Sunsets, a River and a Trail: Goderich and Scenic Huron County

---

With a vantage point high above the picturesque Maitland Valley, this tour begins at the Goderich Airport, then quickly joins a multi-use railbed. Cycling east into the heart of Huron County, you will pass through several wetland areas before riding a logging road south along the Maitland River. At Windy Hill, enjoy a thrilling downhill ride to the blue waters of Little Lakes and a historic bridge crossing at Balls Bridge. Following an undulating county road back into Goderich, the tour completes its loop by rejoining the railtrail as it crosses the mentesetung Bridge and descends to the sandy shores of Lake Huron.

Return Distance: 55 km
No. of recommended legs: 1
Level of Difficulty: 🚲 🚲 🚲
Surface: Re-conditioned railbed, jeep trail,
gravel roads, asphalt

Villages/Towns/Cities: Goderich, Benmiller

Local Highlights: Goderich Historic Gaol, Governor's House, Unique Town Square, Marine Museum, Huron County Pioneer Museum, Tiger Dunlop's Tomb, Goderich Harbour, Maitland Woods Hiking Trails, St. Christopher Beach and Harbour

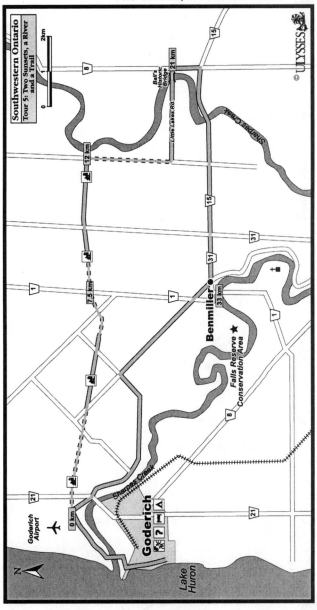

Practical Information

Population:
Goderich: 8,000

 Tourist Information

The Country of Huron Planning and Development Department, Court House Sq, Goderich, Ont, N7A 1M2, (519) 524-2188 or 524-6600, www.huron.org/tctg

 Bicycle Shops

Goderich Cyclery, 625 Pentland Ave, Goderich, Ont, N7A 3X8, (519) 524-4720

 Special Sights and Events

Canada Day Celebrations, Celtic Roots Festival, Goderich Festival of Arts and Crafts, Maritime Heritage Weekend, Blue Water Kennel Obedience Trials, Blyth Rutabaga Festival, Huron Pioneer Threshers Steam Show, Market (on Saturdays, seasonal)

 Accommodations

Hotel/Motel/B&B/Camping

Boardwalk, Menesetung Bridge, Lighthouse Park, The Laithwaite Legacy and Apple Park, Benmmiller Conference Centre, Blyth Festival Summer Theatre, Clinton Railway School on Wheels

Recommended Bicycles: Mountain/Hybrid

Tour Suggestions: A good place to park your car is Goderich airport, located just off Hwy 21 north of the Maitland River. Spend some time cycling the unique downtown core area of Goderich

How to Get There: East of Kitchener take Hwy 401 to Kitchener exit at Hwy 8 and continue to Goderich. From Michigan & Sarnia take Hwy 402 east and Hwy 21 N; from London take Hwy 4 north and Hwy 8 west.

Years ago, visiting royalty called **Goderich** "one of the prettiest towns in Canada," and the same may still be said today. It is a town of tradition, heritage and technology tied together by the expanding rim of its unique hub and spoke-like downtown square. When town founders Dr. William "Tiger" Dunlop and John Galt looked down on Lake Huron from the bluffs in 1827, they were most likely the first new settlers to enjoy a unique Canadian site. Goderich is the only place in Canada where you can see the sun set twice, first from the shores of Lake Huron and then from the bluffs high above the lake. Today Goderich's deep harbour is a busy port of call where massive ocean vessels can bee seen as they are guided to the landing dock for loading by powerful tug boats.

Itinerary: From the Goderich airport parking lot turn [L] (east) onto Airport Rd. Turn [R] just before the modern windmill, which is at the fourth road from the airport. As this gravel road curves to the left, access the Tiger Dunlop and Maitland Trail [RB] via the gate at the bend.

Turn [L] onto the hard-packed [RB] that crosses Hwy 21. Now the [RB] is called the Auburn Rail Trail. The riding surface of the two-lane jeep road is very hard, through extensive use, and can be slippery during the spring.

The first road crossing is 2 km away: You will have noticed that you have been cycling up a slight grade. After passing a barn with two huge and two small silos, the [RB] enters a marshy area, which is a great place to stop and stretch your legs. If your timing is right, you can load up on fresh raspberries that line both sides of the trail.

The [RB] continues to climb, and it turns into single-track just past the third road crossing. As you enter another wetland area known as the McGaw Ponds, the bush closes in over the trail. Look for a windmill and a dilapidated old bridge on your left. Just before the second bridge crossing the [RB] reverts to dual track and becomes a much easier ride.

On this portion of the ride you will come across gravel pits, another road crossing, a railroad siding with tracks and bluebird nesting boxes that lead you first along the trail into a grove of cedar and then through sweet-smelling spruce. Again, the [RB] changes into a jeep trail just before another road crossing.

At Blind Line you have three options. If you turn [L], it is an uphill climb to Cty Rd 25; or you can go straight and the rail trail ends at the Maitland River, which is an excellent spot for a morning break. The third option is to continue the tour. By turning [R] at the Blind Line, you will follow it up and downhill (mostly uphill) over some rough terrain and past a marvellous view of the Maitland River Valley, which leads to Windy Hill. Keeping to the left, enjoy the cooling breeze as you swiftly descend down this gravel road and turn [L] onto aptly named Little Lakes Rd. Enjoy the scenery surrounding these two small inland lakes and take some time to look for the sunbathing turtles.

Before reaching Hwy 8, enjoy a long gradual descent to Balls Historic Bridge. Spared from replacement, this iron bridge still has wooden boards that make up the road and there is nothing quite like the thuddy-d-thud sound of rubber hitting wood when you cross this beautiful section of the Maitland River.

Turn [R] onto Huron Rd 8 for an uphill climb before turning [R] onto Huron Rd 15. The striking scenery includes some dramatic hills and many other breathtaking highlights that can be enjoyed along this road. Just opposite Boundary Bridge, the entrance to the Maitland Trail will be on your right. Take some time to examine some of the old stones marking the site of the Colborne Evangelical Church and Cemetery. Huron Rd 15 turns into Huron Rd 31 just before reaching the hamlet of **Benmiller**.

Follow Huron Rd 31. Keep to your right, and notice the pretty little walking area along Sharpe's Creek opposite the Benmiller Inn and Conference Centre. Continue along Huron Rd 31 to Falls Reserves Conservation area, a red barn, a number of cemeteries and Riverside Park. When the Goderich water tower comes into view just around the next bend you will be treated to a great view of the Maitland River. The river was originally named Menesetung meaning "Laughing Water," by the Chippewa referring to the sound of water running over the rocks. From here, downhill to Goderich – and what a terrific ride! Cross Hwy 21 to what appears to be a dead-end road, but is actually the Tiger Dunlop Heritage Trail. Follow the trail, with the wetlands of the Maitland on your left and the Tiger Dunlop Tomb above you to your right.

Continue up the hill following the trail as it turns into single track. Eventually you will have to carry your bicycle up a short flight of wooden stairs. At the top of the stairs, turn [L] onto the [RB] and follow it to the Menesetung Bridge. Reconditioned by local citizens, the bridge was originally built by the C.P.R. in 1907. It was the longest bridge in Ontario at the time and was in service until 1988. Note the 22-ton commemorative rock on the far side of the bridge.

Cross the bridge and turn [R] onto North Harbour Rd, taking some time to explore the harbour area before rejoining the [RB] to the left of the grain elevators. At the far end of the harbour is the Sifto Salt Mine. Salt was discovered in the area in 1866 by Samuel Platt in what is now referred to as Saltford just upstream across Hwy 21. The mine shafts at the mouth of the river are presently 1700 feet deep, extending westward through a bed of salt that is 30 metres thick and produces over 3.25 million tonnes of salt per year.

To rejoin the [RB], notice a series of cement steps high above you on your left, just before entering the harbour area. Carefully cross the railroad track and carry your bike up the stairs from where you can almost see the top of the grain elevators. Follow the trail to the Goderich Harbour which has been active since 1840. Upon entering the harbour, you will see the C.P.R. Station built in 1907 to link Guelph and Goderich. Cool, refreshing winds off Lake Huron accompany you as you continue to follow the road along the lakeshore. The trail ends at Christopher Beach, where there is lots of sand, clean water and washroom facilities.

Retrace your steps to the Menesetung Bridge. Cross it, and immediately turn [L] onto the Maitland Heritage Tree Trail. At the first split in the trail, keep to the left, eventually arriving at the magnificent heritage red oak tree, which is 30 metres high, three metres around and 218 years old. It is truly a sight to behold! If you turn left here, you will end up at the marina.

There are two different ways to return to the starting point. Either turn [R] at the oak tree and follow the single-track back uphill to the [RB], retracing your steps to the airport, or follow this trail up to the trail access point on your left, which will take you out to Mill Rd. Follow this road to Airport Rd, then turn [R] towards the parking lot.

---

6. Down by the Old Mill Stream:
London and Dorchester

Enjoy a ride on the London Bikeway, which originates in downtown London and makes its way along the Thames River to historic Hamilton Rd. Dip your feet in Dorchester's old mill pond at midday before following the road back into London. Then join the northern portion of the recreational trail to cycle along residential streets, paved trails and single track before returning to Greenway Park.

Return Distance: 55 km
No. of recommended legs: 1
Level of Difficulty: 🚲
Surface: Recreational trail, asphalt roads
and 200 metres of single track

Villages/Towns/Cities: London, Dorchester

Local Highlights: Banting Museum and Education Centre, Eldon House, Fanshawe Conservation Area and Pioneer Village, London Regional Art Gallery, Middlesex County Building, Royal Canadian Regiment Museum, Imax Theatre,

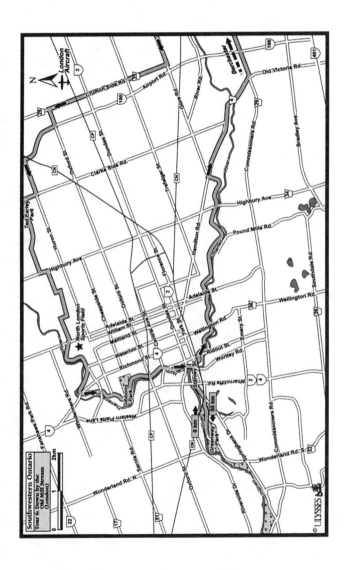

Ska-Nah-Doht Indian Village, Springbank Park, Story Book Gardens, University of Western Ontario, Archival Teaching and Research Museum, Bellamere Country Market, Canadian Medical Hall of Fame, Children's Museum, Grand Theatre, Guy Lombardo Music Centre, Museum of Archaeology, Old Courthouse and Gaol, Victoria Park, Novaks Periscope, Western Fair Raceway

Recommended Bicycles: Touring/Hybrid/Mountain

Tour Suggestions: This is a nice, easy ride that lets you enjoy a picnic lunch along the banks of the Dorchester mill pond.

How To Get There: There are four exits for London from Hwy 401. This tour starts at Greenway Park. To get there, take the Wellington Rd N exit off Hwy 401. At Horton St, turn left and cross Wharncliffe Rd S onto Springbank Dr. Turn right at Greenside Ave and park at the no-charge parking lot on the right.

Colonel John Grave Simcoe founded **London** in 1792 and named it after the great city in England. In 1881, it was the site of one of the worst marine disasters in Canada when the steamboat *Victoria* overturned, taking the lives of 200 people. Today, the city is best known as the home of the University of Western Ontario. Nicknamed the "Forest City" because of its location at the Forks of the Thames River, it has managed to maintain a "green" image thanks to constant conservation efforts and careful urban planning. Currently, the city boasts more than 50,000 trees and over 607 hectares of parks, 405 hectares of which are along the Thames River. London has also kept up with current trends, developing a recreational highway that provides safe cycling routes to almost anywhere in the city.

Itinerary: Facing the Thames River and the recreational trail, turn [R] onto the trail, keeping the river on your left. Ride through the Greg Curnoe tunnel, which exits onto Evergreen Ave. The tunnel was named for artist and cyclist Greg Curnoe, who was killed by a truck while riding with his local club in 1992. Keep left and turn onto Riverview Ave. At O'Brien St, rejoin the trail and ride past Her Majesty's Canadian Ship Prevo, the river; continue along the pathway as it loops left in a clover leaf pattern to join the trail in Ivy Park and the London Peace Gardens below.

Pass under Stanley St and continue along the trail as it merges with the sidewalk at Horton St. Just after the Horton St bridge, swing right and get back onto the recreational pathway. The smell of hops fills the air as you pass the Labatt Brewery. Look for the falls on your right just before crossing Richmond St to join the South Branch Bikeway.

The trail ends at Nelson St; follow it to the end before joining Wellington St. Turn [R], ride across the bridge, and then quickly turn [L] into the Watson St Park. The river is again on your left until you reach the Adelaide St loop.

Cross the bridge at Adelaide St and follow the pathway as it passes under Highbury Ave. At Meadowlily Rd N, the trail continues just to the right of where you exited onto the street. Finally, ending at the Pottersburg Creek Pollution Control Plant, bear [L] and follow the driveway up to Hamilton Rd.

Make a [R] turn onto old Hamilton Rd and ride to the stop lights at Commissioners Rd and Old Victoria Rd. Turn [L] and follow Hamilton Rd through the hamlet of Nilestown into the village of **Dorchester**. The road begins to descend at the Dorchester Golf and Country Club. At the bottom of the hill on your right is the mill silo and above you is the old Mill Pond and Dam. The pond itself is a pretty wetland area that only takes 30 minutes to walk around. Remember to lock up your bicycle. If you get lucky, you just might meet the local gaggle of swans.

The town was first settled in 1820 and was called Edwardsburgh and then Dorchester Station before the name was shortened to Dorchester in 1861. Today, Dorchester is a quiet bedroom community that sits high above the Thames River, but in 1925 the town was in turmoil. Dorchester's Donnybrook Fields was the site of the Ku Klux Klan's first public recruitment campaign ever held in Canada. Apparently, over a 100 residents from nearby London took the oath of the Klan before an altar of flame.

Practical Information

Population:
London: 320,099
Dorchester: 2,756

 Tourist Information

✦ **London:** London Visitor and Convention Bureau, 300 Dufferin Ave, London, Ont, N6B 1Z2, (519) 661-5000 or (519) 661-6156, www.city.london.on.ca;
✦ **Dorchester:** North Dorchester Township Offices, PO Box 209, 4305 Hamilton Rd, Dorchester, Ont, N0L 1G0, (519) 268-7334, www.tnd.on.ca.

Bicycle Shops

✦ **London:** All Seasons Sports & Cycle, 790 Dundas St, N5W 2Z7, (519) 660-6932; Bicycle Planet, 176 Horton St, N6B 1K8, (519) 858-8647; Champion Bicycle Sales & Service, 592 Adelaide St N, N6B 3J8, (519) 679-1266; Cyclepath, 737 Richmond St, N6A 3H6, (519) 432-2208; Cyzzle Cycles, 360 Springbank Dr, N6J 1G5, (519) 657-1729 ; Dirt Devil Brothers, 214 Emerson St, N5Z 3L8, (519) 685-6526; First Cycleworks, 525 First St, N5V 1Z5, (519) 455-9124; Lloyd's Cycle & Repairs, 924 Oxford St E, N5Y 3J9, (519) 452-3881; Missing Link Cycle & Ski, 1283 Commissioners St W, N6K 1C9, (519) 641-5056; To-Wheels, 134 Dundas St, London, Ont, N6A 1G1, (519) 663-9447; Racer Sportif, 353 Clarence St, London, Ont, N6A 3M4, (519) 434-5652; South London Cycle, 479 McGregor Ave, N6J 2S8, (519) 433-4275.

Special Sights and Events

London International Air Show, Canada Day, Balloon Festival, Folk Festival, Rib Fest, Panorama, Pioneer Village seasonal events, Western Fair, The Celtic Gathering

 Accommodations

Hotel/Motel/B&B/Camping.

 Off-Road Cycling

Yes, please refer to "Off-Road Cycling" at the end of this chapter.

Ride back to Hamilton Rd and turn [R], then cycle uphill and make a [L] turn onto Bridge St. Once across the river, turn [L] onto Catherine St (Middlesex 49). Cycle past two churches and the Dorchester Day Use Conservation Area, turn [R] onto Middlesex Rd 32, also known as Shaw Rd.

Ride to Knoch Manufacturing and turn [L] onto Gore Rd. The next several kilometres take you through hydro alley. At Crumlin Side Rd, turn [R] and follow this well-used road past Diamond Aircraft to the four-way stop at the London Airport. Turn [L] onto Oxford St and then turn [R] at the stop lights. Take Airport Rd, and make a [L] turn at the Huron St [T] intersection. Follow the road and merge [R] onto Clarke Rd. Look for Ted Earley Park, opposite LaFarge on your left. Ride across the road and join the northern portion of the London Bikeway.

The trail exits the park onto Cayuga Cresc. Bear left and follow the road until you turn [R] onto Oakville Ave. At Chippewa Dr, turn [L] and ride to Idylwood Rd. Make a [L] turn and then swing [R] onto Jensen Rd. At the Highbury Ave [T]

intersection, turn [L] and then move into the right-hand lane at the stop lights. Turn [R] onto Fuller St and ride past the local ambulance station into residential London. At McNay St turn [L], and then [R] onto Melsandra Ave. Make a [R] turn onto Barker St and cycle to a [L] turn onto Kipps Lane. At the lights, cross Adelaide St and join the recreational trail in the North London Sports Field.

Cycle along a narrow dirt road, and follow it as it bears [R] and joins an asphalt path. Turn [L] onto the path and ride towards a large building that stands majestically high on top of a hill. At an interesting junction where the trail seems to end, keep [L] and cross the large culvert. Ride up the dirt hill that exits to the tennis courts at St. Peters Seminary. Slip up to the driveway next to the church and follow it out onto Huron St. Turn [R] onto Huron St and then turn [R] once again at Waterloo St, riding past Kings College onto Epworth Ave. At Richmond St, turn [R] and follow the road past the entrance to T.J.F. Roth Park. Just before crossing the river, access the path on your right and follow it under the Richmond St Bridge.

This is perhaps the nicest portion of the recreational trail as it makes its way back towards London's downtown core. As the trail exits onto Parkway St, bear [R] and ride to Huron St. Enter the gates by turning [R] onto the trail and ride across a wide-open field into Gibbons Park. Keep [R] at the [Y] intersection and continue to follow the river and trail as it crosses Black Friars St next to the oldest wrought-iron bridge in Ontario, which dates back to 1875.

At John Labatts Park, Harris Park, cross Riverside Dr and continue to follow the trail along the river. When you get back to the Peace Park/Ivy Park, follow the clover leaf back over the walkway used at the beginning of this leg. Once over the bridge, swing [R] and pedal past the familiar HMCS London. Continue to follow the trail as it descends back into Riverforks Park. The trail arcs left, passes the Children's Museum, and then exits onto O'Brien St. Retrace your route from here to get back onto the Terry Fox Pkwy and to Greenway Park.

Optional Side Trip: Once back at Greenway Park, remain on the recreational pathway and ride west, going past the Greenway

Park and the Pollution Control plant. Springbank Park has lots of winding pathways from which you can hear the joyful shouts of children visiting the world-famous Story Book Gardens and the musical merry-go-round along the Thames.

OFF-ROAD CYCLING

Public Trails

Goderich

Tiger Dunlop and G.A.R.T. (12 km)
Surface: Jeep Rd/Loose surface
Beginning: Goderich Airport or Goderich Harbour
Contact: Maitland Trail Association
Box 443
Goderich, Ontario N7A 4C7
☎(519) 524-2188

Sarnia

Howard Watson Nature Trail (16 km)
Surface: Original Railbed
Beginning: Exmouth St to outskirts of Camalachie
Contact: Sarnia-Lambton Chamber of Commerce, 224 North Vidal St, Sarnia, Ontario N7T 5Y3, ☎(519) 336-3232.

Point Edward Waterfront Trail (1 km)
Surface: Loose/hardpacked
Beginning: Waterfront Park (Bluewater Bridge) and Canatara Park
Contact: Village of Point Edward, 36 St. Clair St, Point Edward, Ontario N7V 4G8, ☎(519) 337-3021.

Simcoe

Lynn Valley Trail (8 km)
Surface: Original Railbed/hardpacked
Beginning: Simcoe and Port Dover
Contact: Lynn Valley Trail Association, 137 Decou Rd, Simcoe, Ontario N3Y 4K2, ☎(519) 428-3292.

St. Marys
Grand Trunk Railway Trail
P.O. Box 998, St. Marys, Ontario N4X 1B6, ☎(519) 284-3556.

Windsor (8.5 km)

Ganatchio Trail/Little River Corridor
Surface: Asphalt/some loose surface
Beginning: Tecumseh to Isabelle Place
Contact: City of Windsor Parks and Recreation, 2450 McDougall St., Windsor, Ontario N8X 3N6, ☎(519) 253-2300.

Windsor/Leamington Area to Ruthven

Essex County Greenway (42 km)
Surface: Original Railbed
Beginning: Town of Old Castle and Town of Ruthven
Contact: Essex Region Conservation Authority, 360 Fairview Ave West, Essex, Ontario N8M 1Y6, ☎(519) 255-6530.

Woodstock

The Pines (40 km)
Hickson Trail (12 km)
Grand Truck Railbed (5 km)
Surface: Single track, some technical areas
Beginning: Oxford Rd. 4 and Twp Rd. 4
Contact: City of Woodstock Cycling Club, 590 Dundas St, Woodstock, Ontario N4S 1C8, ☎(519) 539-3681.

Resort and Conservation Trails

Alymer/St. Thomas Area
Archie Coulter Conservation Area (4 km of trail): Catfish Creek Conservation Authority, RR 5, Aylmer, Ontario N5H 2R4, ☎(519) 773-9037.

Grand Bend
Pinery Provincial Park (14 km of trail): RR 2, Grand Bend, Ontario, N0M 1T0, ☎(519) 234-2220.

Long Point/Lake Erie Area
Backus Woods (13 km of trail): Long Point Region Conservation Authority, RR 3, Simcoe, Ontario N3Y 4K2, ☎(519) 428-4623 Backus Woods ☎(905)-586-2201.

London
Boler Mountain: 689 Griffith St, London, Ontario N6K 2S5, ☎(519) 657-8822.

Chatham Area
Rondeau Provincial Park (23 km of trail): Ministry of Natural Resources, P.O. Box 1168, Chatham, Ontario N7M 5L8, ☎(519) 354-7340, Park Office ☎(519) 674-5405.

Exeter Area
Hay Swamp Management Area (38 km of trail): Ausable Bayfield Conservation Authority, P.O. Box 2410, Exeter, Ontario N0M 1S7, ☎(519) 235-2610.

Simcoe/Port Ryerse/ Lake Erie Area
Hay Creek Conservation Area (4 km of trail): Long Point Region Conservation Authority, RR 3, Simcoe, Ontario N3Y 4K2, ☎(519) 428-4623.

Simcoe/Nanticoke Area
Haldimand Conservation Area (3 km of trail): Long Point Region Conservation Authority, RR 3, Simcoe, Ontario N3Y 4K2, ☎(519) 428-4623.

St. Marys
Wildwood Conservation Area (24 km of trails): Upper Thames River Conservation Authority, RR 2, St. Marys, N4X 1C5, ☎(519) 284-2292.

St. Thomas/Aylmer Area
Springwater Conservation Area (12 km of trail):Catfish Creek Conservation Authority, RR 5, Aylmer, Ontario N5H 2R4, ☎(519) 773-9037.

FESTIVAL COUNTRY

Festival Country meanders along the north shore of Lake Erie from Port Rowan to Fort Erie, passing through the fruit and wine producing region of Niagara, and finally touching the time-honoured traditions of Ontario's Mennonite community.

THE TOURS

7. Quarries and Cataracts: Elora to Cataract Rail Trail Adventure

Like a good story, this ride begins dramatically in Elora, and follows an interesting and varied path through the countryside that concludes in a thrilling finale at the thundering falls of Cataract. Try to imagine what it was like to ride the rails in late 1800s as you cycle along this former branch line of the Credit Valley Railway. In 1879, the railway ran from Elora to Cataract Junction acting as a primary feeder line for the main line from Toronto to Orangeville.

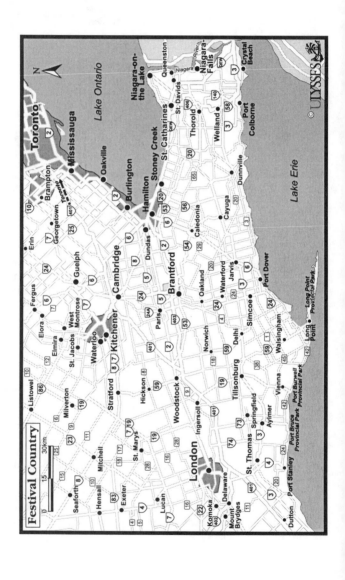

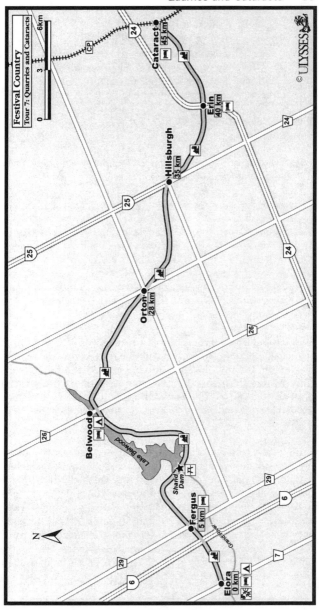

Return Distance: 92 km
No. of recommended legs: 2
Level of Difficulty: 🚲 🚲
(slightly rough terrain in some sections)
Surface: Reconditioned railbed, slightly loose to
hard packed, some undeveloped portions, jeep trail

Villages/Towns/Cities: Elora, Fergus, Belwood, Orton, Erin, Cataract

Local Highlights: Elora Gorge & Quarries, Cataract Falls, portions of the Niagara Peninsula

Recommended Bicycles: Mountain/Hybrid/(Touring)

Tour Suggestions: The tour can be completed in one day by strong riders or by travelling with two vehicles and leaving them at opposite ends of the railbed. If you decide to do the tour in two legs, cycle from Elora to Cataract on the first day, overnighting on the way back in Belwood or Fergus. Complete the return ride to Elora on the following day leaving plenty of time to enjoy this unique village.

How To Get There: From Hwy 401 take Hwy 6 N (exit 295) to the village of Elora. At the stoplights turn [R] onto Metcalfe St and follow the road, keeping to your left. At the traffic lights turn [R] onto Mill St, and travel approximately 1.5 km. After passing the quarries, take the next [L], Gerrie Road; a 20-vehicle parking lot is located a short distance from the Highway on your right.

Elora is a place with some amazing and extreme physical features that include a dramatically carved gorge, caves, rock ledges, islet rocks and natural waterfalls. Originally called Irvine but was better known by its nickname "City of Rocks," the town was first settled in the winter of 1817 by Roswell Matthew. This pioneer had cleared 30 acres of land by 1832 before selling out to William Gilkison. Renaming the town "Elora" after his brother's ship, which was named after the famous Cave Temples of India, Gilkison made his influence felt across the province when he assisted in the drafting of human

Practical Information

Population:
Elora: 3000
Fergus: 6,900
Erin: 2500

 Tourist Information

✦ **Elora:** The Elora & District Chamber of Commerce, 1 MacDonald Sq, PO Box 814, Elora, Ont, N0B 1S0, (519) 846-9841
✦ **Fergus:** 100 Queen St, PO Box 3, Fergus, Ont, N1M 2W7, (519) 843-5140
✦ **Erin:** Town of Erin, PO Box 250, Hillsburg, Ont, N0B 1Z0, (519) 855-4407.

 Bicycle Shops

✦ **Elora:** Salem Cyclery, 11 Mill St E, Elora, Ont, N0B 1S0, (519) 846-8446
✦ **Fergus:** Stryder Sports, 216 St. Andrew St W, Fergus, Ont, N1M 1N7, (519) 843-5773

 Special Sights and Events

✦ **Elora:** Elora Festival - A Celebration in Song (July/ August), Elora Gorge Conservation Area, Elora Quarry Conservation Area, Islet Rock, Wellington County Museum and Archives
✦ **Fergus:** Scottish Festival, Fergus Fall Fair, Summer Theatre, unique Saturday & Sunday Market, Richlyn Botanical Gardens
✦ **Erin:** Cruise & Bloomin Fest.

Accommodations

✦ **Elora and Fergus:** Camping/B&B/Motel
✦ **Erin:** B&B/Motels.

right statements that include representation by population and
the secret ballot.

Itinerary: The [RB] at Elora has recently been reconditioned and
is hard packed. Three cyclists can ride side by side. Travelling
east for half a kilometre from the trail head, look for a cattle
crossing sign and be prepared to stop if these gentle beasts are
encountered. Notice the abundant wood rail fencing and the
gentle aroma of the nearby cedar trees.

When the GSW water tower appears, you are close to **Fergus**.
Entering town, the water tower is on your [L] and the [RB] exits
onto Hill St. Follow Hill St turning [L] onto Maiden Lane, look
for the four-armed tree next to the stop sign at Garafraxa St.
Turn [R] and proceed [E] along Garafraxa St crossing Hwy 6
(St. Davids St North).

Initially called Little Falls, Fergus was renamed after a Scottish
lawyer. Many of the town's original buildings (circa 1850s) in
the downtown area and along the Grand River have survived.
Your time is well spent exploring the village. Fergus is also
home to the oldest curling club in Ontario, and to the pauper's
grave of drunkard George Celphane who is best remembered
for the gospel song "The Ninety and Nine."

Following Garafraxa St, turn [L] onto Gartshore and watch for
the broadcasting tower. Rejoin the [RB] on your right just
before the industrial park. Small information centres at various
spots along this trail reveal tidbits of information about the area
and local wildlife, as well as the Conservation Ontario Motto:
"Leave Tracks not Trash."

Over the last 6 km, the elevation has been rising. A great deal
of planning has gone into designing this greenway. There are
gates at most of the [RB] access points to the road, but it is

still recommended to approach these areas with caution, especially when cycling with children.

A keen eye and good hearing will find plenty to see along the way: a triangular corral, dog kennels, broken windmills and far off in the distance, a castle. Actually, the castle is the 50-year-old Shand Dam. Built in 1942 as Canada's first flood control project, the dam created the Belwood Conservation Area. A beautiful lake is on your left, but on your right is a 75-metre-drop to the Grand River. Make use of the park's comfortable rest area and washrooms on the far side of the dam.

Continue towards the park's entrance; the [RB] is to the left of the gate booth. This section of the trail is multi-use and you will encounter hikers, walkers and horseback riders during nice weather. There is a direction post a short distance past the park entrance. A word of advice: stick to the [RB] because most directions are for snowmobilers and cross private land so they are not recommended for cyclists in the summer months.

Hugging the lake's shoreline, the [RB] passes an old mill at the 18 km trail mark. Cross Cty Rd 26, which emerges just to the south of Belwood. Some camping and B&B facilities can be found in this pretty little town.

Now the [RB] dwindles to little more than a cattle trail. Hard packed, sometimes double track, and often overgrown, it is apparent that it has only recently begun to be used again. This problem will disappear as more and more of the railbed is reconditioned. Notice the two large homes high above you on your right as the railbed climbs and then descends to the White Pines of Springhill Farms. Single track draws you forward, and by the time you reach the 20 dead trees on your left, you have gained 150 metres in elevation. As you approach Cty Rd 3, take a few minutes to admire a perfect scene for a painter's canvas: an old stone house, a pond and a worn-out, upside-down rowboat. Keep an eye out for a rather large, wild potbelly pig that might be wandering the trail. As you approach a blue greystone house standing guard, the [RB] once again has become double track. The elevation starts to fall allowing you to coast by a house that looks like a red-roofed barn, into the village of **Orton**. Fresh baked goods and coffee are available at the General Store.

At Orton, the [RB] changes back into hard-packed single track that feels as though it's rolling up and down. Arriving in Hillsburgh, you will notice a very unique pond to your left that is only a few inches deep; on your right is Morett's Fine Furniture. Follow the [RB] over a wooden bridge crossing Hwy 25, then cycle through some loose, sandy stretches before crossing Cty Rd 22 onto an improved hard pack railbed.

This portion of the trail is an excellent ride that takes you past a sand and gravel operation, the ruins of an old stone barn and through a corridor of sweet-smelling cedar. Listen carefully for a babbling brook. The odour of burning steel lets you know that the town of **Erin** is nearby. Spend some time in this interesting little village poetically named after Ireland. At Hwy 24 the [RB] is under construction for about a kilometre, but quickly changes back to an excellent riding surface and then becomes a well-worn jeep road. You will pass by some rusty farm implements on your left, a cattle crossing sign and a stagnant pond. Cross Mississauga Road to enter one of Ontario's best kept secrets, the Forks of the Credit Provincial Park.

The [RB] is well used and hard packed but, be careful; as you travel further into the park, the [RB] is beginning to wash away in some spots. You will come across a spectacular view of the valley – try and pick out the fast flowing Credit River. If you are lucky, you might see a train making its way up towards the [RB]. At the [T] junction, turn left down into the valley, then cross a wooden bridge and follow the path to Cataract Falls. It's well worthwhile to explore this area. Notice the striking and rugged exposed rock of the Niagara Escarpment and the massive rolling topography created by glacial deposits. Turning right at the [T] junction leads you out of the park and into the village of **Cataract**, where you will find a quaint little English-style inn.

8. Dundas Valley and the Niagara Escarpment (including Webster and Tew's Falls)

Find hidden treasure in the heart of industrial Ontario! To the towering heights of the Niagara Escarpment, which surrounds and protects the dramatically formed Dundas Valley, this area of the province offers cyclists a little bit of everything; awesome single track, reclaimed railbed and wildly winding roads that descend into a developed, urban transportation system that has been designed to accommodate cyclists' needs. Here country meets the city – and it works!

Return Distance: 40 km
No. of recommended legs: 1
Level of Difficulty: 🚲 🚲 🚲,
(a few steep hills to climb)
Surface: Asphalt, hard-packed railbed

Villages/Towns/Cities: Dundas, Hamilton, Flamborough

Local Highlights: Royal Botanical Gardens, Dundurn Castle, Canadian Warplane Heritage Museum, Hamilton Place, Dyment's Pumpkin Patch, Copp's Coliseum, Whitehern, Museum of Steam & Technology, Westfield Heritage Centre, Hess Village, Battlefield House, Art Gallery of Hamilton, Dundas Valley Rail Trail System

Recommended Bicycles: Hybrid/Mountain/Touring

Tour Suggestions: Since the tour starts at Webster's Falls in Dundas, pack a lunch and plan to spend some time cycling some of the 40 km of trail in the Dundas Valley.

How To Get There: Take Hwy 403 to Main St W/Hwy 2/8, then turn left onto King St/Hwy 8 which turns into Brock Rd. Turn right onto Harvest Rd then right onto Short Rd, following it to the Spencer Gorge parking lot. There may be a small parking fee.

Often referred to as "Valley Town" because of its location, **Dundas** was first settled in 1787 by Anne Morden, an United

Empire Loyalist widow who along with her family was granted a large piece of land that now amounts to the north half of the town. Originally named Coote's Paradise after Capt. Thomas Coote who often hunted in the area, the town has seen prosperity come and go over the years. In 1837, the opening of the Dejardins Canal encouraged shipping by linking Dundas to Lake Ontario. The area's rapid development quickly levelled out with the advent of rail transportation in 1853. Today, the town tucked away in the shadow of Hamilton and its billowing smoke stacks, still has a strong sense of community and provides a unique natural playground for the surrounding population.

Itinerary: To the left of the parking lot entrance are a number of interesting gravestones and the entrance to the Bruce Trail. Turn [R], and proceed to an opening in the wire fence. Keeping right on the trail, and watch the wooden steps as the trail descends to Webster Falls. Exiting onto an open field, cross the stone bridge; to the right is Webster's Falls Road, while Webster's Falls is to the left. Look for the stairs that invite you to explore the Webster's Falls gorge.

Follow Webster's Falls Road as it exits out onto Hwy 8, then turn [R] and follow the road north as it turns into Brock Road, turning [L] onto Crooks Hollow Rd (Old Brock Road)/Harvest Road. As it bends to the right and starts to climb, bear [L] keeping near the creek. Enjoy the rolling hills and scenic stops along Crooks Hollow Road, which include the remains of Canada's first paper mill, the Darney Grist Mill and the huge Christie Reservoir further upstream.

Legs will be burning as this rolling road offers up some short stiff climbs. Turn [R] onto Hwy 8 and [L] onto Weirs Lane. As you pass the Free Reform Church, the road becomes somewhat worn and rough in spots. At Governor's Road turn [L], then [R] onto Sulphur Springs Rd. Notice the warning sign for the gravel road ahead. It is twisting and hilly, but the road has been oiled so many times, that it rides as though it were asphalt.

The entrance to the Brantford-Hamilton railbed is located approximately 10 km west of this tour's starting point at the bottom of a hill. Turn [L] onto the railbed's hard-packed calcium

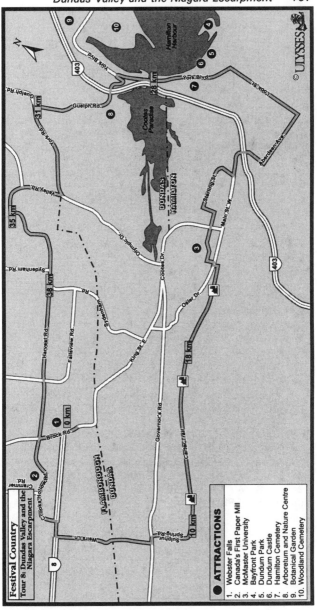

Festival Country
Tour 8: Dundas Valley and the
Niagara Escarpment

© ULYSSES

ATTRACTIONS

1. Webster Falls
2. Canada's First Paper Mill
3. McMaster University
4. Bayfront Park
5. Dundurn Park
6. Dundurn Castle
7. Hamilton Cemetery
8. Arboretum and Nature Centre
9. Botanical Garden
10. Woodland Cemetery

Practical Information

Population:
Dundas: 20,500
Hamilton: 308,000
Flamborough: 27,200

 Tourist Information

✦ **Hamilton:** Tourism and Convention Services, Regional Municipality of Hamilton-Wentworth, 1 James St S, 3rd Floor, Hamilton, Ont, L8P 4R5, (905) 546-4222, Bike Line (905) 546-2453
✦ **Dundas:** Dundas Valley Information – Hamilton Region Conservation Authority, PO Box 7099, 838 Mineral Springs Rd, Ancaster, Ont, L9G 3L3, (905) 648-4427, (905) 525-2181

 Bicycle Shops

✦ **Hamilton:** Cycle Path-Hamilton, 503 Concession St, Hamilton, Ont, L9A 1C1, (905) 574-1102, (905) 574-1127; Main Cycle, 1461 Main St E, Hamilton, Ont, L8K 1C5, (905) 544-0338; Mountain Top Bicycles, 525 Mohawk Rd E at Upper Sherman, Hamilton, Ont, L8V 2J5, (905) 575-8773, (905) 575-4354; Scattolon Cycle & Sports, Unit No. 20, 1527 Upper Ottawa St, Hamilton, Ont, L8W 3J4, (905) 574-6778, (905) 574-9292; Springy's, 1048 Barton St E, Hamilton, Ont, L8L 3E5, (905) 544-2657
✦ **Dundas:** Spin Cycle, 242 Governor's Road, Dundas, Ontario L9H 3K2, (905) 627-5658; Freewheel Cycle, 9 King St W, Dundas, Ont, L9H 1T5, (905) 628-5123, (905) 628-5585

Special Sights and Events

Tiger Cats Football, The Model Engineering Show, Maple Syrup Tapping, Battle of Stoney Creek, Hamilton International Air show, Greater Hamilton Tattoo, Earthsong, Royal Botanical Gardens Floral Festival, Steaming Days, Tulip Festival, Festitalia, Steel City Oktoberfest, Summer Music Festival, American Civil War Re-enactment, Festival of Friends, The Around-the-Bay Marathon/Bobby Kerr Marathon, Christie Conservation area, Confederation Park, Devil's Punch Bowl, Felkers Falls, Fifty Point Conservation Area

 Accommodations

Hotel/Motel/B&B/Hostel/Camping

riding surface, and cycle to the Dundas Valley "Trail Centre." Officially known as the Toronto, Hamilton & Buffalo Railway, the T, H & B was often called "To Hell and Back" and went into service in 1895. The rail line was abandoned in 1986 and its rails were torn up after Brantford's Colborne St landslide. The Hamilton Region and the Grand River Conservation Authorities purchased the trail in 1988 and are currently working to complete the greenway, the master development plan for the railbed is on display at the trail centre.

An afternoon of great riding can be found around the "Trail Centre." This restored train station, flanked on the north and south by 400-million-year-old rocks, offers weary travellers a place to rest. It is also the starting place for over 40 kilometres of hiking and cycling trails that pass over streams and through forests, marshlands and the fields of Dundas Valley.

As you continue east along the [RB], which is almost 100 metres below the level of Lake Ontario, caution is advised as you cross Ancaster Road and Lynden Ave. The "thuddy-d-thud" of wood and rubber brings pleasure to your ears as you cross the 275-metre Binkley Hollow ravine. In the fall, the sight of the brilliant colours of the ravine's many varieties of trees can be invigorating. Look for an information sign pointing out their location.

French explorers who passed through this area in the 17th century knew of the escarpment by native description as "The Head of the Lake." Following the American Revolution, the British purchased land in the vicinity from the Mississauga Indians to provide homes for Loyalists. **Hamilton** was known first as Burlington Bay, then as King's Head after a local inn and in 1813 it was renamed after George Hamilton. Over the years, it was nicknamed the "Ambitious City" due to its rapid and continued growth.

Cross Main St W and turn [L] onto Ewen Road. Walter Jakes and Son will be to your right. Turn [R] when rejoining Main St W, then turn [L] onto West Park Avenue. Turning [R] onto a very wide Saunders Blvd (the railtrail continues to your left at Cootes Drive), cross Cootes Drive and enter the McMaster University Campus. Following the campus road as it curves to the left, turn [R] onto the next street, Sterling St and follow it to the traffic lights (first city in Canada to have them) at King St W. Cross King St onto Newton Ave, turning [L] onto Main St W. Take the next [R] onto Longwood Road South, turning left onto Aberdeen Ave. Continue until you turn [L] onto Lock St. Cross Main St and King St, then turn [L] onto York Blvd. At the entrance to Dundurn Castle, which was home to Canada's first Prime Minister, rejoin the multi-use trail of Dundurn Park.

On your left, enjoy the inspiring view of Hamilton Harbour, the Burlington Skyway and Hamilton's Bayfront and Pier 4 waterfront developments. Cross the York St high-level bridge built in 1931, replacing the first bridge built on this site in 1896. A little further down, York St turns into Plains Road West where the many original floral displays of the Royal Botanical Gardens may be found.

Just after the bridge, turn [L] onto Old Guelph Road which rapidly descends to and under Hwy 403. The road begins to climb immediately once clear of the underpass; the Royal

Botanical Nature Centre and Arboretum is halfway up the hill on your left.

Turn [L] onto York Road; when the Valley Road pumping station comes into view, turn right. Be prepared for a steady climb as you wind your way back up the escarpment to the Town of **Flamborough** where every fire hydrant has its own flag! At the Rock Chapel Road turn [L], and continue past the Rock Chapel Falls Lookout and Piccioni Mushroom Farm. Keep to your right as Sydenham Road joins Harvest Road. After you pass a radio tower on your right and an old farm harrow on your left, it is just a short distance to the railway bridge underpass and Tews Falls. Once you clear the bridge turn [L] into the parking lot and cycle to an inspiring view of the escarpment and Tews Falls, which are only a few metres shorter than Niagara Falls. Two viewing platforms offer different perspectives, and a walking trail to the left of the falls follows the Bruce Trail to Dundas Peak and other spectacular lookout points.

Rejoin Harvest Road, pass Greensville School, and turn [L] onto Short Road returning to the Spencer Gorge Parking lot on Fallsview Road.

---

9. Elmira and St. Jacob's Countryside Tour

Beginning in the Mennonite town of Elmira, this route includes such sights as a local buggy factory, the fires of a St. Jacobs blacksmith's forge and a ride through a 60-metre foot Mennonite Buggy Bridge.

Return Distance: 60 km
Number of recommended legs: 1
Difficulty: 🚲
Surface: Asphalt and gravel, some single track

Villages/Towns/Cities: Elmira, West Montrose, Winterbourne, Conestogo, St. Jacobs, Hawkesville, Wallenstein

Local Highlights: Maple Syrup Museum of Canada, The Meeting Place, St. Jacobs Farmers Market & Flea Market, St. Jacobs School House Theatre, Fifties Steam Liner, Horse-Drawn Trolley Tours, St. Jacobs Main St, Elmira Raceway

Recommended Bicycles: Hybrid/Mountain/Touring

Tour Suggestions: A full day's ride, but lunch can be made from the local farm produce available at the St. Jacobs Farmers Market.

How To Get There: From Hwy 401, follow Hwy 6, known as the Hanlon Expressway. Turn left onto Hwy 7 and then right onto Regional Rd 86, the Elmira Road. Starting point for the tour is at the Crossroads Restaurant located on the left side of Regional Rd 86. Park your vehicle under the lone maple tree next to the old cemetery.

The town of **Elmira** was settled in the early 1800s and was known first as Bristow's Corners, then as West Woolwich. In 1867, the name was changed to Elmira after the city in New York State. Many of the area's first settlers were Mennonites from Pennsylvania. Today, Elmira is a subdued little town that has managed to hold on to its traditions of yesteryear. While riding along the main street, notice how it has been designed to accommodate a horse and buggy, the traditional transportation of the local population. Mostly old order Mennonites live in this area. The order originated under reformer Menno Simons, a Roman Catholic priest who led the Anabaptist movement in the Netherlands and northern Germany in the 1530s. The first Mennonites belonged to a church in Zurich, Switzerland and arrived in the state of Pennsylvania, where William Penn offered them religious liberty, in 1683. The Amish, who followed the teachings of Jacob Ammann, broke away from the Swiss Mennonites in 1690, primarily because of disagreements with church doctrine regarding the practice of shunning. Amish people can be found in 23 states as well as in Ontario. The Amish are pacifists, do not swear oaths and will not hold an office that implicates them in the use of force.

Itinerary: Turning [L] out of the Crossroads parking lot, cycle north along Arthur St into downtown Elmira. Take a few

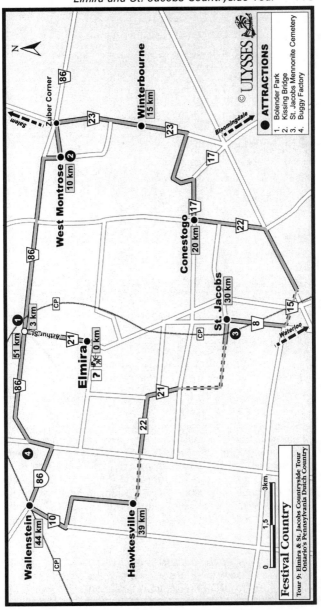

Festival Country
Tour 9: Elmira & St. Jacobs Countryside Tour
Ontario's Pennsylvania Dutch Country

ATTRACTIONS
1. Bolender Park
2. Kissing Bridge
3. St. Jacobs Mennonite Cemetery
4. Buggy Factory

© ULYSSES

Practical Information

Population:
Elmira: 7,300
St. Jacobs: 1,525
Wallenstein: 265

 Tourist Information

Elmira and Woolwich Chamber of Commerce, 5 First St E, Elmira, N3B 2E3 (519) 669-2605, www.elmiramaplesyrup.com.

 Bicycle Shops

Central Source For Sports, 48 Arthur St South, Elmira, NAB 2M6, (519)669-2706

 Special Sights and Events

Elmira Maple Syrup Festival, Elmira Quilt Auction, Elmira Country Fair

moments to visit the Gore Park Bandstand in the downtown core. The bandstand's base was built in 1892 by Henry Zilliax and was located behind his Inn (near the present-day Royal Bank). The roof that protects the band from rain was added in 1912. Continue along Arthur St as it climbs through the town's retail section to the Church St stop lights. Make a [R] turn and follow Regional Rd 86, past Bolender Park and two local cemeteries.

Enjoy the ride through some of this province's richest agricultural land. Along this road are some very impressive looking farms. At Waterloo Rd 22 (the Salem Road), a generous cycling lane has recently been incorporated into the road. A short distance past the **West Montrose** sign, make a [R] turn onto Church St. Coasting downhill, ride by the stone-built United Church and continue following the road as it passes by the front of the general store and then descends into the Grand River Valley. At the bottom of the hill is the 60-metre-long West Montrose Buggy Bridge, better known as the Kissing Bridge. The bridge was built in 1881 at a cost of $3,100. Today it is one of the province's last original covered bridges. The name "kissing bridge" comes from the early days when it had no windows and was lighted by coal oil lamps. The darkness proved to be the perfect hiding place for romantic young couples. Crossing the Grand River via the bridge, turn [L] and follow the road along the river. Swinging to the right, the road begins to climb past a restored 1874 home to Wellington Rd 23. Make a [R] turn at the corner and ride past the very unique fluorescent green school crossing sign and the West Montrose one-room school house.

Take Wellington Rd 23 into the Scottish settlement of **Winterbourne**. Just past the welcome sign, the road descends and crosses Cox Creek. Looking to the left of the bridge, notice the pretty little pond and conservation area while there is rushing water to the right. At the village centre is a very old church. Built in 1870, Chalmers Church continues to serve the needs of the local townsfolk. Making good time on the predominately flat road, ride past the Presbyterian Cemetery and Cribit's Seeds. Turn [R] onto Woolwich Rd 45 and enjoy a leisurely ride along one of Ontario's prettiest roads.

At the stop sign, turn [L] and cycle past the local golf course. The road swings sharply to the left at the river and joins Wellington Rd 17. Turn [R] and cross back over the Grand River, cycling uphill past a large mill and the Black Forest Inn. Continue along the colourful main street of **Conestogo**, which is lined with many little boutiques and craft shops. Make a left turn onto Wellington Rd 22 and ride south into the southern portion of the Conestogo River Valley.

Cycling past the remains of an old railway bridge, and pile upon pile of firewood, make a [R] turn onto Woolwich Rd 38 (Country Squire Rd). This gravel road cuts across the north end of Waterloo, and it is here that the country meets the city. At the stop sign, swing [R]. Now riding on asphalt, continue following Country Squire Road to Wellington Rd 15 (King St). Turn [R] and take Hwy 86 to a set of lights. Now follow Waterloo Rd 8 past the Farmers Market and Outlet Mall into downtown **St. Jacobs**.

In contrast to Elmira, St. Jacobs has developed commercially and has thus become a beehive of activity. First called Jacobstettel by the German and Pennsylvania Dutch settlers who came here in the 1840s, the name was changed to its present one in 1852 to honour two local residents, Jacob Snider and Jacob Eby, who were early millers. Today, St. Jacobs has become one of Ontario's most famous tourist attractions, drawing people from far and wide. Walking along its main street, you can hear the sounds of a blacksmith at work, feel the heat of a glass blower's oven and savour the aroma of freshly baked bread.

Note: Just behind the St. Jacobs Country Mill and the Old Mill Shed is a little bridge that crosses the river and leads to some single track. Follow the Mill Race trail along the creek. It's a lovely ride that exits at Krammer's Buggy Bridge. The bridge was built by a local Mennonite to allow a road crossing at the St. Jacobs Mill Race Pond and Dam.

To finish the ride in Mennonite Country, retrace your path on King St (Waterloo Rd 8) back towards Waterloo. At Henry St, turn [R] and ride past the Head Office for Home Hardware and the local buggy washing booth and parking lot. Crossing a set of railway tracks, proceed to the [T] intersection at Township Rd 32. Turn [R] and follow the road as it swings to the left. Immediately after riding over a bridge, the road becomes gravel. As you pass the local Mennonite church and cemetery, notice how the cemetery stone inscriptions all face west. Cross Woolwich Rd 17 and follow Cty Rd 21 north.

Riding past the St. Jacobs Mennonite Cemetery and Three Bridges Public School, look for the home of a local Mennonite who outsmarted the township's building inspector. As the story goes, the local farmer wanted to build a granny flat next to the main part of his home. The township gave him permission to go ahead as long as the new building was attached to the original. Of course, when it was built and wasn't attached, the building inspector became quite upset. The quick-thinking farmer saved the day by taking a beam of wood and attaching it to the two separate buildings. Thus, he complied in a roundabout way with the township's requirement.

At the farm of Elias Martin, notice the windmill that rocks back and forth. Just a few metres ahead, turn [L] onto Woolwich Rd 22. The road immediately descends to Donald Creek and cuts through a dramatically sculpted countryside. Continue along Woolwich Rd 22 into the village of **Hawkesville**.

Turn [R] onto the main street, Union St, and ride past the local variety store. Enjoy this stimulating ride as you follow the road along the upper banks of the northern portion of the Conestogo River Valley. At Woolwich Rd 10, turn [R] and begin the ride towards the village of **Wallenstein**.

Every so often, look skyward for gliders from the nearby flying club. The groans and squeaks of several windmills along this road fill the air as you cycle north. The Martins, a local Mennonite clan, own most of the property in the area – as you can see by the names listed on the mailboxes along the road. At the junction of Hwy 86, turn [R] and cycle east toward Elmira.

Riding past the Wallenstein General Store and Wallenstein Brick Company, you will find that Regional Rd 86 is quite busy. When Waterloo 86 begins to arc left, do not take the St. Jacobs/Elmira cutoff (shortcut) on the right. A short distance ahead, a dilapidated silver building appears on the horizon. Take a few moments to cross the road and visit with the proprietor of this timeless building, which is home to the Elmira Buggy Works.

Now Waterloo 86 swings sharply to the right. In the late afternoon on Saturdays, it is quite common to see the black buggies of local Mennonites heading into town for church. Cycling past the Elmira Mennonite Church and its very large cemetery, turn [R] at the stop lights onto Arthur St. As you make your way back to the Crossroads parking lot, take a few minutes to relax at the Gore Park Bandstand and try to imagine how the band would have sounded back in 1892.

---

10. Elora Gorge Adventure (Guelph to Elora)

This tour is ideal for a beginner's first outing. It's great for the first ride of the season and also makes an excellent fall colour tour. Cycling north from Guelph, the ride is an easy one. Only a few climbs are encountered on the way to the Elora gorge. The day slips away quickly as you follow the trail along the gorge past the "Tooth of Time" and into downtown Elora. Enjoy Elora's historic downtown and explore the dramatic gorge before riding out to the famous cool "Quarry" waters.

Return Distance: 50 km
No. of recommended legs: 1
Level of Difficulty: 🚲 🚲
Surface: Asphalt

Villages/Towns/Cities: Guelph, Elora

Local Highlights: Elora Gorge Conservation Area, Islet Rock, The Arboretum, Church of Our Lady, Guelph Civic Centre, Guelph Civic Museum, Guelph Lake Conservation Area, Kortright Waterfowl Park, MacDonald Stewart Art Centre, McCrae House, Riverside Park, Town Lattice-covered Footbridge

Recommended Bicycles: Touring/Hybrid/Mountain

Tour Suggestions: Pack a lunch and make a full day of it. Be careful when walking along the gorge; a number of people have fallen down it.

How To Get There: From the north and south, Elora can be reached via Hwy 6. From the east, it can be reached by taking Hwys 9 & 24 and from the west, Hwy 86. This tour starts in Guelph. From the Hwy 401, take Hwy 6, also called the Hanlan Expressway, north to Hwy 7. Turn right and then immediately

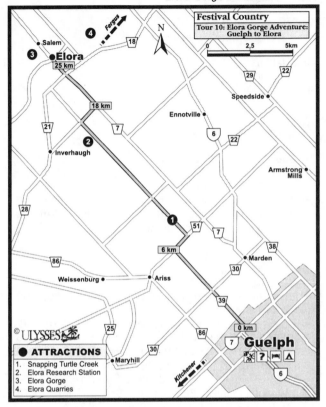

turn left onto the Silver Creek Parkway. Begin the tour from the TSC parking lot on your left.

Beginning at Guelph's northern outskirts, just a short distance to the southeast, at the confluence of the Speed and Eramosa Rivers, is the city proper. Founded in 1827 the town was named after the British Royal Family by Scottish novelist John Galt, who planned it according to a unique radial street pattern. The town kept its nickname as "The Royal City," over the years because no other city in the entire Commonwealth has the name of Guelph. The city was also the home of Colonel John McCrae, who was the WWI physician who wrote the immortal

Practical Information

Population
Guelph: 90,000
Elora: 3,300

 Tourist Information

✦ **Guelph:** Guelph Chamber of Commerce, PO Box 1268,
485 Silvercreek Pkwy N, Guelph, Ont, N1H 7K5,
(519) 822-8081, www.city.guelph.on.ca
✦ **Elora:** Elora Chamber of Commerce, PO Box 814,
1 MacDonald Sq, Elora, Ont, N0B 1S0, (519) 846-984,
www.eic.elora.on.ca/index.html

 Bicycle Shops

✦ **Elora:** Salem Cyclery, 11 Mill St E, Elora, Ont, N0B 1S0,
(519) 846-8446
✦ **Guelph:** Bicycles Etc., 116 Woolwich St, N1H 3V2,
(519) 763-3325; Bits & Bikes, 170 Woolwich St, N1H 3V5,
(519) 824-0866; George Vettor Cycle & Sport, RR 6,
N1H 6J3, (519) 824-5829; Paramount Ski & Sports,
4-35 Harvard Rd, N1G 3A2, (519) 822-1767;
PI Manufacturing, 86 Arthur St N, N1E 4T8,
(519) 824-3869; Revolutions Bicycles, 43 Cork St E,
N1H 2W7, (519) 766-4082; Speed River Bicycle,
135 Wyndham St N, N1H 4E9, (519) 824-9371

 Special Sights and Events

Annual Fall Fair, Canada Day, Guelph Jazz Festival, Guelph
Premier Art show, Hillside Festival

Accommodations

Hotel/Motel/B&B/Camping

 Off-Road Cycling

Yes, refer to "Off-Road Cycling" at the back of this section

poem "In Flanders Fields." Today, Guelph is home to the highly regarded Ontario Veterinary College and the Ontario Agriculture College.

Itinerary: Turn [R] out of the TSC parking lot and cycle north on the Silvercreek Parkway. Riding past the recently renovated School House No.4, you quickly leave the city behind. Wellington Rd 39 becomes a comfortable and interesting ride after you cross Wellington Rd 30, since at this point motor vehicle traffic virtually disappears. At the Schuett's Corners [T] intersection, turn [R] onto Wellington Rd 51. Ride past the abandoned railbed and make a [L] turn at the next road, 2nd Line East. The road climbs, then levels out and passes through a marshy area known as Snapping Turtle Creek. Be careful in the spring as these "hardshells" will be crossing the road in numbers. Just past Side Road 14 is the Ponsonby Conservation Area and Ball Park. Tucked away in a dilapidated drive shed a few metres past Side Road 14 is an old bi-wing airplane.

The road goes uphill past a farm tractor graveyard before it levels out and reaches the Elora Research Station complex. It then descends through a wetland. Make a [R] turn onto Side Road 7 and enjoy a short ride through the Elora Highlands before turning [L] onto Wellington Road 7, which leads into Elora. Continue past the stop lights and follow the road as it descends to the bridge lookout. Walk out onto the bridge to take in the dramatic view of the gorge's tall walls, rocks, crevices and caves.

Join the single track trail on the right, just before the bridge, and ride along the top of the gorge towards downtown Elora. There are many side trails to explore, all of which access the river below. If you go down to the river, it is best to dismount and walk to the bottom of the gorge. The way is steep and treacherous and there are often other trail users on the path. As you ride into Elora, the heritage buildings, bridges and the impressive Islet Rock come into view. Look for the rope suspended over the rushing waters of the Grand River; it offers adventurers a chance to test their mountain climbing skills. The trail exits onto the street at Little Folk Ltd. Ride across the wooden Victoria Walkway into downtown Elora.

The Elora Gorge was formed by two separate geological events, separated by almost 300 million years. The Elora Gorge begins at the Irvine Creek low level bridge west of town, and extends all the way back to the Islet Rock. The gorge also continues up the Irvine Creek to the village of Salem, where it ends at a waterfall under the highway bridge. The village of Elora was not settled until the winter of 1817, when Roswell Matthews walked from Niagara to Elora to begin construction of his log home. The town was named "Elora" after the ship owned by the brother of the town benefactor, Captain Gilkison.

Turn [L] and follow Mill St into the Old Mill Restaurant parking lot and to the stable lookout. A [R] turn will take you to the Elora Quarries. At the old grist mill entrance, follow the road to the right to get to the path along the upper portion of the gorge and a set of stairs that leads into it. Today, the village of Elora is building on its past, so be sure to spend some riding time exploring old Elora along the Grand River. Here you will find a town that is blessed with many magnificent old homes and stone churches.

The Elora Quarries are an excellent place to finish off the day. Although it is possible to walk completely around the top, be extremely careful as the trail is only as wide as your hand at the section at the back. To return to Guelph, simply retrace the route back to Hwy 7 and the Silvercreek Parkway.

11. Paris to Cambridge Rail Trail

The bicycle ride from Paris to Cambridge along the abandoned lake Erie & Northern Railway has to be one of the prettiest single-day outings in the province. It's a leisurely ride that is complimented by the stunning backdrop of the Grand River Valley.

Return Distance: 38 km
No. of recommended legs: 1
Level of Difficulty: 🚲
Surface: Crushed gravel

Villages/Town/Cities: Paris, Glen Morris, Cambridge

Local Highlights: Adelaide Hunter Hoodless Homestead, Bell Homestead, Brant County Museum & Archives, Royal Chapel of the Mohawks, Paris Cobblestone Architecture, Antique Market, Canning Perennials, Churchill Park, African Lion Safari, Cambridge Arts Theatre. Cambridge Galleries, Bi-Annual Can-American Games, Cambridge Riverfest, Fat Tire Festival, Mill Race Festival, Downtown Funfest, Cambridge Fall Fair

Recommended Bicycles: Hybrid/Mountain/Touring

Tour Suggestions: This is a great family ride and a great fall colours outing. Pack a picnic lunch and spend part of the day in Churchill Park.

How to Get There: Paris can be reached from the east and west by following Hwy 2 and from the north and south by Hwy 24. Start from the Paris Lions Park (free parking) to get a great view of the Grand River. The park is located just off Hwy 2, at the top of the hill before the junction of Hwy 2 and the Grand River Road. At the cemetery, follow the park road down to the river. Take the wooden walkway across the Nith River to the main street, Grand River Road. Turn [L] and, upon reaching the stop lights, turn [R] and cross the Grand River. Turn [L] immediately after the bridge and join the trail that runs along the river. The trail exits onto East River Road;

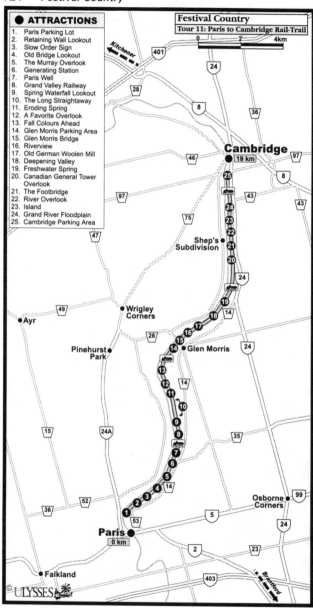

● ATTRACTIONS

1. Paris Parking Lot
2. Retaining Wall Lookout
3. Slow Order Sign
4. Old Bridge Lookout
5. The Murray Overlook
6. Generating Station
7. Paris Well
8. Grand Valley Railway
9. Spring Waterfall Lookout
10. The Long Straightaway
11. Eroding Spring
12. A Favorite Overlook
13. Fall Colours Ahead
14. Glen Morris Parking Area
15. Glen Morris Bridge
16. Riverview
17. Old German Woolen Mill
18. Deepening Valley
19. Freshwater Spring
20. Canadian General Tower Overlook
21. The Footbridge
22. River Overlook
23. Island
24. Grand River Floodplain
25. Cambridge Parking Area

Festival Country
Tour 11: Paris to Cambridge Rail-Trail

0   2   4km

← Kitchener
401
24
28
8
36
46
97
8
43
43
Cambridge
19 km
25
24
23
22
21
20
75
Shep's Subdivision
47
49
Wrigley Corners
28
24
19
18
14
16 17
15
14 Glen Morris
13
12
11
10
9
8
● Ayr
Pinehurst Park
35
7
6
5
4 14
3
2
1
53
15
24A
Paris
0 km
52
36
5
Osborne Corners
99
24
● Falkland
2
23
403
← Brantford

© ULYSSES

Practical Information

Population:
Paris: 8,100
Cambridge: 95,000

 Tourist Information

✦ **Paris:** Town of Paris, 66 Grand River St N, Paris, Ont, N3L 2M2, (519) 442-6324, www.execulink.com/~creed/Paris.html, www.ontariotowns.on.ca/paris/paris.html
✦ **Cambridge:** Cambridge Visitor and Convention Bureau, 531 King St E, N3H 3N4, www.cambridge.in.on.ca; Paris to Cambridge Rail-Trail, Grand River Conservation Authority, Box 729, N1R 5W6, (519) 621-2761, www.mgl.ca/~wemiller/lentrail.htm

 Bicycle Shops

✦ **Paris:** Paris Sporting Goods, 52 Grand River N, Paris, Ont, N3L 2M2, (519) 442-6843
✦ **Cambridge:** Bikes At Rivers 'n Trails, 22 Queen St W, N3C 1G1, (519) 658-2155; Cycle Cambridge, 505 Hespeler Rd, N1R 6J2, (519) 740-8766; Galt Re-Cycle Sports, 79 Dickson St, N1R 7A5, (519) 740-3194; Gears & Grills, 410 Hespeler Rd, N1R 6J6, (519) 624-5814; Ontario Sports Distributors, 653 King St E, N3H 3N7, (519) 653-4651

 Special Sights and Events

Canada Week and Parade, Springtime in Paris, St. James Annual Miniature Show, Paris Country Fair, Annual Steam Show, Cambridge Highland Games

Accommodations

Motel/B&B/Camping

 Off-Road Cycling

Yes, refer to "Off-Road Cycling" section at the back of this chapter.

 Market Days

Farmers Market held on Saturdays from May to late fall

continue riding north. A short distance ahead, on the right, is the Paris Pavilion and parking lot for the Grand River Trail. Turn right into the parking lot and join the rail-bed.

Paris is possibly the second most important town in the County of Brant. Located at the confluence of the Grand and Nith Rivers, it is one of Ontario's most picturesque and inviting spots. Settled by immigrants in 1821, it was known as "The Forks of the Grand River." The settlement was officially named Paris after the large plaster-of-paris beds developed by its founder, Vermont native Hiram Capron, in 1828. Paris also played a role in Alexander Graham Bell's first long distance telephone call, which took place on August 10, 1876. As you ride along the main street, you are surrounded by cobblestone buildings. Paris is home to Canada's largest number of cobblestone buildings, featuring a total of 11 homes and 2 churches.

Itinerary: There are several lookouts along the railbed, that should not be missed. The Spring Waterfall Lookout is sometimes hard to locate. Approximately one kilometre past the Paris Well, the falls can be heard and found along the left side of the trail. They are hidden from view by overgrown bushes, so look for the entrance carefully.

Another interesting spot is the old German Woolen Mill, which is a short distance past the **Glen Morris** parking lot. Be careful here as the old stone walls may be unstable. The mill is on private property, so respect the rights of the owner. If you are ready for a water refill, line up at the freshwater spring (one of many along the trail) and enjoy a cold invigorating drink.

The trail passes the Cambridge Water Treatment Plant and exits onto Hwy 24 near a gas station and Churchill Park. Churchill Park is the second largest in **Cambridge** and has deer, bird pens, washrooms, picnic and limited camping facilities. Churchill Park is a great place to stop for a break before returning back to Paris along the river trail.

Optional Side Trip: The more adventurous can follow Hwy 24 to Concession St. Cross the Grand River and turn [R] joining the Cambridge River Bank System. Follow this network of pathways along the river through numerous parks to the 70-foot-high Devil's Creek Waterfall and Devil's Cave.

---

12. Welland Canal Explorer:
Port Dalhousie, St. Catharines and Welland

Beginning in Port Dalhousie, the first leg is an adventurous ride along the Merritt Trail as it follows a portion of the original canal and the rushing white waters of Twelve Mile Creek. The route visits Lock 7 in the city of Thorold for a close up view of the large ocean freighters, and ends in the city of Welland. Leg 2 begins by taking in Welland's many large murals before crossing Merritt Island to join the Welland Canal Parkway Trail. The highlight of this much easier return leg is the Lock 3 Visitor's Centre and the waterfront trail from Port Weller to Port Dalhousie.

Return Distance: 108 km (58 km, 50 km)
No. of recommended legs: 2
Level of Difficulty: 🚲 🚲 🚲
Surface: Asphalt, single track,
jeep road, loose gravel

Villages/Towns/Cities: Port Dalhousie, St. Catharines, Thorold, Port Weller

Local Highlights: Welland Canal Locks 7 & 3, Brock University, British Methodist Episcopal Church, Happy Rolph Bird Sanctuary, Morningstar Mill and Decew Falls, Rodman Hall Arts Centre, Stokes Seeds, Port Dalhousie Mercantile District, Lakeside Park Carousel, Hernder Estate Wines, Henry of Pelham Family Estate, Battle of Beaverdams Park, Welland Historical Museum, Welland Recreational Canal, The Wine Route, Wiley Brothers Farms

Recommended Bicycles: Mountain/Hybrid

Tour Suggestions: The tour can be completed in a day, but staying in Welland overnight makes it much more interesting and relaxing.

How to Get There: From the east or west take the Queen Elizabeth Way, and get off at the Ontario St exit. From the south, follow Hwy 58/406 to Ontario St, then turn left onto Lakeport Road and follow it into Port Dalhousie's Lakeside Park.

As the starting point for the first Welland canals, almost 170 years ago, **Port Dalhousie** has tried to preserved much of its heritage. Here, along the shores of the lake, are two lighthouses from the early 1800s and an antique hand-carved 1898 indoor carousel, brought here from Rhode Island in 1921. As well, just a short distance from the beach and attracting much attention, are two English-style double-decker buses and some intriguing sailing vessels hailing from many different ports of call.

Itinerary: Leg 1 (Welland to Port Dalhousie, 58 km). First take a few moments to ride out on the pier, then exit the parking lot and go past the red double-decker buses onto Hogans Alley. Turn [L] onto Lock St, then make a [R] turn onto Main St. Follow the tree-lined boulevard past the Anne St memorial statue, Martindale Road and the three armed-tree, then make a [L] turn onto Third St S.

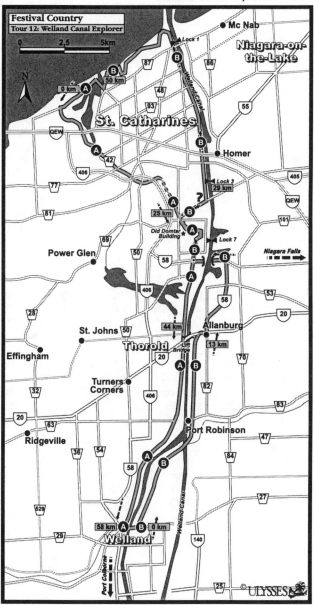

Practical Information

Population:
St. Catharines: 129,300
Welland: 47,900

 Tourist Information

✦ **St. Catharines:** St. Catharines Chamber of Commerce, PO Box 940, 1 St. Pauls St, L2R 6Z4, (905) 684-2361, www.st.catharines.com
✦ **Welland:** Greater Welland Chamber of Commerce, 32 Main St, L3B 3W3, (905) 732-7515, www.callwelland.com

 Bicycle Shops

✦ **St. Catharines:** Liberty Bicycles, 40 St. Paul St, L2R 3M2, (905) 682-1454; Ski Pro Shop, 278 Geneva St, L2N 2E8, (905) 934-2682; Bikefit, 184 Scott St, L2N 1H1, (905) 646-9396; Buckner's Sports Centres, 120 Welland Ave, L2R 2N3, (905) 641-0066; Rapid City Cycle, 331 St. Paul St, L2R 3N1, (905) 684-9111; Glauco Bicycle Sales & Repairs, 107 Welland St, L2R 5P9, (905) 984-6661; Uptown Sports, 363 St. Paul St, L2R 3N1, (905) 685-4535
✦ **Thorold:** Clarkson Cycle & Fitness, 1 Wellington St N, L2V 1P8, (905) 227-0810
✦ **Welland:** Thorton's Cycle & Sports Centre, 300 Lincoln St, Lincoln Plaza, Welland, Ont, L3B 4N4, (905) 732-4770; Buckner's Sports Centres, 545 Niagara St, L3C 1L7, (905) 734-6422; Goods Service & Cycle, 17 Southworth St N, L3B 1X8, (905) 732-5535

Special Sights and Events

✦ **St. Catherines:** Niagara Grape & Wine Festival, Oktoberfest, Ontario Sausage Festival, Royal Canadian Henley Regatta, Salmon Derby, Folks Arts Festival, Strawberry Festival, Summer Solstice Festival

✦ **Welland:** Canadian Canoeing Championships, Niagara Food Festival, Niagara Regional Exhibition, Soiree Traditionelle, Welland Folklore Festival, Welland Rose Festival

 Accommodations

✦ **St. Catharines:** Hotel/Motel/B&B/Camping

 Off-Road Cycling:

✦ **St. Catharines:** Yes, several in the area. Refer to the "Off-Road Cycling" section at the end of this chapter.

 Market Days

✦ **St. Catharines:** Located behind the Old Court House. Year round on Tuesdays, Thursdays and Saturdays

---

A short distance past the tree nursery, swing [L] onto the Green Ribbon Trail, which is dedicated to all missing children. Descending quickly, the trail crosses a class one wetland before exiting onto Martindale Road. Cycling past the Martindale Pond and over the Queen Elizabeth Way, and prepare for a [L] turn onto the Merritt Trail. As you approach Huntington Square Mall, the trail entrance is on your left, just before reaching Erion Rd.

Descending quickly to Old Welland Canal, also known as Twelve Mile Creek, the trail appears to be below water level, and in the spring this area may be wet. You can hear plenty of rushing water and noise as the canal exits at Welland Avenue on the Niagara College Business Campus. Turn [L], cross the canal and follow Welland Avenue/Vale Road about halfway uphill, and rejoin the trail by going through the gate on your right. The trail is now high above the canal's deep green waters which are still noisily churning and frothing. On the right is a unique salmon-coloured firehouse. Exit onto a paved cul-de-sac, continue straight, and rejoin the trail at the far end as it descends to Burgoyne Bridge. Climbing, look for the rocks indicating the trail direction, and go straight as the trail parallels the road. At McGuire St and St. Pauls Crescent, turn [R] onto the walkway and cross Hwy 406.

Descending off the walkway, bear [L] and follow the Merritt Trail to the stop lights at Carlisle St and Westchester Avenue. Turn [L] onto Westchester Avenue and follow this four-lane road across Hwy 406 to the Captain Scott Misner section of the Merritt Trail. The trail entrance is on the right, just before stop lights at Oakdale Avenue.

Turning [R], the trail immediately descends and quickly arrives at a split in the road; make a [L] turn, cross the wooden bridge, and follow the crushed gravel surface to Moffatt St where it ends. Cross Disher St onto Moffat St and rejoin the trail on the left. Both trail and canal are ascending. There is a very large smoke stack which dominates the skyline on the left. The trail eventually reaches a bridge and crosses the canal. Turn [R] off the bridge and follow the road over the railway tracks. Warning signs indicate that this is an active railway line, so proceed with caution. As the trail changes into gravel, it exits onto Glendale Avenue. Take note of the Johansson's Bar on the left, and visit the remains of the old Domtar building across the road.

As a suggestion, it will be safer and much quicker to walk across Glendale Avenue into Mountain Locks Park or onto Mountain St. Once across the road, there are two ways to join the trail: either take the path on the other side of the trees at the park entrance, or go past the historical plaque just a short distance down Mountain St, on the left. This section is a lot of fun to ride as it dips and dives, twists and turns, and finally exits out on Bradley St. Notice the yellow trail marking signs on the telephone posts as you follow Bradley St to the [T] intersection at Town Line Rd W. Turning [L], the road crosses the canal via an old bridge. At Front St, turn [R] and cycle into downtown **Thorold**. The town was named after Sir John Thorold, and during the War of 1812, a mighty battle was fought here, at Beaverdams Park. This battle was a major loss for the Americans who were defeated by a much smaller contingent of native soldiers led by Major William Johnson Kerr.

Turn [L] onto Clairmont St, cross Ormond St S, and pass two very impressive churches to the stop sign at the Chapel St [T] intersection. Turn [R] and then [L] onto Flight Locks Road, which will bring you alongside Lock 7 of the Welland Canal. Here you can almost reach over the fence and touch the ships as they travel through the last lift over the Niagara Escarpment. The canal was built to bypass Niagara Falls which connect Lake Ontario to Lake Erie. The first canal was built in 1829, and the first leg of this journey began and will end alongside one of the original canals. The present-day canal, which you are now standing near, has seven locks each with a height gain of 14.2 metres (46.5 ft).

Return to Chapel St, turn [L] and then [R] onto Portland St. When you come to a golden Mosque at Ormond St, turn [L]. Follow Ormond, keeping left, and go past Beaverdams Road until you reach a set of gates. Proceed through the gates and follow the upper jeep road, keeping the canal on the left. Ahead in the distance are two black towers that cross the canal. They disappear from view as you turn at the small, fenced-in hydro power station located a short distance past the fluorescent green markings on both sides of the canal. Turn [R] on the jeep trail on the far side of the station and follow it across some abandoned railway tracks to a [T] intersection. Turn [L] and continue to the first trail on the right, which leads down and across the old waterway.

Once across the water, swing [L] and continue following the sandy old jeep roads to a railway bridge. Turn [R], and cross the bridge to join the jeep road on the other side. As the trail approaches a water-control dam, watch for glass – now is not the time for a flat! Leave the dam by following the road back to the canal and the twin towers of lift bridge No. 11.

The constant twanging sound of the bridge's guy wires fills the air as the jeep road enters Allanburg Park. Exit the park and turn [R] onto Niagara Regional Rd 20. After crossing a small bridge, turn [L] onto Princess St, cycle uphill and join the trail on your left. Be careful as this is single-track. Keep your wits about you as this section of trail is somewhat difficult. Exiting out along the canal, keep right following the deep green water to a [T] intersection. Swing [R] and follow the jeep road up a slight grade moving away from the canal into a wooded area. The trail exits out onto a cul-de-sac and then descends past some large rafts along the canal and around a gate at Fox Road. Ride through the steel yard and cross the railway tracks. This 4th section of the Welland canal is no longer used for shipping, but for recreational purposes.

The trail quickly changes from loose gravel to asphalt and then back into gravel as it enters a green area along the canal. After passing Notre Dame College School, join the single-track path on your left which leads back to the canal and Main St. At Main St, turn [L], cross the old Welland Canal and make an immediate [L] turn onto Boardwalk St.

The "Rose City", **Welland** has always been prosperous due to its proximity to the canal. The original settlement was called Aqueduct, and the name only changed to Merrittsville in 1842, in honour of William Hamilton Merritt, the financial agent for the Welland Canal. In 1858, upon its incorporation, Lt. Gov. Simcoe renamed the settlement Welland after the river in Lincolnshire, England.

Itinerary: Leg 2 (Welland to Port Dalhousie, 50 km). Take a few minutes to explore Welland's famous mural on the back streets that branch off Main St. Within a four-block radius of your present location, there are over 27 giant outdoor murals painted by some of Canada's finest artists.

A short distance along Boardwalk St at the S-bend, get on the pathway as it passes between some cedars on the left side of the road. Riding along the canal into Merritt Island Park, keep to the left and follow the paved pathway as it goes under one bridge, over another and changes into a crushed gravel trail just before arriving at a set of railway tracks. At the railway tracks, turn [L] and cross the canal. On the far side of the bridge, turn [R] and rejoin the trail you were on earlier.

To get to the best spot along the canal to view ships in motion, cross the train tracks and follow the jeep road to the canals [Y] junction located where the road swings sharply to right. Here, the ships heading for Lake Erie can be seen as they send tall plumes of steam into the air.

Follow the trail back to Niagara Regional Rd 20, turn [R] and walk your bicycle across the lift bridge. Turn [L] onto Regional Rd 58/Davis Road and cycle to the stop lights at Thorold Stone Road. Immediately after crossing the lights, turn [L] and join the bicycle path which goes under the canal into the Thorold Tunnel. This was the first tunnel built under the Welland Canal. After passing through the tunnel, at the top of the hill, turn [R] onto Ormond St and ride to St. David St. Turn [L] and then [R] onto Front St, and cycle back to Mountain Locks Park. At Glendale Ave turn [R] and pedal to the Welland Canal Parkway Trail.

Do not cross the canal. Once on the canal trail, the cycling is much easier. The first stop along the Welland Canal Parkway Trail is the visitors centre at Lock 3. The main information centre for the canal (washroom facilities and refreshments available), the visitors centre houses many historical artifacts. There are also an elevated observation deck and the Lacrosse Hall of Fame. Lacrosse is Canada's national sport – not hockey as many people tend to think. The observation deck is an ideal place to stop and see the ocean-going freighters make their way across the Niagara escarpment. The trail for the most part runs parallel to Government Road. Ride under Queenston St, past Lock 2 and then Lock 1 at Lakeshore Road before entering Malcomson Park. At the Port Weller Municipal Beach, the trail swings left and turns into the Waterfront Trail, which runs from Niagara Falls to Gananoque. Follow the Waterfront Trail signs as they guide you along Arthur St into Cherrie Road Park. For the most part, the trail hugs the Lake Ontario shoreline and passes through Spring Garden Park and Belmont Park before following a few back streets into Westcliffe Park. After the old lighthouse, the trail rounds the harbour and finally returns to the starting point at Port Dalhousie's Lakeside Park.

13. Myths, Miracles and Pathways

This tour begins in Niagara-on-the Lake, the first capital of Upper Canada, and travels through Queenston Heights, one of the province's oldest towns. Passing under the shadow of Brock's Monument, it follows the Niagara Recreational Trail along the Niagara River. It then climbs high above the rapids at the Niagara Generating Station, and to the Seventh Wonder of the World, Niagara Falls.

Return Distance: 55 km
No. of recommended legs: 1
Level of Difficulty: 橲橲
Surface: Asphalt, very little gravel

Villages/Towns/Cities: Niagara-on-the-Lake, Queenston Heights, Virgil, Niagara Falls

Local Highlights: Casino Niagara, Great Gorge Adventures, The Guinness Book of World Records, Journey Behind the Falls, Louis Tussaud's Waxworks, Lundy's Lane Historical Museum, Maid of the Mist, Marineland, Minolta Tower, Mount Carmel & St. Therese Shrine, Niagara Falls Art Gallery, Niagara Falls Museum, Niagara Helicopters Ride, Niagara Parks Butterfly Conservatory and Greenhouses, Queenston Heights Park, Air-Combat Canada, Fort George National Historic Park, Laura Secord Homestead, Mackenzie Heritage Printery, McFarland House, Niagara Historical Society Museum, Niagara Parkway, Shaw Festival, Samuel E. Weir Library, eleven local wineries

Recommend Bicycles: Touring/Hybrid/Mountain

Tour Suggestions: Pack a lunch to enjoy on the tour.

How to Get There: Get off the Queens Elizabeth Way at the exit for Hwy 55 and follow it to Niagara-on-the-Lake. Start the

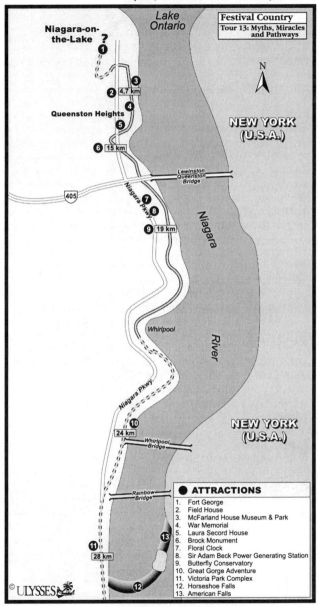

Lake Ontario

Festival Country
Tour 13: Myths, Miracles and Pathways

Niagara-on-the-Lake ?

N

4,7 km

Queenston Heights

15 km

NEW YORK (U.S.A.)

405

Lewinston Queenston Bridge

Niagara Pkwy

19 km

Niagara River

Whirlpool

Niagara Pkwy.

24 km

Whirlpool Bridge

NEW YORK (U.S.A.)

Rainbow Bridge

28 km

● **ATTRACTIONS**

1. Fort George
2. Field House
3. McFarland House Museum & Park
4. War Memorial
5. Laura Secord House
6. Brock Monument
7. Floral Clock
8. Sir Adam Beck Power Generating Station
9. Butterfly Conservatory
10. Great Gorge Adventure
11. Victoria Park Complex
12. Horseshoe Falls
13. American Falls

© ULYSSES

Practical Information

Population:
Niagara-on-the-Lake: 12,700
Niagara Falls: 75,000

 Tourist Information

✦ **Niagara-on-the-Lake:** Niagara-on-the-Lake Chamber of Commerce, PO Box 1043, 153 King St, Niagara-on-the-Lake, Ontario, L0S 1J0, (905) 468-4263, www.niagaraonthelake.com
✦ **Niagara Falls:** Niagara Falls Chamber of Commerce, 4458 Queen St, Niagara Falls, Ontario, L2E 6H1, (905) 374-3666, www.niagaraparks.com

 Bicycle Shops

✦ **Niagara-on-the-Lake:** The Bike Shop, 996 Lakeshore Rd, Niagara-on-the-Lake, Ontario, (905) 934-3815
✦ **Niagara Falls:** Pedlar Bicycle Shop, 4547 Queen St, Niagara Falls, Ontario, (905) 357-1273;   Cupolo's, 5510 Ferry, Niagara Falls, Ontario, (905) 356-4850; E & R Lawn & Garden Equipment, 4374 Drummond, Niagara Falls, Ontario, (905) 358-0729; Steve's Place Bicycles and Repair, 181 Niagara Blvd., Niagara Falls, Ontario 1-888-649-2453

 Special Sights and Events

✦ **Niagara-on-the-Lake:** Virgil Stampede, Tour of Homes, Hillebrand Vineyard Strings, Strawberry Festival, Wine Auction, Society Garden Tour, Artistry by the Lake, Canada Day, St. Mark's Cherry Festival, Hike of Parks Day, Potato People Family Festival, Peach Celebration, Apple Festival, Sotheby's Heirloom Discovery Days.

✦ **Niagara Falls** Star Traveller, May Blossom Festival, Police Pipes and Drums Tattoo, Festival of Lights, Seasonal flower shows at the Niagara Greenhouses, Kings' Birthday, Garden Party, American Garrison Day, Friendship Festival, Living History Weekend, Blues in the Park, All Hallow's Eve, Chrysanthemum Show, McFarland Christmas

Accommodations

✦   **N i a g a r a - o n - t h e - L a k e**   and   **N i a g a r a Falls**: Hotel/Motel/Inn/B&B/Camping

trip at the Fort George parking lot on the Niagara Parkway. Parking is free and it is safe to park there. As the Niagara River Recreational trail winds its way through the region's fruit belt, you will pass many historical landmarks and enjoy the breathtaking scenery of the Niagara River gorge. The highlight of this ride are the impressive American and Canadian Falls. Here, the myths of the past are only surpassed by the falls' stunning beauty and the legendary barrel riders who have braved its thundering water to the bottom of the gorge.

Itinerary: Facing historic Fort George, which was built in 1796, turn [R], and [R] again, and follow the Niagara Recreational Trail across Queen's Parade, and past modern replicas of period barracks and cannons. After arcing to the left and passing the vine-covered fences along John St, the trail crosses the parkway, follows the Niagara River and soon arrives at the back door of a well-preserved Georgian brick house. This was the home of His Majesty's Boat Builder, James McFarland. A short distance ahead, on the other side of the road, just after Line 2, is the "Field House," now a private residence. Built in the 1800s, it is one of the oldest brick buildings in the province. The trail crosses many wooden bridges and passes several local wineries as it makes its way to the spot where Roger Woodward, at the age of seven, was the first person to be swept over the falls unprotected and survive!

Just a short distance ahead of the adjacent Inniskillin water tower, the trail enters a residential area. Remember to yield the right of way to cars and other trail users. At the first driveway past the water tower, turn [L] and follow the trail into the woods instead of proceeding along the parkway portion of the trail. This is a lovely ride that offers some refreshing shade on a hot day. The trail climbs back up to the parkway, where you are rewarded with a pretty view of the Niagara River. The river is approximately 56 kilometres long and moves along at a respectable 64 kilometres per hour.

After passing some intricate residential stone fences, the trail leaves the parkway and descends into the town of **Queenston**. Coast downhill past a pillared Georgian mansion known as Willowbank. Built for Alexander Hamilton in 1833, it served as the area's first post office. To the left of the mansion is a laneway that leads down to an excellent view of the Niagara River. At the bottom of the valley, an exhilarating climb begins on Queenston St as you cycle past the 1842 Queenston Baptist Church and Laura Secord's homestead. As the road swings to the right, notice the glass-enclosed bronze statue of Sir Isaac Brock's horse. At the Niagara Parkway, turn [L] and then [R] onto York St and access the trail on your left. Then it's a long climb to the top of the Niagara Escarpment. At the top of the hill, the trail enters Roy Terrace, where the Niagara River Gorge begins. To the right are 260 steps leading to Queenston Heights Park, and to the left is the Niagara Parkway. Take the easier way into the park by following the parkway to the park's entrance. Since one of the most important battles of the War of 1812 took place here, a 210-foot monument dedicated to the battle's hero, Sir Isaac Brock, dominates the park and the valley below. To the left of the statue, enjoy a fantastic view of the Niagara River as it flows into Lake Ontario. Here, the Bruce Trail begins its long 693-kilometre journey across the province to the tip of the Bruce Peninsula.

Rejoin the trail by exiting the parking lot, crossing the parkway, and accessing the trail entrance on the left. The trail crosses a parking lot, and goes under the Lewiston Queenston Bridge. On the far side of the road is one of the world's largest floral clocks (12 m in diameter), built by Ontario Hydro in 1950. The face of the clock is now a landmark, covered with

19,000 plants and maintained by the gardeners and students of the Niagara Parks Commission.

The trail rounds a bend and arrives at the Sir Adam Beck Power Generating Station. Here, it passes under a row of hydro towers and overlooks the rapids on the Niagara River far below. After the ivy-covered Hall of Memory, the trail exits into a large parking lot. Keep left as you ride along the gorge, and follow the trail across the Niagara Parkway. After passing the Butterfly Conservatory and the Niagara Parks School of Horticulture, you will notice the Niagara Glen Picnic and Nature Area on the opposite side of the parkway. Its unique nature store makes for an interesting stop. The trail crosses back over the parkway just after Niagara Glen, and enters Thompson Point. This is an excellent rest spot where you can watch a cable car cross the gorge that separates Canada from the United States.

The trail enters a grove of gnarled pine trees, and follows what used to be the double track bed of the electric Niagara Falls Park and River Railway. As you ride past the helicopter landing pad, the Minolta Tower is clearly visible in the distance. The trail ends at the Whirlpool Rapids Lookout and the Spanish Aero Car ride which dangles its riders some 1,800 feet above the swirling whirlpools of **Niagara Falls**.

At this point, the trail joins the parkway and the spectacular gorge fades into the distance. We suggest you walk your bicycle along the sidewalk for the next several kilometres, as the view is just too good to miss.

Ahead is the Great Gorge Adventure and the Whirlpool Bridge. As you pass the magnificent stonework of Christ Church, you can feel the mist off the American Falls spray your face. The gorge is much wider here, and the water movement has slowed considerably. Just after passing under the Rainbow Bridge, you can see both the 56-metre-high American Bridal Falls and 54-metre-high Canadian Horseshoe Falls. The Rainbow Bridge marks the beginning of Queen Victoria Park. One of North America's most prestigious gardens, it encompasses 154 acres of rock and rose gardens, stately trees and over 500,000 daffodils that bloom in the spring. On the right is the new Casino and just ahead is the Victoria Park Restaurant and the Maid of the Mist Complex. There are so many people that it is much easier to get around by walking your bicycle. This recreational trail continues all the way to Fort Erie, but with so much to explore it is perhaps best to leave that trip for another day.

The return ride to Niagara-on-the-Lake is much safer and quicker if you take the road rejoining the trail at the Spanish Aero Cars. As the trail approaches Thomson Park, look for a single-track trail to the right. Follow this old Indian trail to one of the best lookouts on the river. Be careful: just before it rejoins the recreational trail, it drops dramatically over several tree roots. After passing Vrooman's Battery, continue following the river trail along the parkway to Brown's Point instead of descending along the tree-lined path taken earlier. Finally, keep to the right following the trail along the gorge through a grove of stately oaks and French thorn trees. On this return leg, the trail you have been following exits onto the Parkway behind Fort George. Turn [R] onto the road and follow it as it descends to the Navy hall and the refurbished steamship SS Pumper. At Melville St, turn [L] and pedal uphill to a [L] turn onto Byron St. After riding past the front doors of Queens Landing, join the path at the end of the road and return to the Fort George parking lot.

---

14. Wineries and Vineyards

The quiet backroads of the picturesque Niagara Escarpment and the surrounding vineyards and countryside provide the picturesque backdrop for this tour. Occasional stops along the route allow you to experience the traditions and hospitality of a number of world class wine producers.

Return Distance: 56 km
No. of recommended legs: 1
Level of Difficulty: ۶۶
Surface: Asphalt, very little gravel

Villages/Towns/Cities: Niagara-on-the-Lake, Queenston Heights, Virgil, Niagara Falls

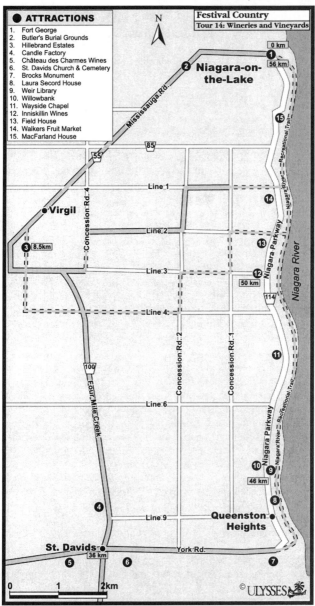

● ATTRACTIONS

1. Fort George
2. Butler's Burial Grounds
3. Hillebrand Estates
4. Candle Factory
5. Château des Charmes Wines
6. St. Davids Church & Cemetery
7. Brocks Monument
8. Laura Secord House
9. Weir Library
10. Willowbank
11. Wayside Chapel
12. Inniskillin Wines
13. Field House
14. Walkers Fruit Market
15. MacFarland House

N

Festival Country
Tour 14: Wineries and Vineyards

0 km
1
56 km

Mississauga Rd.

2 Niagara-on-
the-Lake

15

85

55

Line 1

Virgil

Concession Rd. 4

14

Line 2

13

3 8.5km

Line 3

12
50 km

Line 4

114

Concession Rd. 2

Concession Rd. 1

11

100

Four Mile Creek

Niagara Parkway
Niagara River = Recreational Trail

Niagara River

Line 6

10 9
46 km

8

4

Line 9

Queenston
Heights

St. Davids
36 km
5   6

York Rd.

7

0   1   2km

©ULYSSES

Practical Information

See also Tour 13. Myths, Miracles and Pathways

 Local Wineries:

✦ **Niagara-on-the-Lake:** Hillebrand Estate Wineries, Hwy 55, (905) 468-7123; Chateau des Charmes Wines, York Road, (905) 262-5202; Inniskillin Wines, Niagara Parkway at Line 3, RR 1, L0S 1J0, (905) 468-3554; Stone Chruch Vineyards, 1270 Irvine Road, RR 5, L0S 1J0, (905)935-3535; Marynissen Estates, 1208 Concession 1, L0S 1J0, (905) 468-7270; Pillitteri Estates Winery, 1696 Hwy 55, L0S 1J0, (905) 468-3147; Reif Estate Winery, 15608 Niagara Parkway, RR 1, L0S 1J0, (905) 468-7738; Sunnybrook Farm Estate Winery, 1425 Lakeshore Road, RR 3, L0S 1J0, (905) 468-1122; Joseph's Estates Wines, 1811 Hwy 55, RR 3, L0S 1J0, (905) 468-1259; Konzelmann Estate Winery, 1096 Lakeshore Road, L0S 1J0, (905) 935-2866, Strewn Winery, 1339 Lakeshore Road, L0S 1J0, (905) 468-1229

Local Highlights: Casino Niagara, Great Gorge Adventures, The Guinness Book of World Records, Journey Behind the Falls, Louis Tussaud's Waxworks, Lundy's Lane Historical Museum, Maid of the Mist, Marineland, Minolta Tower, Mount Carmel & St. Therese Shrine, Niagara Falls Art Gallery, Niagara Falls Museum, Niagara Helicopters Ride, Niagara Parks Butterfly Conservatory and Greenhouses, Queenston Heights Park, Air-Combat Canada, Fort George National Historic Park, Laura Secord Homestead, Mackenzie Heritage Printery, McFarland House, Niagara Historical Society Museum, Niagara Parkway, Shaw Festival, Samuel E. Weir Library, eleven local wineries

Recommend Bicycles: Touring/Hybrid/Mountain

Tour Suggestions: Pack a lunch to enjoy on the tour. The Vineyard Bicycle Tour at Hillebrand Estates is very enjoyable and educational.

How to Get There: Get off the Queen Elizabeth Way at the exit for Hwy 55 and follow it to Niagara-on-the-Lake. Start the trip at the Fort George parking lot on the Niagara Parkway. Parking is free, and it is safe to park there.

Following the wine route along the rolling roads in the Niagara Peninsula is a soothing experience. There are eleven wine makers in the immediate area around Niagara-on-the-Lake, three of which will be visited during this tour. These wineries lie on the same latitude as Florence, Italy and parts of France, and produce excellent Chardonnay, Riesling, Pinot Noir and Ice Wine. It is difficult to choose which winery to tour. Most winery tours visit the vineyards, the barrel-aging room, and the underground cellar, and include a sampling of their most popular wines.

Itinerary: Exit the Fort George parking lot by turning [R] onto Queens Parade, which changes into Picton St just after passing the Shaw Festival at Wellington St. Just before reaching the 1921 clock tower, located right in the middle of the road, turn [L] onto King St. Once past the Prince of Wales Hotel, turn [R] onto Mary St. At the Mississauga St stop lights, turn [L] and follow Regional Rd 55 out of **Niagara-on-the-Lake**.

Cycling through the heart of the Niagara wine country, you will pass a number of benchtop and estate wineries. Although all of these wineries use similar varieties of grapes, they each produce a wine with a taste that is unique to itself. Most of the wineries in the area offer tours and are required by law to charge a nominal fee for their wine tasting. Also, wine cannot be served until 11am. Since most of your riding will take place under the hot afternoon sun, pack plenty of water.

Continue straight through **Virgil** – the town of many names. It was originally known as Four Mile Creek, then as Cross Roads, and then Lawrenceville before the post office established its present name in 1895. Once past the second set of stop lights, be careful as the road's shoulder drops at least six inches. Just ahead, turn [L] into Hillebrand Estates Winery. The region's largest wine producer, it offers many different ways to experience the art of wine making.

Hillebrand is a good place to start a day of cycling in wine country. Beginning next to their Vineyard Cafe, exit the grounds via their back entrance. Turn [R] out of the parking lot onto Niagara Line 3, and at St. Michael's School turn [L] onto Niagara Concession Road 6. As you cycle past row upon row of grape vines, you will notice that these rows are planted north to south, allowing for even lighting on both sides of the vines. At Line 4, turn [L], cross Four Mile Creek Road, and turn [L] onto Concession Road 2. After passing a greenhouse complex, make a [R] turn onto Line 3 and follow it to Concession Road 1. Turn [L], cycle past a field of grapes that has been planted east to west because of poor land drainage. Notice that the type of grapes grown here are quite different from the varieties seen earlier. At Line 2, turn [R] and look for Brock's Monument in the distance.

Upon reaching the Niagara Parkway, turn [L] onto the Niagara River Recreation Trail, and return to the road at Walkers Fruit Market. Turn [L] onto Line 1 and follow this gravel road across Concession Road 1. At this point, Line 1 is paved once more, and if you are in the right place at the right time, you can enjoy a cooling shower compliments of the local irrigation pumps. At Concession Road 2, turn [L], go past a man-made dam and irrigation ditch, and make a [R] turn onto Line 2. Just past the cow-in-the-mail-box, turn [L] onto Concession Road 4. What begins as a fairly good gravel road, quickly becomes quite rough. At the [T] intersection turn [R] onto Line 3 and ride back to Four Mile Creek Road. At this point, the road along Line 3 passes an excellent lunch stop at the Upper Virgil Dam and the back entrance to the Hillebrand Estates.

Turn [L] onto Four Mile Creek Road and go past the Niagara Nut Grove. Here, many species of nut trees, such as the American Chestnut, Black Walnut, Butternut, Chinese Chestnut and European Filbert, are grown. A few kilometres further, the road passes Nabisco and a candle factory before climbing into the village of St. Davids. At the stop sign turn [R] onto York Road, and cycle past the old fire hall and the Burning of St. Davids plaque. At the green-roofed mansion, turn [L] into Chateau des Charmes Wines. This winery uses state-of-the-art equipment, but like all wineries, it still ages its wine in oak barrels.

Return to St. Davids, cross Four Mile Creek Road and go past St. Davids United Church and cemetery with its large grave stones. Major David Secord, St. Davids' namesake and brother-in-law to Laura Secord, is buried here. Cycle downhill on the Niagara Parkway, turn [L], and then [R] and follow Queenston St as it rapidly descends into **Queenston**.

After climbing uphill past the Weir Library, join the Niagara Recreational trail and follow it to a split in the river trail. Bear right and follow the trail down and through a wooded area along the Niagara River. The trail eventually returns to the parkway. At this point, instead of joining the recreational trail, ride on the parkway and make a [L] turn at the bridge onto Line 3. You'll easily spot the water tower of the Inniskillin Winery just up the road. This winery offers guided and self-guided tours, and has a unique wine-tasting facility where you step right up to the bar.

Return to the Niagara Parkway and resume your ride on the Niagara River Trail. Cycle past Reif Estate Winery on your left. Follow the river back to Fort George and the **Niagara-on-the-Lake** tourist information booth.

If time permits, cycle around the delightful Edwardian town of Niagara-on-the-Lake. Originally, this area was the Neutral Indian village of Onghiara. When it was settled by Loyalists, it became known as Newark. It was the first capital of Upper Canada, and the site of some important battles during the War of 1812, including one that burned the town to the ground in 1813. Today, Niagara-on-the-Lake is best known for the Shaw summer theatre festival. The plays are staged in an 822-seat proscenium arch theatre, the only one in the world solely devoted to presenting the works of George Bernard Shaw. Other building highlights in town are the St. Vincent de Paul Roman Catholic Church and the St. Andrews Presbyterian Church. One stop that should not be missed is a visit to the Niagara Apothecary, the oldest pharmacy still in operation in Canada. The picturesque back streets of this 19th-century community are steeped in history and make for a relaxing ride after a day in the country.

OFF-ROAD CYCLING

Public Trails

Cambridge

Cambridge Heritage River Trail (18 km)
Surface: Asphalt/loose surface
Beginning: Churchill Park to Blackridge Road and Townline Road
Contact: Cambridge Visitor and Convention Bureau, 532 King
St East, Cambridge, Ontario N3H 3N4, ☎(519) 653-1424.

Cambridge to Paris Rail Trail (18.7 km)
Surface: gravel/hard packed
Beginning: Cambridge or Paris
Contact: Grand River Conservation Authority, 400 Clyde Road,
Box 729, Cambridge, Ontario N1R 5W6, ☎(519) 621-2761.

Dryden Tract & Sudden Tract (20 km)
Surface: Technical Single Track
Beginning: Cambridge (Alps Road)
Contact: Grand River Conservation Authority, 400 Clyde Road,
Box 729, Cambridge, Ontario N1R 5W6, ☎(519) 621-2761.

Elora

Elora Cataract Trailway (47 km)
Surface: Original Railbed/hardpacked
Beginning: Elora and Cataract
Contact: Grand River Conservation Authority, 400 Clyde Road,
Box 729, Cambridge, Ontario N1R 5W6, ☎(519) 621-2761.

Fonthill

Fonthill Spur Trail/Stop '19' (4.5 km)
Surface: Original Railbed/hardpacked
Beginning: City boundary and Welland River

Contact: Welland Community Planner, City of Welland, 411 East Main St, Welland, Ontario L3B 3X4, ☎(905) 732-7515.

Guelph

Guelph Spurline (1.6 km; part of 20 km Royal Recreation Trail)
Surface: Loose surface/hardpacked
Beginning: Dufferin/George St to London Road
Contact: OALA, Park Technician, Recreation and Parks Department, 1 Carden St Guelph, Ontario N1H 3A1, ☎(519) 837-5618.

Hamilton Area

Hamilton to Brantford Rail Trail (37 km)
Surface: Loose surface/hardpacked
Beginning: Brantford and Hamilton
Contact: Halton Region Conservation Authority,, 838 Mineral Springs Road, P.O. Box 7099, Ancaster, Ontario L9G 3L3, ☎(905) 648-4427.

Waterdown Trails (25 km)
Surface: Technical Single Track
Beginning: Waterdown
Contact: Halton Region Conservation Authority, 838 Mineral Springs Road, P.O. Box 7099, Ancaster, Ontario L9G 3L3, ☎(905) 648-4427.

Chedoke Radial Trail (2.5 km)
Surface: Paved/loose surface
Beginning: West Hamilton to Ancaster
Contact: Parks Division, The Regional Municipality of Hamilton, 1 James St South, 3rd Floor, Hamilton, Ontario, L8P 4R5, ☎(905) 546-2409.

Escarpment Rail Trail (7 km)
Surface: crushed gravel
Beginning: Hamilton Core to East Mountain

Contact: Parks Division, The Regional Municipality of Hamilton, 1 James St South, 3rd Floor, Hamilton, Ontario L8P 4R5, ☎(905) 546-2409.

Cootes Dr. Trail (2.5 km)
Surface: Paved
Beginning: McMaster University to Dundas
Contact: Parks Division, The Regional Municipality of Hamilton, 1 James St South, 3rd Floor, Hamilton, Ontario L8P 4R5, ☎(905) 546-2409.

Niagara

Upper Canada Trail (10.6 km)
Surface: Original Railbed/hard packed
Beginning: Regional Road 81 and Land River
Contact: Upper Canada Trail-Property Officer, 2201 St. David's Road, P.O. Box 1042, Thorold, Ontario L2V 4T7, ☎(905) 984-3630.

St. Catharines Area

Participark Trail (4 km of trail)
Merritt Trail (26 km)
Terry Fox Trail (3 km)
Walker's Creek Trail (5 km)
Burgoyne Woods
Welland Canal Parkway Trail
Green Ribbon Trail
Participark
Contact: Parks and Recreation Department, 320 Geneva St, St. Catharines, Ontario L2R 7C2, ☎(905) 937-7210.

Resort and Conservation Trails

Alton/Caledon Area
Alton Trail (10 km of trail): Terra Cotta Conservation Area, ☎(905) 877-9650.

Backus Heritage Conservation Area
RR 1, Port Rowan, Ontario, N0E 1M0, ☎(519) 586-2201.

Bolton Area
Albion Hills Conservation Area (27 km of trail): Metro Toronto Region Conservation Authority, 5 Shoreham Drive, Downsview, Ontario M3N 1S4, ☎(416) 661-6600.

Chicopee Ski Hill
396 Morrison Road, Kitchener, Ontario N2A 2Z6, ☎(519) 894-5610.

Guelph/Milton Area
Hilton Falls Conservation Area (16 km of trail): Halton Region Conservation Authority, 2596 Britannia Road West, RR 2, Milton, Ontario L9T 2X6, ☎(905) 336-1158.

Hamilton
Dundas Valley Trails (41 km of trail): Hamilton Region Conservation Authority, P.O Box 7099, 838 Mineral Springs Road, Ancaster, Ontario L9G 3L3, ☎(905) 525-2181.

Milton Area
Kelso Conservation Area (10 km of trail): Halton Region Conservation Authority, 2596 Britannia Road West, RR 2, Milton, Ontario L9T 2X6, ☎(905) 336-1158.

St. Catharines/Thorold Area
Short Hills Provincial Park (13 km of trail): Ministry of Natural Resources, P.O. Box 1070, Fonthill, Ontario L0S 1E0, ☎(905) 892-2656.

Turkey Point Provincial Park
PO Box 5, Turkey Point, Ontario, N0E 1TO, ☎(519) 426-3239.

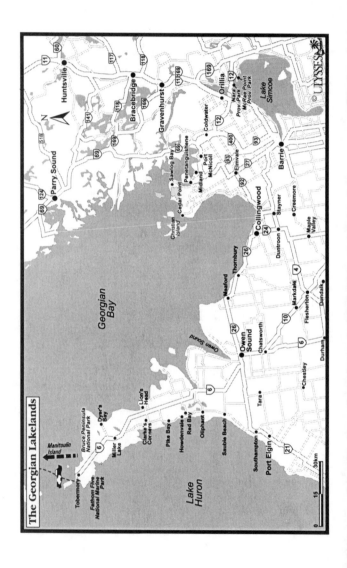

The Georgian Lakelands

THE GEORGIAN LAKELANDS

T he Georgian Lakelands embrace the maple lined streets of Port Elgin, the inviting waters of Lake Huron and the majestic limestone cliffs of Georgian Bay. Cycling this area of the province can take your breath away in more ways than one. Enjoy spectacular scenery, awe-inspiring wildlife and some great single-track. All roads in this part of the province follow the Bruce Trail to Tobermory's famous Five Fathom Underwater Park.

THE TOURS

15. Breweries, Sulfur Springs and Boxing: Cycling in the Queen's Bush

If quiet country roads winding through engaging scenery dotted with hamlets of German and Scottish heritage appeal to you, a bicycle adventure in Ontario's Saugeen Country is an experience you don't want to miss.

Return Distance: 68 km
No. of recommended legs: 1
Difficulty: 🚲 🚲
Surface: Asphalt and some gravel

Villages/Towns/Cities: Hanover, Carlsruhe, Neustadt, Mildmay, Walkerton, Formosa

Local Highlights: John G. Diefenbaker Home, Neustadt Springs Brewery, Mildmay Artesian Spring, Formosa Springs Brewery, Stoneyground Gardens

Recommended Bicycles: Hybrid/Mountain/Touring

Tour Suggestions: There are two different routes from Formosa to Walkerton.

How To get There: From the Kitchener area, take Hwy 401 to exit 295, and follow Hwy 6 N to Arthur, make a [L] turn onto Hwy 9, at Walkerton, turn [R] and follow Hwy 4 into Hanover. From the London area, take Hwy 401 to exit 177, and follow Hwy 4 N, make a [R] and then turn [L] onto Hwy 23; at Hwy 9 turn [L], turn [R] at Walkerton on Hwy 4 and follow the road to Hanover.

The Queen's Bush or the Huron Tract, was one of the last areas in the province to be colonized. Extensive tracts of forest and fertile land waiting to be put to good use could still be found along the Saugeen River in the 1850s. This land was free for the taking for people with strong backs and a lot of determination and settlers from eastern Ontario and countries overseas rushed to settle the area. As the Queen's Bush developed, nationalities and groups of particular religious beliefs settled close together creating distinct Irish, French and German communities. There is a long tradition of country inns, which continue to play an important role in this area of the province. Abraham Buck was one of the first settlers in the region, and the predominately German town that grew up around his inn in 1848 became known as Buck's Crossing. It must have been somewhat confusing for map makers at the time, as the town was renamed several times, (Adamstown and Slabtown) before deciding on its current name, **Hanover**. Even

ATTRACTIONS
1. Historic Carlsruhe Brewery
2. Neustadt Brewery
3. House of John George Diefenbaker
4. Flowing Artesian Spring
5. Formosa Springs Brewery
6. Old School House and Stoney Ground Gardens
7. Vertical-Slot Fishway

The Georgian Lakelands
Tour 15: Breweries, Sulfur Springs and Boxing

© ULYSSES

today, Hanover is known for its furniture production and for the accomplishments of one of its early citizens, Noah Brusso, better known as Tommy Burns. He became the first Canadian Heavyweight Champion in 1906.

Itinerary: The starting point is the Hanover Town Park located on Bruce Rd 10, which is north of Bruce Rd 4 (10th Street/Hwy 4). Free parking, as well as washroom and picnic facilities, can be found here. Exit the parking lot, turn [R] onto 7th Ave/(Bruce Rd 10) and cross Bruce Rd 4. After passing the Piano Man on your right and the Hanover Convention Centre on your left, keep right following 7th Ave at the [Y] junction. The memorial plaque for Tommy Burns is on your left and further ahead is the Hanover Hospital and Cemetery. As the road curves to the right it becomes Southline Rd, which descends, and once it crosses the Saugeen River, the road becomes Concession Road 2. Climbing uphill, the Allan

Practical Information

Population:
Hanover: 6,400
Mildmay: 981
Walkerton: 4,700

 Tourist Information

✦ **Hanover:** Hanover Library at the Civic Centre, 451 10th Ave., Hanover, Ontario N4N 2P1, (519) 364-1420
✦ **Mildmay:** Village of Mildmay, P.O. Box 128, Mildmay, Ontario, N0G 2J0, (519) 367-2617
✦ **Walkerton:** Town of Walkerton, P.O. Box 68, Walkerton, Ontario N0G 2V0, (519) 881-2223.

 Bicycle Shops

✦ **Hanover:** Mako Sports, 294 10th Street, Hanover, Ontario N4N 1P2, (519) 364-1019
✦ **Mildmay:** Liesemer's Home Hardware Cycle & Sports, 98 Elora Street, Mildmay, Ontario N0G 2J0, (519) 367-5314
✦ **Walkerton:** Joy Source for Sports, 435 Durham E, Walkerton, Ontario N0G 1V0, (519) 881-2046.

 Special Sights and Events

✦ **Hanover:** Ringette Craft Fair, Fall Fair
✦ **Mildmay:** Mildmay-Carrick Fall Fair, Rotary Park walking trails, Artesian Spring
✦ **Walkerton:** Midwestern Ontario Festival, County Town Weekend, Little Royal Winter Fair, Heritage Fair, Seasonal Market, Saugeen River Trail, Vertical Slot Fishway, Stoneyground Gardens.

🛏 **Accommodations**

✦ **Hanover:** Motel/B&B/Camping
✦ **Mildmay:** Camping/Motel in Formosa
✦ **Walkerton:** Hotel/Motel/B&B/Camping

Poechman firewood farm is on your left. Turn [L] onto
Sideroad 30S, coast down into a pretty valley, then climb to
the historic village of **Carlsruhe**. To the left of the main
intersection on Concession Rd 14, is the original and somewhat
dilapidated Carlsruhe Brewery.

Resume your journey along Sideroad 30S, which turns into a
gentle gravel downhill. Your swift descent will take you past a
wood rail fence, wild raspberry canes and what appears to be
an old stone fort on your right. Caution is recommended as you
approach Concession Rd. 12. Listen for the forlorn *baas* of
sheep grazing amid the marsh on your right and enjoy the
cooling shade of an overgrown woodlot before reaching the
Haack gravel pit and Bruce Rd 16.

Turn [L] onto paved Bruce Rd 16 (there is no cycling lane) and
travel east towards the birthplace of the 13th Prime Minister of
Canada, John George Diefenbaker. Diefenbaker's yellow brick
home is still standing, and is located just northeast of Mill
Street. It is a quick descent to the main intersection of
Neustadt. Turn [R] onto Mill St. and take some time to
appreciate the towns many unique and historic mercantile.
Along Mill Street, the Neustadt Tavern and Restaurant are on
your left, the Neustadt Spring Brewery is on your right and the
impressive St. Peter's Lutheran Church is at the top of the hill.
Tours of the brewery caverns are available during business
hours and individual bottles of the Neustadt Brewer's unique
blend be purchased here.

Continue along Mill Street past the brewery and the water
tower. Turn [R] onto Concession Rd. 8 and follow this little
used road as it undulates, dramatically at times, to the hamlet
of Deemerton at Sideroad 20. Take some time to explore the

area on your left where you will find a magnificent old church built in 1872, the pastors home, a stable with a hardwood floor and a large, ancient cemetery.

Resume your trek along Concession Rd 8. Enter the "Lamplighter Village," Mildmay, on Absalom Street, turning [R] at the lights onto Elora Street/Bruce 9. Notice the old commercial hotel which still has separate men and women's entrances. The spires you saw in the distance as you approached **Mildmay** are those of the Sacred Heart Catholic Church that is found here. On the banks of Otter Creek, just a short distance ahead, is the Rotary Spring Park, which offers a full service rest area. Originally named Shield's Corner after a local innkeeper, then Mernersville after a well-known town benefactor, the town was renamed in 1868 for Mildmay Park in Scotland. At the park, look for the natural flowing artesian spring from which you can refill water bottles with fresh cool water.

Leaving the park, turn [L] onto Bruce Rd 9, towards downtown. Turn [R] onto Bruce Rd 3; it has no cycling lane but is reasonably wide. Enjoy this winding road for several kilometres as it passes a gravel pit and the Carrick Township sheds. Once past Bruce Rd 15 and Country Gardens Antiques, look for the "Elora Road Meat" sign, a red striped silo, a white silo and a radio tower. At the top of the hill turn [L] onto Beeline Road, which is a hard-packed gravel road. Descend to the [T] intersection, turn [R] and then [L] onto Council Road. Notice the lucky 911 number (13) at the first house on your left. Watch for moose ("beware of moose" sign) as you descend into the village of **Formosa**. Arriving at the [T] intersection of Bruce Rd. 12, the Formosa Springs Brewery is to your left.

Turn [R] and follow Bruce Rd 12 up a difficult climb. The magnificent Immaculate Conception Roman Catholic Church is at the top of the hill. Follow Bruce 12 for the next 5 km until reaching a [Y] junction of roads on your immediate right (Carrick Brant West Road and Tower Road). At this point you have two routing choices to Walkerton: for Hybrid or Mountain Bikes only, turn [R] onto Carrick Brant West Road, an old jeep road, that is very rough in spots. You will join Bruce Rd 3 after riding a wicked downhill stretch of washouts and ruts. Turn [L] onto Bruce Rd 3 and follow it to Bruce Rd 4/Hwy 4/9. Turning [R], cycle to a [T] intersection and turn [L] following the road past the old jail to downtown Walkerton. Turn [R] onto Durham Street/Bruce Rd 4. The other alternative is continue along Bruce Rd 12, cross Bruce Rd 4/Hwy4/9, and follow the road that is now called the Greenock-Brant Rd. Turn [R] onto North Durham Road at the large silos. Cross over Bruce Rd 3, then cycle past an old school house and Stoneyground Gardens, and take Durham Street into the town of **Walkerton**.

Follow Durham Street past the local bicycle shop and over the Saugeen River. Walkerton is also home to the Traux Dam which is the only vertical-slot fishway east of the Rockies, a type of fish ladder that allows rainbow trout to "climb" the dam, and swim upstream to their spawning grounds. The newly resurfaced road has a nice wide cycling lane as you follow this portion of Bruce Rd. 4 toward Hanover,. A short distance past the truck inspection station turn [L] onto Bruce Rd. 22, which takes you past the local airport. At the stop sign turn [R] onto Concession Rd. 2 NDR. Follow it east between Rosalind and Marl Lakes. At Bruce Rd. 10/7th Ave. turn right and make your way back to the starting point at the Hanover Town Park.

---

16. Cycling the Bruce Peninsula: Owen Sound, Tobermory and Sauble Falls

---

Cycling the Bruce is an exceptional tour. The ride follows the dramatic shores of Georgian Bay northwards and then heads south along the tree-lined roads and sandy beaches of Lake Huron. Begin in the shipping port of Owen Sound and cycle along the quiet country roads into the heart of the Bruce. Since this is a leisurely ride, you will have enough time to stop at many of the area's impressive lookouts and enjoy the view from there. Hike to the Bruce Caves, visit Wiarton Willy and see the breathtaking beauty of Lion's Head. Other highlights include a walk along the Bruce Trail to the unique cairns at Cypress Lake, and a search for shipwrecks in Fathom Five National Marine Park. The return legs cut through the centre of the peninsula and swing right to join the warmer waters of Lake Huron. After cycling through dense forest, wetland and the port towns of Pikes Bay and Howdenvale, the highlight of the return trip will be the refreshing rushing waters at Sauble Falls.

Return Distance: 306 km (56 km, 40 km,
54 km, 67 km, 54 km, 35 km)
No. of recommended legs: 6
Level of Difficulty: 🚲 🚲 🚲 🚲
Surface: Asphalt and gravel country roads

Villages/Towns/Cities: Owen Sound, Big Bay, Wiarton, Hope Bay, Lion's Head, Tobermory, Stokes Bay, Pike Bay, Howdenvale, Sauble Falls, Sauble Beach, Shallow Lake

Local Highlights: Billy Bishop Heritage Museum, Jones and Indian Falls, County of Grey-Owen Sound Museum, Harrison Park, Hibou Conservation Area, Inglis Falls Conservation Area, Owen Sound Marine & Rail Heritage Centre, The Roxy Theatre, Tom Thomson Memorial Art Gallery, Cape Croker - Chippewa of Nawash First Nations, Bruce's Caves Conservation Area, Spirit Rock Conservation Area, Movie set for "Quest for Fire," Bruce Trail in Lion's Head, Big Tub Lighthouse, Larkwhistle Garden-Dyer's Bay, Bruce Peninsula National Park, Fathom Five National Marine Park, Flowerpot Island, St. Edmund's Museum, Glass Bottom Boat Cruises, Ferry to Manitoulin Island, Sauble Falls, Saugeen Rail Trail

Recommended Bicycles: Hybrid/Mountain/Touring

Tour Suggestions: Allow one complete day in the Tobermory area for the Cypress Lake walking trails and a Tobermory glass bottom boat cruise. While cycling in the upper Bruce Peninsula, watch for black bears and poisonous Eastern Massassauga rattlesnakes which inhabit the area. Inexpensive overnight parking can be arranged at the K.O.A. campgrounds in Owen Sound.

How to Get There: From the north, Owen Sound can be reached by Highway 6; from the south by Highways 21, 6 and 10; from the west by Highway 21 and from the east by Highway 26.

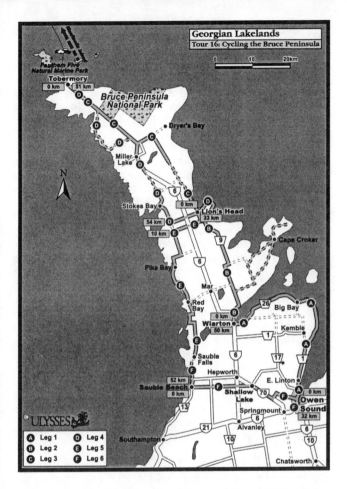

ⒶLeg 1	ⒹLeg 4
ⒷLeg 2	ⒺLeg 5
ⒸLeg 3	ⒻLeg 6

Because of its location in the Sydenham River Valley, Owen Sound has several good-sized hills to cycle. Owen Sound was a busy shipping centre in the 1800s due to its natural harbour. The town is also the birthplace of two of Canada's famous Group of Seven artists and WWI flying ace, Billy Bishop.

Itinerary: Leg 1 (Owen Sound to Wiarton, 56 km). Begin at the war memorial on the banks of the Sydenham River, at the corner of 8th Street West and 1st Ave West. Cycle north with the river on the your right, cross 9th Street and join the road. Cross 10th Street and rejoin the trail at Mr. Transmission.

Swing [L] onto the river boardwalk, and cycle to the bay. On the far side of the river, you can't miss the *Nindawayma,* the sister ship of the Chi-Cheemaun. At one time this ship was supposed to have provided ferry service from Tobermory to Manitoulin Island – but it never left the docks.

The trail passes numerous information plaques, the Marine Rail Museum, and by a large skateboard park. Then it crosses a small parking lot and turns left onto a private roadway that leads to some large grain elevators. Turn [R] and join the trail to the left of the road. Cross a wooden bridge into the lower end of Kelso Park, pass the large outdoor amphitheatre and swimming beach, and ride into the Rusty Gull Marina parking lot. Next, exit the parking lot and turn [R] onto 3rd Ave W (Eddy Sargent Parkway) and follow it north as it changes into Grey Rd. 1.

After riding past the historic Royal Orange Lodge, turn [L] onto Grey Rd. 26 and descend back towards the water and into Gravelly Bay. At the bottom of the hill, the road arcs to the left and follows the clear waters of Georgian Bay towards Wiarton. It is interesting to read some of the unique and bizarre cottage names along Island View Drive. Now climbing above the bay, look for the entrance to Centennial Park on the right. The park is a good spot to rest, and probably the best place in the world for skipping stones. Be careful as it is a very steep ride down into the park. When walking on the stone beach, it sounds like broken pieces of china are being rubbed together.

After Whippoorwill Marsh, Grey Rd. 26 descends into the charming community of **Big Bay**. On your right, at the main intersection, is the lake and a welcoming hello from the local fry shack at the boat launching dock. To the left is the general store and delicatessen, and you can even find some spare bicycle parts here.

Leaving Big Bay, cycle up the first of three hills. The road levels out after this first hill, and the ditches alongside have been planted with colourful Snapdragons. After Cedar Park, Grey Rd. 26 swings sharply to the left and then climbs dramatically. Once at the top, take a break and turn around and look back. The view makes the uphill ride well worth the struggle. Now

Practical Information

Population:
Owen Sound: 21,700
Wiarton: 2,291
Lion's Head: 500
Tobermory: 960
Sauble Beach: 517

 Tourist Information

✦ **Owen Sound:** Owen Sound Visitor Information Centre, 1155 1 St. Avenue West, N4K 4K8, (519) 371-9833, www.city.owen-sound.on.ca
✦ **Wiarton:** Town of Wiarton, Box 310, 315 George Street, Wiarton, Ontario, (519) 534-1400, www.wiarton-willie.org / South Bruce Chamber of Commerce, Box 269, N0H 2T0, (519) 534-1400
✦ **Lion's Head:** Bruce Peninsula Tourism, Box 269, N0H 2T0, (519) 793-4734, www.brucepeninsula.org
✦ **Tobermory:** Tobermory Chamber of Commerce, Box 250, N0H 2R0, (519) 596-2452, www.tobermory.org
✦ **Sauble Beach:** Chamber of Commerce Sauble Falls (519) 422-3300, www.saublebeach.com

Bicycle Shops

✦ **Owen Sound:** Terry's Cycle & Repair Shop, 101 10th Street East, N4K 1S1, (519) 376-0766;Todd's Sporting Goods, 80 9th Street East, N4K 1N4, (519) 376-0575

Special Sights and Events

✦ **Owen Sound:** All Breed Champion Dog Show,

Artist Studio Tour, Grey-Sauble Conservation Authority Craft and Garden Fair, Owen Sound Family Day, Highland Dance Competition, Canada Day, Roxy Theatre, A Tour of Secret Gardens, Spoke and Bustle, Harbour Heat Waves, Owen Sound Fall Fair, Festival of Northern Lights, Eddie Sargent Memorial "Cross the Bay Swim"

✦ **Wiarton:** Groundhog Festival Weekend

✦ **Lion's Head:** Escarpment Climbing, Glass Bottom Boat Cruise

✦ **Tobermory:** Glass Bottom Boats, Chi-Cheemaun Spring Cruise, Annual Chi-Cheemaun Festival Weekend, Canada Day, National Parks Day Celebrations of Flowerpot Island Light Station, Marine Heritage Weekend, Ceiledh Festival Weekend

✦ **Sauble Beach:** Summer Stock Car Racing, Chantry Chinook Classic Fishing Derby, Sauble Rock Festival with "No One You Know & Friends," Street Dance, Sandfest and Sandcastle Building Competition, Sauble Open Football Tournament, Oktoberfest

 Accommodations:

✦ **Owen Sound:** Hotel/Motel/Resort/B&B/Camping
✦ **Wiarton:** Cottages/Motel/B&B/Camping
✦ **Lion's Head:** Motel/Inn/B&B/Camping
✦ **Tobermory:** Hotel/Motel/Inn/B&B/Camping
✦ **Sauble Beach:** Cottages/Motel/B&B/Camping

 Off Road Cycling:

✦ **Owen Sound:** Yes, refer to the "Off Road Cycling" section at the end of this chapter.

 Market Days:

✦ **Lion's Head:** Every Saturday Morning

high above the bay, the large parking lot of Skinners Bluff is just ahead. From Colpoys Lookout, the islands of White Cloud, Hay and Griffith are just a small part of the spectacular view that looks across the bay to Colpoys Bluff.

Suddenly, an escarpment appears out of nowhere on your left – this is the last hill to climb before reaching the Bruce Caves Conservation Area. At the top of the hill, make a [L] turn; the caves parking lot is one kilometre down a gravel road. Because the area is cool, damp and moss covered, it has been nicknamed "Fern Capital of the World." Many different fern species are found here, including some that are endangered. Walking ferns, slender Cliffbrake and Holy ferns are native to the area. Lock your bicycle up at the visitor pavilion, then hike another kilometre to the caves which were created by the erosion of glacial Lake Algonquin almost 8,000 years ago.

Continuing along Cty. Rd. 26, enter **Wiarton** on Frank Street. A right turn will take you into downtown Wiarton and the campground and beaches on Colpoys Bay. A left turn leads to accommodations on the south side of the city. Wiarton's mascot is world famous. Born on the Bruce Peninsula, exactly on the 45th parallel, "Wiarton Willy" is an albino groundhog who has been predicting the coming of spring every February 2nd since 1956. If he see his shadow, there will be six more weeks of hard winter. No shadow means an early spring, and believe it or not, he has been right 90% of the time.

Itinerary: Leg 2 (Wiarton to Lion's Head, 40 km). At the corner of Cty. Rd 26 and Hwy 6, ride north through downtown Wiarton. Climb a long steep hill out of town and continue to the turn off for Cty. Rd 9. About a kilometre out of town, turn [R] into the Spirt Rock Conservation Area. This road leads to the burned-out ruins of the 1882 McNeil Mansion. Look for the spiral staircase that leads down the cliff to the water.

Back on Hwy. 6, make a [R] turn onto Cty. Rd. 9. The road swings left and descends to Colpoys Bay. Notice the "Old Factory" on the shores of the bay. At the Mallory Beach boat launching pier, keep following the road as it swings left and climbs past the local cemetery. For the next several kilometres, this road passes through some useless, boulder-encrusted farmland. At Bruce Rd. 18, you can make an optional [R] turn which will take you to the Cape Croker Camp Grounds in the Chippewa of Nawash First Nations Reserve. The return loop around the reserve is approximately 40 km.

Cape Croker Side Trip: The Cape Croker Indian Reserve is home to 600 Ojibways. It was established in the early 1800's after the inhabitants of the Nawash Indian Reserve surrendered their land on the west side of Owen Sound Bay. The reserve's population has travelled from as far as Wisconsin, Michigan, Chicago and Manitoulin Island. Turn [R] onto Bruce Rd. 18, ride past Artargan Saw and Lumber Mill and follow the road until it appears to end at a gravel laneway. Stay on the asphalt by turning [L] onto Purple Valley Road, and cycle through the hamlet of Purple Valley. Ride to the second road and turn [R] onto McIver Road. A short distance ahead is a spectacular view of the McGregor Bay, and the Cape Croker Campground is on your left. As the road descends from one of the highest points on the Peninsula, it turns into gravel. Cycle along the bay and follow the road past the water tower. It climbs once more before descending into the village of Cape Croker. Directly across the street from the stop sign is the 1892 United Church. Spend some time exploring the immediate area. It shouldn't take you long to find the only stone house on the reservation. It was built in the 1880s for the first Indian Agent. Also look for the 1907 Roman Catholic Church. Nearby is another old church, built in the 1860s, which is the area's oldest landmark. For the more adventurous, visit the Cape Croker Lighthouse. To get there, continue straight and follow the road as it swings to the left. At the second road, turn [R] and ride through Nayausheeng. Continue along the gravel road and bear right until you reach a [T] intersection. Turn [L] and follow this rough road out to the Cape Croker lighthouse. (On the return route do not make any turns, follow the road back to the United Church.) To complete the Cape Croker loop turn [R] at the stop sign; the United Church is now on your left. Pedal to another [R] turn at the end of the street. As you leave the village, notice the many wooden homes. You are now travelling through an area known as Cape Croker Prairie. The towering walls of the Niagara Escarpment are on the left and Coveneys Road climbs for a kilometre before it ends at Purple Valley Road. Turn [R] and cycle back to Bruce Rd. 9.

You could miss the hamlet of Adamsville in the blink of an eye; it is only discernable by the modern log house on the left. From here, Bruce Rd. 9 begins a series of gradual climbs and descents. At the top of the next rise after Adair Quarries, a large stone block cutting company, is Hope Bay Road. Turn [R] here and enjoy a quick descent into **Hope Bay**. Cliffs and blue water dominate the view at the bottom of the hill. It is pleasant to stroll along the bay, whose water is not much higher than your knees. Further up are the caves and pot holes of the Hope Bay Forest Provincial Nature Reserve.

Back on Cty. Rd. 9 at the Hopeness and Jackson's Cove Road you can embark upon another enjoyable excursion to the Greig Caves. To get there turn [R] onto the gravel road and follow it to the first [T] intersection, turn [L] and ride past the CKCO-TV tower to a laneway with a gate. Continue onto the laneway and follow the road to a trail along the escarpment. From here, hike the escarpment to the many caves used in the movie "Quest for Fire."

Once back on Bruce Rd 9, the road passes the old Barrow Bay mill. Exploring the bridge across from the mill reveals a hidden waterfall, to the right.

Bruce Road 9 climbs out of Barrel Bay and passes Cemetery Road twice before descending into **Lion's Head**. At the bottom of the hill, turn [R] and ride into the municipal park and campgrounds. The frigid, crystal blue waters of Isthmus Bay and the massive cliffs of the lion's mane fill the horizon. To the right of the park entrance, walk up to the bay. When the water is very still, the rotting, wooden ribs of a large ship are visible. Further out, by the floating shallow water marker, another ship can be seen at the bottom of the bay. Lion's Head was known as Point Hangcliffe in the late 1870s. When ships entered the bay from the lake, sailors noticed that the steep cliffs surrounding it resembled the head of a lion, hence its present name.

While in Lion's Head, take a hike on the Bruce Trail. From the municipal campgrounds, follow Webster Street to Helen Street. Turn [R] and cycle to Moore Street. Turn [L] and follow the road past the hospital and the numerous resort cottages until the road comes to a dead end. Lock up your bicycle and follow the trail to the right, then turn [L] onto an old jeep road. As you enter the Lion's Head Provincial Nature Reserve, notice the rusting cars just before the white trail markers of the Bruce Trail. Join the trail and follow it to the top of the Lion's Head escarpment and then down and around to Georgian Bay.

Itinerary: Leg 3 (Lion's Head - Tobermory, 54 km). Starting from the park, follow Webster Street to Main Street. Turn [R] onto Main Street and cycle north out of town. With Isthmus Bay on your right, the road climbs past the rocky 45th Parallel park (the halfway point between the North Pole and equator) and descends to a pretty ride along Whippoorwill Bay.

The waters of Georgian Bay are so clear that flat limestone rocks can be seen many feet under the water. When Isthmus Bay Road swings sharply to the right, it immediately changes into a winding gravel road. Now cycling along 40 hills, this portion of the tour quickly becomes one of those more memorable rides. Narrowing, it twists and turns, rises and falls through thick cedar forests, and feels a lot like a slow roller coaster ride. At East Road, the road changes back to asphalt and continues through open countryside. Upon arriving at Cape Chin, take a few minutes to visit the St. Margaret's Historical Chapel. Then cycle to Chin Road North and turn [L]. From here, it is only a short ride to the local Tea Room. Continue along East Road to Brinkman's Corner. Turn [L] and ride past Shouldice Lake Road to Hwy 6. If you turn right at Brinkman's Corner, an adventurous road lies ahead, which will take you out to the Dyers Bay lighthouse and world famous Larkwhistle Gardens.

Turn [R] onto Hwy 6; a short distance ahead is the Crane River Conservation and Rest Area. Hwy 6 can be very busy when the ferries arrive and depart, but with a little planning, the ride on this highway can be a relaxing experience. Cycling past a local Indian artifact dealer, the road descends and goes past a newly renovated gas station with showers. There are no showers in the National Park at the Cypress Lake campgrounds, and the showers at the gas station are five kilometres away. Continue past Cypress Lake. On the left are the Singing Sands Provincial Park and the shallow waters of Dorcas Bay.

By the time you get to **Tobermory** the locals will have warned you about the black bears and rattlesnakes. If encountered along the route, give these creatures a wide berth. There are seven more kilometres of climbs through cedar forests and several sections of wet, boggy countryside. Upon entering Tobermory, the St. Edmunds Township Museum and the local tourist booth are on the right. Just past the tourist office, turn [R] into the bustling tourist community of Little Tub Harbour. Tobermory is where the Bruce Tail ends its 633-kilometre journey from Queenston Heights near Niagara Falls. The town has two harbours, which offer safe anchorage in bad weather. Originally named Big Tub in 1871, it was renamed Tobermory ten years later after its twin fishing port on Scotland's Isle of Mull. Today it is a hot spot for divers to explore Canada's first national marine park with its 21 sunken sail and steam vessels. Glass bottom boats offer excursions to view the ship wrecks, and hikers flock here in order to explore the Cape Hurd Island system which includes Flower Pot Island.

Itinerary: Leg 4 (Tobermory to Lion's Head, 67 km). Returning to Lion's Head along the shores of Lake Huron is less demanding than the previous route taken. Follow Hwy 6 south and make a [R] turn onto Dorcas Bay Road. Ride through a man-made cedar tunnel, past the Singing Sands campground and the beaches of Dorcas Bay. The view over the next 20 kilometres is monotonous at times. The never-ending colour of green cedar is occasionally broken by a splash of colour on some of the local cottage signs or by the blue waters of Lake Huron. At the Johnson Harbour Rd. [T] intersection, swing [R] and have fun riding the next several kilometres on the only winding hills on this return leg.

Finally back on Hwy 6, turn [R], cross the Crane River and ride past Dyers Bay Road. Continue past the Miller Lake Road "Drift In" variety store and a colourful artist's fence. As the road begins to arc left at Lindsay Road 30, keep right and take the Ira Lake Road cutoff. This gravel road has little traffic and rides through a wetland area before zig zagging its way around Lake Ira. At Clarks Corners, cycle past the Colonel Clarke Tavern onto a smooth asphalt surface. The Stokes Bay Road swings sharply to the right as it enters Stokes Bay. Just before the turn, look for a forgotten stone address marker leaning up against an elderly cedar tree. Just before turning [L] at the Copper Kettle Restaurant, ride to the end of the street and look at the baby rattlers next to the telephone booth.

Cycle past the cheering at the Celtic Sports Camp and the tantalizing aroma of the local bake shop just up the road. At Bruce Rd. 9, turn [L], cross Hwy 6 at Ferndale, and return to Lion's Head.

Itinerary: Leg 5 (Lion's Head to Sauble Beach, 54 km). Following Bruce 9 south out of Lion's Head, retracing a portion of the route taken on Leg 2. Turn [R] onto Cemetery Road, cycle across the peninsula to the village of Spry and make a [L] turn onto West Road. Once you cross Little Pike Bay Road, the next several kilometres are gravel. At Pikes Bay Road (Harbour Road) turn [R] and then make a [L] turn onto Bellmore Lane. Join Sutter Road by turning [R] and then follow the Lake Huron Shoreline Sucker Creek Road. Turn [L] and ride into **Howdenvale**.

At the next [T] intersection, turn [L] and then [R] onto Huron Road. At Spry Lake Road turn [R] and, as you approach the lake, swing [L] onto Shoreline Road. Now on gravel, ride past a boardwalk crossing a marsh before entering the village of Oliphant. At Mary Street, continue straight and follow Bay Street along the lakeshore. Once at South Oliphant Road, turn [L], and turn [R] at the Sauble Falls Parkway/Bruce Rd 21. Cycle a few kilometres past the "Welcome to Sauble Beach" sign into **Sauble Falls**. Years ago along the falls, there were a saw mill and a hydro-electric power station. The ruins of these two building can be still be found on the north side of the river. Today the falls are a great place to have fun, so take off your shoes and try to walk across the rushing water. A short distance past the falls, turn [R] onto Lakeshore Road and follow the dunes and hundreds of colourful bathing suits into **Sauble Beach**.

Itinerary: Leg 6 (Sauble Beach to Owen Sound, 35 km). This final leg is a short one, leaving plenty of time to enjoy the warm Lake Huron waters. The last leg begins at the corner of Bruce Rd. 8 and the Sauble Falls Parkway. Ride south as Sauble Falls Parkway changes into the Southhampton Parkway.

At Silver Lake Road turn [L]; the road immediately begins to climb and passes the local "adopt-a-toad" sign. It's a peaceful ride through cottage country. Crossing Bruce Rd. 10 onto Shouldice Road, turn [R] at Hwy 6 and cycle through downtown **Shallow Lake** past the Harley Davidson dealership and the Wayside Chapel.

This portion of Hwy 6 is busy, but it has a wide cycling lane, so the trip is reasonably comfortable cycling experience. Further down the road, look for the Red Cardinal Bird Seed sign and prepare for a left turn. A short distance past Ledgerock Rd and the Log Cabin Guest House, about halfway down the hill, turn [L] onto Wilcox Rd and follow it to Girl Guide Rd. Turn [R] and cycle to another [T] intersection at West Street. From here, the City of Owen Sound dominates the skyline. Turn [L] and enjoy a long downhill ride on 24th St. Bending to the right, 24th St becomes 4th Ave W. At 23rd St W, turn [L] and cycle along the Eddie Sargent Pkwy. Turn [R] and ride until the Kelso Beach stop lights. Make a [L] turn into the park and follow the trail back to the beginning of Leg 1.

---

17. Beaver Valley Explorer: Thornbury, Meaford and Markdale (including Eugenia Falls)

Beginning in the southern reaches of the Georgian Triangle, this ride climbs up to the top of the Niagara Escarpment, travels to the rushing waters of Eugenia Falls, and descends into the Beaver Valley. Riding north along the valley through the villages of Kimberly and Heathcote, the first leg joins the recreational trail in Thornbury and follows it along the shoreline of Georgian Bay to the village of Meaford. The second leg has many difficult climbs that are always followed by thrilling downhills. It starts with a climb, and then follows the escarpment's upper rim, then descends back into the heart of the valley. Passing through the city of Markdale, this stretch is completed by following the Old Durham Road back into the Saugeen Valley.

Return Distance: 180 km (84 km, 75 km)
No. of recommended legs: 2
Level of Difficulty: 🚲 🚲 🚲 🚲
Surface: Asphalt roads

Villages/Towns/Cities: Durham, Flesherton, Eugenia, Kimberly, Heathcote, Thornbury, Meaford, Markdale

Local Highlights: Durham Art Gallery, Welbeck Sawmill, Eugenia Falls, South Grey Museum, The Georgian Theatre Festival, Georgian Bay, Georgian Trail bike path, Meaford Tank Training Centre, Walters Falls, Old Baldy Lookout, Epping Lookout, Paul's Hotel Mural, Meaford Museum, Thornbury Dam and Fish Lock

Recommended Bicycles: Touring/Hybrid/Mountain

Tour Suggestions: Some of the hills are quite steep, but with a little effort each of these hills can be conquered. Pack extra water as there are only a few places to refill on route.

How To Get There: Durham can be reached from the north and south by following Hwy 6 and from the east and west by travelling along Hwy 4. A good location to begin the trip is from the Saugeen Valley Conservation Area. Follow Hwy 6 North and turn right onto Old Durham. There is a small fee for parking a car overnight.

Back in 1842, a group of settlers followed Archibald Hunter as he travelled north from Arthur on the Garafraxa Colonization Road (Hwy 6). They built a log cabin and the founded settlement that became known as Bentinck. The name was changed to **Durham** twelve years later, after land agent George Jackson's hometown in England. In recent years, Durham has become known for its annual Wood Show and the growing number of murals painted on its storefronts.

Itinerary: Leg 1 (Durham to Meaford, 84 km). Turn [R] out of the Saugeen Valley Conservation Area onto Old Durham Road. In the mid 1850s, this road made it possible to clear much of the land between Kincardine and Walkerton. At the [T] intersection of Concession 2, turn [R] and then [L] to and join Hwy 4 in the middle of a bend. For the next several kilometres, this undulating road begins a series of climbs and dips. Each time the top of the next hill is reached, the overall altitude will have increased by a few metres. Riding past a large gravel pit operation and a small art studio in a wooden barn, you may

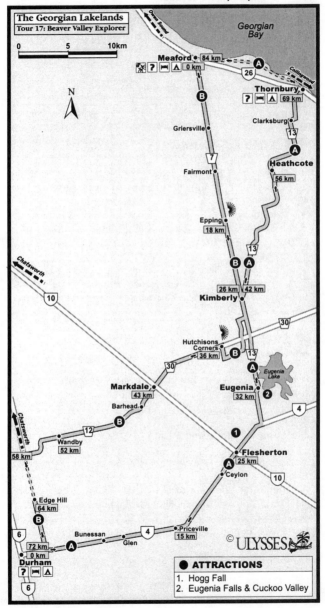

The Georgian Lakelands
Tour 17: Beaver Valley Explorer

0   5   10km

Georgian Bay

Owen Sound

Collingwood

Meaford 84 km
0 km

26

Thornbury
69 km

Clarksburg

13

Griersville

Heathcote
56 km

7

Fairmont

Chatsworth

10

Epping
18 km

13

B A
26 km 42 km

Kimberly

30

Hutchisons
Corners
36 km

B
13

Eugenia
Lake

Markdale
43 km

30

A

Barhead

Eugenia
32 km

2

4

Chatsworth

12

B

Wandby
52 km

1

58 km

Flesherton
25 km

A

Ceylon

10

Edge Hill
64 km

B

6

72 km
0 km

Bunessan

Priceville
15 km

4

Glen

© ULYSSES

Durham

6

● ATTRACTIONS
1. Hogg Fall
2. Eugenia Falls & Cuckoo Valley

Practical Information

Population:
Durham: 2,500
Thornbury: 1,458
Meaford: 4,400

 Tourist Information

✦ **Durham:**   Durham Town Office, 137 Garafraxa
Street North, P.O. Box 639, Durham, Ontario, N0G 1R0,
(519) 369-2200, www.town.durham.on.ca
✦ **Thornbury:**   Georgian Triangle Tourist Association,
601 First Street, Collingwood, Ontario, L9Y 4L2,
(705)   445-7722,   www.georgiantriangle.org,
www.thornbury.net
✦ **Meaford:**   Georgian Triangle Tourist Association,
601 First Street, Collingwood, Ontario, L9Y 4L2,
(705)   445-7722,   www.georgiantriangle.org,
www.meaford.net

 Bicycle Shops

✦ **Meaford:** Jolley's Cycle Centre, RR 1, Meaford, Ontario,
N4L 1W5, (519) 538-3000

 Special Sights and Events

✦ **Durham:** Herb Fair, Antique Car Show, Durham Wood
Show
✦ **Thornbury:** Blessing of the Boats, Georgian Bay Sailing
Regatta, Thornbury Apple Harvest Festival
✦ **Meaford:** Military Appreciation Day, Meaford Run/Walk,
Summer Concert Series, Meaford Salmon Derby, Great
Scarecrow Invasion, Apple Harvest

🛏️ **Accommodations**

+ **Durham:** B&B/Camping
+ **Thornbury:** Inns/Cottages/B&B/Camping
+ **Meaford:** Motel/Cottages/B&B/Camping

---

notice that the ditches running along the road are all full of water. This is due to runoff from the nearby escarpment. At the white barn, look for the old 1889 McKenzie Cemetery. A short distance ahead, the road enters the village of Priceville. Apart from the few homes, the most striking buildings are the General Store and the 1888 Presbyterian Church. Behind the church is a little park and cenotaph with a German Field Machine Gun and. Upon closer inspection, you will notice that the church has been used by many different denominations.

Hwy 4 descends as it enters **Flesherton**, passing a small pond and park on the right. Continue straight through town, crossing Hwy 10. Now, the cycling lane disappears and the road is several inches above the shoulder. Originally settled in 1851, the town was given the pretty name of Artemesia. By 1853, it had become known as Flesher's Corners, named after the owner of the local saw and grist mills. In 1867, the name was changed to Flesherton.

Just a short distance from Flesherton is a little-known waterfall called Hogg Falls. It is a worthwhile side trip, but adds about 6 km to the ride. To get there, ride east for 1.5 km from the stop light in Flesherton. Turn [L] onto Lower Valley Rd and cycle north, making a [R] turn onto the next road. Continue riding for approximately 1 km to an unmarked but easily recognizable parking lot. Park your bike and travel on foot, following the path to the falls.

At the red-roofed house on Hwy 4, turn [L] onto Grey Rd 13. Ride uphill until you reach the village of **Eugenia**. Turn [L] onto Tellisier Street at the dilapidated old brick house, and ride down a steep short hill. The village was named after Empress Eugenia, the wife of Napoleon III. Lock your bicycle on one of the many nearby trees (not a pine tree) and walk down to the falls. Be careful as the rocks and exposed roots can be quite slippery. The view of the 23-metre Eugenia Falls and Cuckoo Valley is simply breathtaking. Be sure to explore the area around Eugenia Falls lookout. If there is no water flowing over the falls, Ontario Hydro is probably diverting it into two hydro generators further up the valley.

Continue riding north on Grey Rd 13 as it climbs to the top of the Niagara Escarpment. As you ride past what looks like two booster rockets off the space shuttle and a local deer farm, the hill crests and then immediately descends into Beaver Valley. At the bottom of the hill, with brakes smoking, ride into the ski village of **Kimberly**. Not much is open during the summer months, but in the winter there is plenty of excitement.

Cycle past the Grist Mill Winery and under a bridge, bear left at the [Y] junction of Grey Rd 7, and continue along Grey Rd 13 into the widest part of the Beaver Valley. As you ride past an exposed portion of the escarpment known as "Old Baldy," the road remains fairly flat up to the farm that has many long-eared donkeys. Here, the road begins to meander and, just before arriving in **Heathcote**, passes several bee hives. You are now cycling through the Georgian Triangle apple belt. Notice how the trees are trimmed and tied to wire fences. The road twists and turns as it enters Clarksburg, passing a unique-looking library-lighthouse and the Ministry of Food Inspection Station. Continue along Bruce St. past the stop lights at Arthur St. (Hwy. 26). In the village of **Thornbury**, make a [L] turn onto the recreational trail. The trail entrance is located just before the road bends and begins its descent into the harbour. Take a few moments to relax in town at the little cafe near the rail-trail entrance. There is a very pleasant view of the harbour.

Thornbury is located at the mouth of the Beaver River on the shores of Lake Huron's Nottawasaga Bay. It was named by the town's surveyor in 1833, after his hometown in Somersetshire, England. While in Thornbury, visit the 8-metre dam and fish lock and, in the spawning season, watch the rainbow and chinook salmon leap high in the air as they swim upstream toward their spawning grounds.

The riding is quite easy along this crushed-gravel rail-trail, which runs parallel to Hwy 26 all the way into **Meaford**. At the "Georgian Trail 1989" sign, the trail enters a grove of cedars and crosses two wooden bridges. After passing a lumber company and school, the rail-trail ends at Meaford Harbour. Turn [R] onto Bridge St. and pedal into Meaford's downtown.

Named Pegg's Landing after the first settler's wife, the town's name was later changed to St. Vincent, but was called Meaford by 1858. Nicknamed the "Golden Town", Meaford is always bustling with activity during the warm summer months. It is perhaps best known for the book *Beautiful Joe,* about the rescue of a badly treated mongrel. Meaford was also the home of Sierra Club founder John Muir, and it is thought that this is where he developed many of his ideas for the environmental movement. The town's history is revealed through its many fine heritage buildings. You can learn about fly casting by watching enthusiastic fly-fishers on Big Head River. And you'll learn why this area is known as Apple Country simply by taking a bite of a local apple.

Itinerary: Leg 2 (Meaford to Durham, 74 km). Beginning at the stop light at the corner of Sykes Street and Trowbridge Street, ride east on Sykes Street (Hwy 26) to Grey Rd 7. Turn [L] in front of the car dealership onto the Beaver Valley Road. Many of the climbs and descents on this road are steep and the hill in front of you is one of the steepest.

When exposed limestone rock appears on the left and right of the road, about 8 km into the leg, look for the historic Griersville Rock plaque on the left, hidden among some bushes at the top of the rise. As you ride past the St. James Anglican Church and Cemetery in the village of Fairmont, Grey Rd 7 (Eric Winkler Parkway) has levelled out and the riding is less strenuous. It actually feels as if the road is descending but it is in fact at the same altitude. Several kilometres past the local transformer station, look for the entrance into the Epping Lookout. On a clear day you can see right into the heart of the valley, and "Old Baldy" stands out like a sore thumb. After riding through the small hamlet of Epping, the road begins a long gradual descent, going past some wild-looking trees and the Talisman Ski Resort. At Grey Road 13, make a [R] turn and head into downtown Kimberly.

Just before cycling uphill on Grey Road 13, turn [R] onto Grey Road 30. Descend into the valley, and enjoy the ride past the local ski club and a large home with an airplane sitting in the front yard. Notice the rocket boosters high on top of the escarpment as the road swings to the right and crosses a bridge. The ride out of the valley on Bowles Hill is a difficult one; stop often to catch your breath. In fact, walking your bike will help loosen up those cramped leg muscles. Just imagine what it would be like to ride this hill in a rain storm – it would be more like surfing! At the top of the escarpment, turn [R] at the [T] intersection and continue following Grey Rd 30 as it bears left at Hutchinsons Corners towards **Markdale**.

To add an optional side trip of only a few kilometres, continue straight at Hutchinsons Corners. A short distance ahead is the Beaver Valley Lookout.

Cycling west, the hills quickly disappear in the distance. At Grey Rd 12, turn [L] and ride into Markdale, the home of Chapman's Ice Cream. Markdale is another interesting older town whose name was changed from Cornabus as part of a contractual agreement with the Toronto, Grey and Bruce Railway. Take note of the clock tower just before riding across Hwy 10.

As you leave Markdale, the road is very exciting as it winds its way downhill past a little waterfall. The first half of the ride from Markdale to Wandby is perhaps one of the prettiest autumn rides in the entire province. Grey Rd 12 levels out and passes a little quarry at the village of Wandby. After the local stock yard and a small conservation area, Grey Rd 12 descends and then climbs to Baseline Road (Concession Rd 2), the third road past Wandby.

Turn [L] onto Baseline Road (Concession Rd 2) and follow this gravel road for the next several kilometres. It changes back into asphalt at the Edge Hill Side Rd. Just a wee bit past the Edge Hill Side Rd, look for a herd of black Angus cattle, which is a rare sight these days. The leg is almost complete upon reaching the familiar stop sign at Old Durham Rd. Hwy 4 is right in front of you. Turn [R] and cycle back uphill on Old Durham Road to the Saugeen Valley Conservation Area.

---

18. Cycling to the Big Chute and Back: Midland, Port Severn and Severn Falls

---

There is quite a difference between cycling the eastern and western shores of Georgian Bay. In the Midland area rock formations are more rugged and much more colourful, leaving you with the feeling that much of the land on this side of the lake is still untamed. The first leg begins in the city of Midland and follows the Georgian Bay shoreline. Highlights include the lock at Port Severn and seeing the Marine Railway in action at the Big Chute. The second leg follows an ideal cycling road back into the village of Waubaushene before returning to the blue waters of Severn Sound.

Return Distance: 120 km (72 km, 48 km)
No. of recommended legs: 2
Level of Difficulty: 🚲 🚲 🚲
Surface: Asphalt

Villages/Towns/Cities: Midland, Port McNicoll, Victoria Harbour, Waubaushene, Port Severn, South Bay, Big Chute, Severn Falls

Local Highlights: Wye Marsh, Castle Village and Dracula's Museum, Huronia Museum, Huron Indian Village, Martyrs Shrine, Sainte-Ignace II, Sainte-Marie Among the Hurons, 30,000 Island Cruises, Discovery Harbour, Penetanguishene Centennial Museum, St. Ann's Roman Catholic Church, St. James Garrison Church-On-The-Lines, Octopus Craft Gallery, The Glass Attic, The Historic Murals of Midland, Georgian Bay Islands National Park, Beausoleil Island

Bicycle Types: Touring/Hybrid/Mountain

Tour Suggestions: Pack extra water as this tour does travel through some unpopulated areas.

How to get there: To reach Midland from the south, follow Hwys 400 93 or 12. From the north, take Hwy 400 or 12. From the east follow Hwy 12, and from the west take Hwy 92 or 93. The tour begins from the Midland Harbour on the shores of Severn Sound. The harbour parking lot is free and can be reached by turning right off Hwy 93 onto Young Street and following it to a left turn onto King Street.

Over 500 years ago, the present location of **Midland** and Penetanguishene was the centre of the Huron nation and home to several different Huron villages. In 1639, French Jesuits established the Sainte-Marie Among the Hurons mission and opened the first hospital and church in Ontario. When the post office opened, John Smith, one of the town fathers, named the town Midland because of its location midway between Penetanguishene and Victoria Harbour.

Itinerary: Leg 1 (Midland to Severn Falls, 72 km). Exit the Midland Harbour parking lot by turning [L] onto Bayshore Drive. Enjoy a great view of the bay before the road bends to the right, away from the bay. At this point, the road changes names and becomes William Street. There is a long grade, before William Street crests at a set of stop lights, then descends quickly to Hwy 12.

At the bottom of the hill, turn [L] onto Hwy 12 and pedal uphill past the Martyrs Shrine and the historical village of Sainte-Marie Among the Hurons. At the top of the hill, turn [L] onto Ogden's Beach Road and follow it along Severn Sound and through the village of **Port McNicoll**. Severn Sound has had many different names, including Christendom and Gloucester. In 1872, it was named Munday's Bay after the first settlers off the Midland Railway. Cty Rd 37, the road out of Port McNicoll, becomes quite steep and requires a lot of hard pedalling. At Triple Bay Road, turn [L] and cycle back to Hwy 12.

Turn [L] onto Hwy 12; Hog Bay should be peeking through the trees to the left side of the road. A short distance ahead is a little rest area. Stop for a few minutes to find out why a wooden train-trestle bridge was so important to the area. Ride across Hog Creek to the **Victoria Harbour** Welcome sign, then

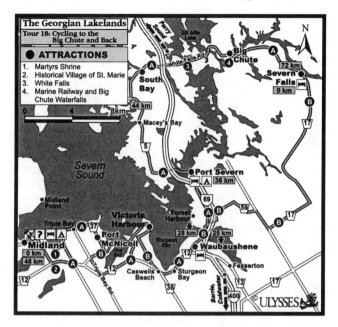

make a [L] turn onto William Street and ride into downtown Victoria Harbour. Originally known as Hog's Bay, the town was soon nicknamed "Canary Town" because most of the houses were once painted canary yellow by the town's major employer, the Victoria Harbour Lumber Company. With the arrival of the Midland Railway in 1871, the town was renamed Victoria Harbour in honour of Queen Victoria. At the stop sign, turn [R] onto Allen Street and follow it around the bay. Make a [L] turn onto Richard Street and pedal past the lights, following the road past Sunset Park and the township offices.

Riding uphill to Hwy 12, turn [L] and follow the highway over the Sturgeon River and past the Waubaushene cemetery. Turn [L] at the next road and ride into village of **Waubaushene** whose name means "meeting of the rocks" or "place of narrows." There is a heritage Bed & Breakfast directly ahead at the Pine Street [T] intersection. Turn [R] off Sturgeon Road and

Practical Information

Population:
Midland: 14,300
Port Severn: 565
Penetanguishene: 6,800

 Tourist Information

✦ **Midland:** Midland Chamber of Commerce, 208 King Street, Midland, Ontario, L4R 3L9, (705) 526-7884, www.town.midland.on.ca;
✦ **Penetanguishene:** Penetanguishene-Tiny Chamber of Commerce, 2 Main Street, Penetanguishene, Ontario, L9M 1T1, (705) 549-2232, www.huronet.com/chamb_commerce

 Bicycle Shops

✦ **Midland:** The Bike Shop, 542 Bay Street, Midland, Ontario, L4R 1L3, (705) 526-5661

 Special Sights and Events

✦ **Midland:** Earth Day, Moon of Wintertime, Wye Marsh Festival, Quilt Rug Fair, Sweetwater Harvest, Thanksgiving Art and Craft Show
✦ **Port Severn:** Christmas on the Bay, Port Severn-Big Chute Cruises
✦ **Penetanguishene:** Lantern Tours, Fall Colour Sail, Halloween Spirit Walk, Sailor's Sunset Evening Sails

 Accommodations

✦ **Midland:** Hotel/Motel/B&B/Camping
✦ **Port Severn:** Lodge/Camping
✦ **Severn Falls:** Motel/B&B/Camping
✦ **Penetanguishene:** B&B/Camping.

then swing quickly [L] onto Coldwater Road and enjoy the downhill ride. Cycling past the local grocery store, turn [R] onto Duck Bay Road. Wait for the green light before riding across the narrow bridge at the mouth of Matchedash Bay.

When you reach Quarry Road, turn [R] and cycle a short distance to a [L] turn onto West Service Road, just before Hwy 69/400. The main highway is on your right as you ride past an old abandoned hotel complex. By now you may have noticed the red colour of the uncovered escarpment rock next to the road. At the Port Severn Road [T] intersection, turn [R] and cross over Hwy 69/400 into **Port Severn**. At the stop sign, turn [L] in front of Rawley Lodge and cycle across another narrow bridge to the Lock 45 Visitor's Centre. The centre is the northern gateway on the Trent-Severn Waterway Canal and one of the most developed service stops on the canal.

Rejoin Muskoka Rd 5 (Honey Harbour Road) and ride up and over Hwy 69. Several kilometres down the road, look for a vacant building that at one time sold all types of watercraft. At South Bay Road, turn [R] and get ready for an enjoyable ride along a very narrow meandering road. At the village of **South Bay**, notice the colour of the water in the pond next to the road, it's almost royal blue.

After the recycling depot, the road begins quite a climb at Service Road 6. The next several kilometres will be spent riding the rolling blacktop of the South Bay Road as it zigzags through fairly dense bush. Crossing Hwy 69 once again, turn [L] onto Muskoka Road 34 (East Service Road).

The landscape here is spectacular, as huge red chunks of granite dominate the skyline. Continue to follow Muskoka Road 34 by turning [R] off the service road onto White Falls Road. After riding across the White Falls bridge, stop for a moment and enjoy the view while listening to the relaxing sound of rushing water as it empties into the Severn River from Six Mile Lake. Have your camera ready as there will be a number of great photo opportunities on the road ahead.

When the road swings sharply to the right, North America's only marine railway and the 18-metre waterfalls of **Big Chute** will come into view. Spend some time looking around the marine railway complex in Big Chute, then walk across the canal bridge and watch the water as it rushes into the river far below. During the summer months, boats are transported via the Marine Railway on a regular basis, and it's quite a sight to see it in operation. As Muskoka Rd 34 crosses the canal, it becomes Simcoe Rd 17 (Upper Chute Road) and an easy ride towards the village of **Severn Falls**.

Itinerary: Leg 2 (Severn Falls to Midland, 48 km) The countryside opens up as Simcoe Rd. 17 arcs south through the Matchedash Valley. Make a [R] turn at the flashing light and ride past the North River General Store to a left-hand bend in the road. Continue straight through at the bend, onto North River Drive. At the [T] intersection, turn [R] onto Quarry Road (Cty Rd 59). Enjoy the peacefulness of Quarry Road as you ride past the Lafarge Quarries, then up and over Hwy 69 to the Duck Bay Road [T] intersection. Turn [L] and retrace your route, riding back across the bay, then get to Hwy 12 via Waubaushene.

Cycling in a westerly direction along Hwy 12, turn [R] upon reaching William Street and return to the marina parking lot on the shores of Severn Sound.

Optional Side Trip: Only 10 kilometres away, the village of Penetanguishene is known for its carved, stone angels and the tall ship, Tecumseth, which is docked for most of the summer at Kings Wharf. From the marina parking lot on Severn Sound, travel north along Harbourview Drive and turn [L] onto Fuller Avenue. Upon arrival in Penetanguishene, simply follow the signs to Discovery Harbour.

---

19. Lake of the Bays and Muskoka Hills

Inspiring and challenging is perhaps the best way to describe this outing into the heart of the Muskokas. Beautiful inland lakes, dense forest and continuous rolling hills coalesce together, making this a cycling adventure to remember.

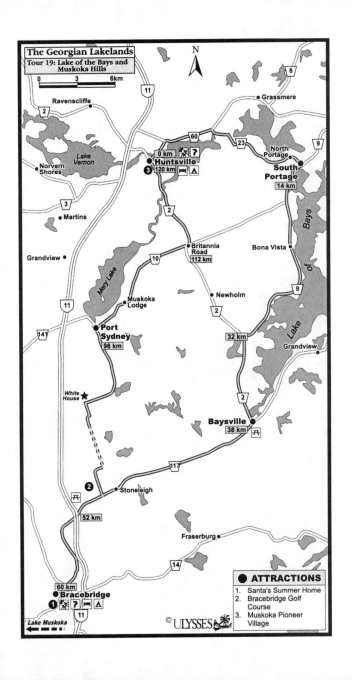

Return Distance: 120 km
No. of recommended legs: 2
Difficulty: 🚲 🚲 🚲 🚲
Surface: Asphalt

Village/Towns/Cities: Huntsville, Portage North, Baysville, Bracebridge, Port Sydney

Local Highlights: Bird Mill Mews Gallery, Bracebridge Bay Park, Lady Muskoka Boat Cruise, Lakes of Muskoka Cottage Brewery, Muskoka Art and Crafts Gallery, Santa's Village and Rudolph's Fun Land, Woodchester Villa, Arrowhead Provincial Park, Dyer Memorial, Madill Church, Muskoka Pioneer Village

Recommended Bicycles: Touring/Hybrid/Mountain

Tour Suggestions: Pack extra water and plan to complete in 2 days as the ride is physically demanding and there is a lot to see. Remember to book accommodations in advance as the cycling season is also the tourist season in the Muskokas.

How to get there: To reach Huntsville from the south, take Hwy 400 to Hwy 11 N; from the north, take Hwy 11 S. From the east, take Hwy 60 W and from the west, take Hwy 141 to Hwy 11 N.

The town of **Huntsville** is the last major community before entering Algonquin Park from the west and is vibrating with excitement. Huntsville may have also been one of the province's first "dry" communities. When the area was surveyed in 1869, teetotaller Capt. George Hunt, the town's namesake, settled in the area, then known as Fairy Lake Junction. Hunt divided his land into lots and sold each lot with a "no drinking" clause written into the deeds. As a result, the town first developed on the hilly west side of the Muskoka River rather than on Hunt's flat lots on the river's east side.

Itinerary: Leg 1 (Huntsville to Bracebridge). Starting from the Canadian Tire Parking lot, east of downtown Huntsville on Main/King William Street (Muskoka Rd 3), turn [R] onto Muskoka Rd 3 and [R] again onto Hwy 60 (Muskoka Rd 60). Caution should be exercised as Hwy 60 can be very busy, and

Practical Information

Population:
Huntsville: 12,320
Bracebridge: 9,968

 Tourist Information

✦ **Huntsville:** Huntsville/Lake of the Bays Chamber of Commerce, 8 West St N, Unit 1, Huntsville, Ontario P1H 2B6, (705) 789-4771/Muskoka Tourism, RR 2, Kilworthy, Ontario P0E 1G0, (705) 689-0660, www.muskoka-tourism.on.ca
✦ **Bracebridge:** Bracebridge Chamber of Commerce, 1-1 Manitoba St, Bracebridge, Ontario P1L 2A8 (705)645-8121, Muskoka Tourism, RR 2, Kilworthy, Ontario P0E 1G0 (705) 689-0660, www.muskoka-tourism.on.ca.

 Bicycle Shops

✦**Huntsville:**Algonquin Cycle Tours, 170 North Waseosa Rd, Huntsville, Ontario, P1H 2J4, (705)789-1500/Muskoka Bicycle Proshop, 14 Main St E, Huntsville, Ontario, P1H 2C9, (705) 789-8344
✦ **Bracebridge:** Campbell Sports, Box 57 Station Main, 7 Manitoba St, Bracebridge, Ontario, P1L 1T5, (705) 645-3131, Ecclestone Cycle Co. 230 Ecclestone Drive, Bracebridge, Ontario, P1L 1G4, (705) 645-1166, Nielsen & Company, 28 Woodglen Cres., Bracebridge, Ontario, P1L 1A1, (705) 645-8534

 Special Sights and Events

✦ **Huntsville:** Bathtub Derby, Music of the Lakes Festival, Canada Day, Huntsville Festival of the Arts, Muskoka Pioneer Village - Pioneer Day and other special events throughout the year

✦ **Bracebridge:** Muskoka Arts and Craft Show, Festival of Falls, Santa Village Seasonal Grand Opening, Canada Day, Muskoka Pioneer Power Association Annual Show, Music of the Lakes Festival, Bracebridge Fall Fair, Festival of Lights

 Accommodations

✦ **Huntsville and Bracebridge:** Motel/Hotel/B&B/Camping.

 Off-Road Cycling

✦ **Huntsville and Bracebridge:** Yes, several in the area. Refer to "Off-Road Cycling" at the back of this section.

picturesque Fairy Lake on your right is sure to be somewhat distracting.

Turn [R] onto Muskoka Rd 23 following it through the countryside. When the Deerhurst golf course comes into view, the road will begin to bend to the left and the Deerhurst Inn Complex will be directly ahead. To remain on Muskoka Rd. 23, turn [R] and follow Foot and Bay Road (the local name for Muskoka Rd 23) to the village of **Portage**. Ever wondered who plans what direction a road will take? Well, when cycling along these Muskoka backroads that question will come to mind many times throughout the day. A ride through the Lake of the Bays region is like being on a roller coaster, the only difference is that you have to do all the work to get to the top of the next exhilarating drop.

As you enter the town of Portage, the Portage Inn is directly in front and the road bends sharply to the right. Continue along Muskoka Rd 23 and turn [R] at the [T] intersection of Muskoka Rd 9. Not quite as hilly, Muskoka Rd 9 can be quite entertaining. With a sharp eye, you may catch a glimpse of the local deer or watch the comical antics of the area's wild grouse. Upon reaching Britannia Rd, the turnoff for Bracebridge is only 18 kilometres further down the road.

After arriving at the **Baysville** [T] intersection, turn [R] onto Muskoka Rd 2. Take a break and check out the local store or enjoy a brief rest at the Parry Falls Park just ahead on your left. Though there isn't a cycling lane on this extremely wide road, you should not have a problem riding. Leaving Baysville behind, the road climbs past a beautiful rock garden on your right before levelling out. At Bonnie Lake Rd, the Bracebridge Golf Course will be on the right. Remember this landmark as it will be your turnoff to Huntsville during leg 2 of this tour.

Cross Hwy 11 via the Baysville Bridge and do not turn onto Hwy 11. Just over the bridge, the Baysville Road is now called Cedar Lane, and on your right is a small but comfortable rest area. A narrow road, Cedar Lane has little traffic and is almost void of hills all the way to Bracebridge. After passing the Cedar Lane Fish Farm Pits and the local public school, turn [R] at Muskoka Rd 42 and cycle into downtown **Bracebridge**.

An interesting town, Bracebridge is distinctive for a number of reasons, the most famous of which is that Bracebridge serves as Santa's summer home. The town also abounds in natural wonders: throughout the city, the relaxing tenor of 22 waterfalls can be heard. Thanks to these falls, Bracebridge became the first municipality in Ontario to own its own hydroelectric station. At night, downtown Bracebridge is lit up with colourful displays and during the day a visit to the Bird's Mill and Woodchester Villa are not to be missed.

Itinerary: Leg 2 (Bracebridge to Huntsville). This leg begins by retracing your steps along Cedar Lane, crossing Hwy 11 and cycling to the Bracebridge Golf Club. Upon reaching the golf course, turn [L] onto Muskoka Rd 46 (Bonnie Lake Rd). Twisting its way through the countryside, Muskoka Rd 46 is a most delightful ride. As you approach a [T] intersection, a white house will be directly in front; turn [R] and continue following Muskoka Rd 46.

If you're up to a little exploring, turn left at the [T] intersection and cycle for a short distance to the little wooden bridge that crosses Sage Creek, which makes a great place to stop for a short break.

Muskoka Rd 46 is a funny little road and it seems as if it is heading in the wrong direction. Hang on: eventually it begins to head north, passing Faun Lake and Clear Lake Roads and arriving at the Muskoka Rd 10 [T] intersection.

Note: turning left will take you into the village of **Port Sydney**, on the picturesque shores of Mary Lake.

Turn [R] at the [T] intersection and follow the delightfully hilly Muskoka 10 along the south shore of Mary Lake. Passing some interesting side-roads, like Candy Town Lane and West Point Sands Road, a rest stop will be in order when arriving at the Muskoka Baptist Conference Centre.

At the junction of Muskoka 2, turn [L] and make your way into Huntsville. Once past the Treble Clef and the Muskoka Pioneer Village, downtown Huntsville is only a short distance away. At the [T] intersection, turn [R] and return to where this unforgettable ride began.

OFF-ROAD CYCLING

Public Trails

Barrie Area

Floss Corridor/ North Simcoe Rail Trail (14.5 km)
Surface: Original Railbed
Beginning: Cty Rd 22 Horseshoe Valley Road to Essa Transformer Station near Hwy 90
Contact: North Simcoe Railtrail, RR 2, Minesing, Ontario, L0L 1Y0, ☎(705) 728-9621.

Georgian Trail (32 km)
Surface: loose/hardpacked
Beginning: Collingwood and Meaford
Contact: Secretary, Georgian Cycle and Ski Trail Association, 601 First Street, Collingwood, Ontario L9Y 4L2, ☎(705) 445-7722.

Bracebridge Area

South Monck Trail (7.5 km)
Surface: hardpacked
Contact: Bracebridge Chamber of Commerce, 1-1 Manitoba Street, Bracebridge, Ontario, P1L 2A8, ☎(705) 645-8121.

Midland Area

Tiny Trail (22 km)
Surface: Original Railbed/sandy sections
Beginning: Cty Rd 26 to Hwy 27

Orillia

Lightfoot Trail (6.5 km)
Surface: Asphalt/loose surface
Beginning: Wilsons Point to Forest Avenue
Contact: Director of Parks and Recreation, City of Orillia, Opera House Building, P.O. Box 966, Orillia, Ontario L3V 6K8, ☎(705) 326-4424.

Uhthoff Trail (11 km)
Surface: loose surface/hardpacked
Beginning: North River(no access) to Wilson Point Road
Contact: Orillia Naturalist Club, P.0 Box 2381, Orillia, Ontario L3V 6V7, ☎(705) 326-4424.

Port Elgin

Saugeen Rail Trail (6 km)
Surface: Original Railbed/ hard packed
Beginning: Port Elgin and Southampton
Contact: Public Relations, Saugeen Rail Trail, 599 Elgin Street, Port Elgin, Ontario N0H 2C0 or The Saugeen Rail Trail Association, Box 2313, Port Elgin, Ontario N0H 2C0, ☎(519) 832-6443.

Resort and Conservation Trails

Santa's Village
Bracebridge, Ontario, PO Box 398, Bracebridge, Ontario, P1L
1T7, ☎(705) 645-2512.

Blue Mountain Resort
RR 3, Collingwood, Ontario L9Y 3Z2, ☎(705) 445-0231.

Talisman Mountain Resort
General Delivery, Kimberley, Ontario, N0C 1G0, ☎(519) 599-
2420.

Harwood Hills (36 km downhill ski trails, 45 km single track)
RR 1, Oro Station, Ontario L0L 2E0, ☎(705) 487-3775.

Horseshoe Resort
Simcoe Road 22, Horseshoe Valley, Ontario, ☎(705) 835-2790.

Kalapore Trails
University of Toronto Outing Club Inc., Box 6647, Station A,
Toronto, Ontario M5W 1X4; or Georgian Triangle Tourist
Association, 601 Front Street, Collingwood, Ontario L9Y 4L2,
☎(705) 445-7722; trail maps available at the general store in
Ravenna.

M.O.C. Mountain Bike Centre (30 km single and double
track trails)
Box 95, Mansfield, Ontario L0N 1M0, ☎(705) 435-4479.

Port Elgin Area
MacGregor Point Provincial Park (24 km of trail): District
Manager, Ministry of Natural Resources, 611 Ninth Street East,
Owen Sound, Ontario N4K 3E4, ☎(519) 376-3860 or Park
Office ☎(519) 389-9056.

Wingham Area
Wawanosh Valley Conservation Area (4 km of trail): Maitland
Valley Conservation Authority, P.O. Box 127, Wroxeter, Ontario
N0G 2X0, ☎(519) 335-3557.

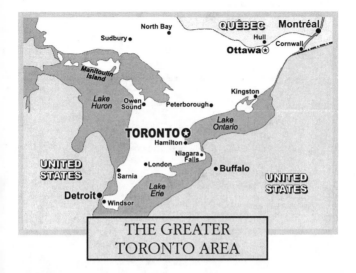

THE GREATER TORONTO AREA

The Greater Toronto Area has something for everyone: excellent off-road cycling, a well-developed waterfront and world class entertainment. When combined with its renowned intercity cycling network, it is no wonder Toronto happens to be one of the most cycling friendly cities in the world.

THE TOURS

20. Toronto Islands, Lakeshore and Beaches

Don't be intimidated by the fact that it is Canada's largest city, because **Toronto** is a wonderful place to visit by bicycle. The waterfront trail along Lake Ontario, a ferry ride to the picturesque Toronto Islands and beautiful East Beach are only a few of the highlights that make this trip a wonderful experience!

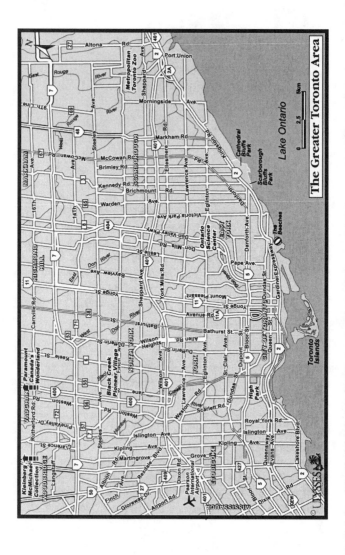

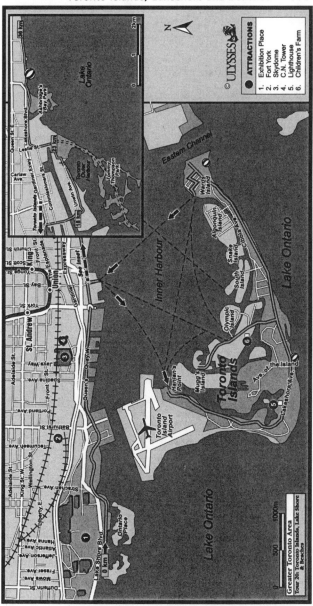

Lake Ontario

Ashbridge's Bay Park

Queen St. E

Leslie St.

Lakeshore Blvd.

Carlaw Ave.

36 km

21 km

13 km

Toronto Outer Harbour

Tommy Thompson Park

Commissioners St.

Toronto Islands Ferries

100 km

© ULYSSES

ATTRACTIONS
1. Exhibition Place
2. Fort York
3. Skydome
4. C.N. Tower
5. Lighthouse
6. Children's Farm

N

Eastern Channel

Ward's Island

Algonquin Island

Snake Island

South Island

Cibola Ave.

Olympic Island

Toronto Islands

Lake Ontario

Inner Harbour

Church St.

Scott St.

King St.

Yonge St.

Bay St.

Union

See Inset

St. Andrew

York St.

Adelaide St.

Spadina Ave.

Queen's Quay W.

Front St.

Jays Way

Portland Ave.

Bathurst St.

Tecumseh Ave.

Adelaide St. W

King St. W

Wellington

Stadium Ave.

Hanlan's Point

Mugg's Island

Toronto Island Airport

Ave. of the Island

Lakeshore Ave.

Lake Ontario

Ontario Place

Lake Shore Blvd

Strachan Ave.

Liberty St.

Hanna Ave.

Atlantic Ave.

Fraser Ave.

Mowa Ave.

Jefferson Ave.

Dufferin St.

0 km

500   1000m

Greater Toronto Area

Tour 20: Toronto Islands, Lake Shore & Beaches

Return Distance: 60 km
No. of recommended legs: 1
Difficulty: ♿
Surface: Waterfront trail and city streets

Villages/Towns/Cities: Toronto

Local Highlights: Allan Botanical Gardens, Art Gallery of Ontario, The Grange, Bay of Spirits Gallery, Campbell House, CN Tower, Canadian Sports Hall of Fame, Casa Loma, Centreville Amusement Park, Fort York, Harbourfront Centre, Colborne Lodge, Hockey Hall of Fame, Mackenzie House, Market Gallery, Ontario Parliament Buildings, Osgoode Hall, SkyDome, Toronto's first post office, Toronto Stock Exchange, Upper Canada Brewing Company, Bata Shoe Museum, Canadian Broadcast Centre and Museum, George R. Gardiner Museum of Ceramic Art, HMCS Haida Naval Museum, Marine Museum of Upper Canada, Police Museum, Museum for Textiles, Redpath Sugar Museum, Royal Ontario Museum, Spadina House and Gardens, Theatre District

Cycling Pathways within the City: The Waterfront Trail, Rosedale Valley and Don River Trail, Willet Creek Trail, Humber River Valley, Mimico Creek, Cedarvale Ravine, High Park, Warden Woods and Taylor Creek, Highland Creek, Leslie Street Spit

Recommended Bicycles: Touring/Hybrid/Mountain

Tour Suggestions: This trip can be combined with the tour of Olde Town Toronto (Tour 21).

How to Get There: From the east and west, take Hwy 401; from the north, follow Hwy 400 south; and from the south, take the Queen Elizabeth Way (QEW) to Hwy 403. Begin Tour 26 at Ontario Place where the parking charges are very reasonable. Ontario Place is located on Toronto's lakefront between Dufferin and Strachan Avenues. Leave the Gardiner Expressway at the Spadina exit and keep right, driving west along Lake Shore Boulevard; then turn left at Strachan Avenue.

Practical Information

Population:
Toronto: 2.9 million

 Tourist Information

Tourism Toronto, PO Box 126, 207 Queens Quay W, Suite 90, Toronto, M5J 1A7, (416) 203-2600 or (800) 363-1990, www.tourism-toronto.com / Metro Cycling Trail Information: Metro Parks and Culture, 24th Floor, Metro Hall, 55 John St, Toronto, M5V 3C6, (416) 392-8186, www.metrotor.on.ca.

 Bicycle Shops

Hogtown Skateboard & Snowboard Shop, 401 King St W, Toronto, M5V 1K1, (416) 598-4192; Trail Blazer Cycles, 1282 Danforth Ave, M4J 1M6, (416) 463-0431; Broadway Cycle, 1185 Bloor St W, M6H 1M9, (416) 531-1028; Curbside Bike Repair, 412 Bloor St W, M5S 1X5, (416) 920-4933; Bathurst Cycle 913 Bathurst St, M5R 3G4, (416) 533-7510; Beaches Cyclery, 1882 Queen St E, M4L 1H2, (416) 699-1461; The Bike Place, 3096 Dundas St W, M6P 1Z8, (416) 766-1085; The Bike Ranch, 216 Adelaide St W, M5H 1W7, (416) 595-1576; Bikes On Wheels Workers Co-Op, 309 Augusta Ave, M5T 2M2, (416) 966-2453; Bloor Cycle, 950 College, M6H 1A5, (416) 536-7107; Bloor Cycle, 2081 Yonge Street, M4S 2A2, (416) 545-1557; Cabbagetown Sports & Cycle, 444 Parliament, M5A 3A2, (416) 927-7499; Cycle Logic, 935 Mt. Pleasant Rd, M4P 2L7, (416) 488-2453; The Cycle Shoppe, 630-A Queen W, M6J 1E4, (416) 703-9990; Cyclemania, 113 Danforth Ave, M4K 1N2 (416) 466-0330; Cyclemania, 945 Bloor Street West, M6H 1L5,

(416) 533-0080; Cyclepath, 1204 Bloor St W, M6H 1N2, (416) 533-4481; Dave Fix My Bike, 130 Harbord Street, M5S 1G8, (416) 944-2453 Downtown Cycle, 368 College St, M5T 1S6, (416) 923-8189; Duke's Cycle, 625 Queen St W, M6J 1E4, (416) 504-6138; Grove Cycle & Sports, 335 College St, M5T 1S2, (416) 923-9633; Hi Speed Cycle & Sports, 923 Danforth Ave, M4J 1L8, (416) 778-1447; The Hilltop Bicycle Company, 855-A Bloor St W, M6G 1M3, (416) 533-2400; L & J Cycle, 1144 Davenport Rd, M6G 2C6, (416) 656-5293; La Bicicletta, 2109 Bloor St W, M6S 1M5, (416) 762-2679; McBride Cycle, 2797 Dundas St W, M6P 1Y6, (416) 763-5651; Mountain Bike Specialists, 935 Mt. Pleasant Rd, M4P 2L7, (416) 488-2453; Racer Sportif, 2214 Bloor St W, M6S 4Y7, (416) 769-5731; Street City Bikes, 1178 Queen St E, M4M 1L4, (416) 466-7492; Velotique, 1592 Queen St E, M4L 1G1, (416)466-3171; Warren Cycle Works, 890 Queen St E, M4M 1J3, (416)466-6958

 Special Sights and Events

Sunday Market, Toronto Home Show, Canadian International Auto Show, Toronto Bicycle Show, Sportsman Show, Canadian National Exhibition, Dragon Boat Race, Symphony of Fire Fireworks Display, Downtown Jazz Festival, Renaissance Festival, Molson Indy, Caribana, International Film Festival, Canadian Open, International Marathon, Festival of Authors, Toronto Blue Jays Baseball, Toronto Maple Leafs Hockey, Toronto Raptors Basketball, Royal Winter Agricultural Fair

 Accommodations: Hotel/Motel/B&B/Camping.

 Off-Road Cycling: Yes, refer to "Off-Road Cycling" at the back of this chapter.

Over 300 years ago, the Hurons referred to this area as "Toronto" which means "place of meeting." In the late 1790s, the English called it York. When the town became a city, it reverted back to its aboriginal name. As Ontario's capital city, Toronto has developed into a true multiethnic community where you can experience the "old world" neighbourhoods of Little Italy, Chinatown, and Danforth (Greektown). Toronto has also worked hard to accommodate the needs of cyclists, creating extensive public transportation networks, that reduce the amount of traffic, and thus make the city a reasonably safe and enjoyable place to ride a bicycle.

Itinerary: Starting from the Molson Amphitheater at Ontario Place, ride east past the *HMCS Haida* warship towards the CN Tower. Once you join the waterfront trail, you will see hundreds of sailboats bobbing up and down at the Alexandra and National Yacht Club, a short distance ahead. The trail takes you through Coronation Park, where the pathway is divided by green and blue lines. The colours indicate the general direction of the path: west is green and east is blue. Keep riding as the trail swings to the right and around the HMCS York Department of National Defence building. Back along the lake, the trail crosses Stadium Road to join the Queens Quay West.

Stay on this road for the next couple of kilometres, which take you past the CN Tower, the world-famous SkyDome and the Spadina Gardens. Just before the Harbour Weston Hotel and Conference Centre, turn [R] at the Bay Street stop lights. Join the pathway immediately to your right and ride across the hotel's underground parking lot to the Toronto Island Ferry Docks. For a small fee, board the ferry to Hanlon's Point and enjoy the 15-minute ride across Toronto Harbour to Gibraltar Point.

Once on the island, follow the road as it arcs left around the harbour. Take a few minutes to look around the old haunted lighthouse opposite the Natural Science school, which was built in 1808. A short distance ahead is an old crane boat, next to the Metro Works Marine Yard. Upon reaching Centre Island, there is a path through the gardens on your left, which leads across the bridge to Centre Island Amusement Park and the

Centre Island Ferry. On the right is the Dock Inn and pier where four-passenger bicycles can be rented.

Continue along the main road, keeping right, and join the wooden boardwalk along the lake. Just before the trail ends (it turns into gravel), turn [L] onto First Street. Spend some time cycling around the enchanting narrow cottage-lined streets of Ward Island. The pathway eventually emerges to reveal a striking view of Toronto's skyline. Board the Ward Island ferry and return to the mainland.

Once off the ferry, turn [R] onto Queens Quay East and ride past the Harbour Castle, Captain John's Seafood Ship and the Redpath Sugar Museum. Join the trail a short distance ahead to the right, which parallels the Queens Quay, and later the Lake Shore Boulevard. Swing [R] and follow the trail over the Cherry Street Bridge. Cross the intersection of Commissioner and Cherry Street, at the Toronto Hydro Electric building, to join the trail on the left side of the road. The trail passes Clarke Beach and the docks of the Toronto Wind Surfing Club as it meanders eastward. Exit onto Unwin Ave; at the ship building facility, keep right and cross the bridge to a [T] intersection at Leslie Street. Turn [L] and continue following the trail.

Optional Side Trip: A [R] turn at Leslie Street takes you to Tommy Thompson Park and the Leslie Street Spit. The spit is a manmade landmass that makes for an interesting ride. The road into the park ends at the Tommy Thompson lighthouse. Be careful when riding around the lighthouse as the road crosses an old dump and the rate of tire punctures is rather high in this area!

Watch out for roller bladers coming around a sharp right-hand bend in the trail at Lake Shore Boulevard. At the stop lights, swing [R] and then turn [L] into Ashbridge Park. You will have to ride past a number of food concessions and an outdoor theatre before arriving at Beaches Park and the Woodbine Bathing Station. The trail ends one kilometre ahead at Fernwood Park Avenue. If time and weather permit, don your bathing suit and enjoy a refreshing dip in Lake Ontario before returning to Ontario Place.

---

21. Olde Town Toronto

Toronto is one of North America's most exciting cities, and this ride takes you along the bustling streets of the old downtown. This urban adventure will take you across electric streetcar tracks and past the city's most important historic and modern landmarks. The sights include the unique flat iron building, Casa Loma, the University of Toronto, the CN Tower and Fort York.

Return Distance: 26 km
No. of recommended legs: 1
Difficulty: ڶ
Surface: Asphalt and paved recreational trail

Villages/Towns/Cities: Toronto

Local Highlights: Allan Botanical Gardens, Art Gallery of Ontario, The Grange, Bay of Spirits Gallery, Campbell House, CN Tower, Canadian Sports Hall of Fame, Casa Loma, Centreville Amusement Park, Fort York, Harbourfront Centre, Colborne Lodge, Hockey Hall of Fame, Mackenzie House, Market Gallery, Ontario Parliament Buildings, Osgoode Hall, SkyDome, Toronto's first post office, Toronto Stock Exchange, Upper Canada Brewing Company, Bata Shoe Museum, Canadian Broadcast Centre and Museum, George R. Gardiner Museum of Ceramic Art, HMCS Haida Naval Museum, Marine Museum of Upper Canada, Police Museum, Museum for Textiles, Redpath Sugar Museum, Royal Ontario Museum, Spadina House and Gardens, Theatre District

Cycling Pathways within the City: The Waterfront Trail, Rosedale Valley and Don River Trail, Willet Creek Trail, Humber River Valley, Mimico Creek, Cedarvale Ravine, High Park, Warden Woods and Taylor Creek, Highland Creek, Leslie Street Spit

Recommended Bicycles: Touring/Hybrid/Mountain

Tour Suggestions: Saturday seems to attract fewer people to the Big Smoke (Toronto), so this is the best day to do both of these tours along the shores of Lake Ontario. This trip can be combined with the tour of Toronto's Islands (Tour 20). Caution should always be exercised when crossing the electric streetcar tracks.

How to Get There: From the east and west, take Hwy 401; from the north, follow Hwy 400 south; and from the south, take the Queen Elizabeth Way (QEW) to Hwy 403. Begin Tour 26 at Ontario Place where the parking charges are very reasonable. Ontario Place is located on Toronto's lakefront between Dufferin and Strachan Avenue. Leave the Gardiner Expressway at the Spadina exit and keep right, driving west along Lake Shore Boulevard; then turn left at Strachan Avenue.

Itinerary: Begin in front of the SkyDome, under the bronzed adoring fans, ride down Blue Jays Way and turn [R] onto Front Street. The SkyDome has the world's first retractable roof that opens in under 20 minutes. You can see the CN Tower over your right shoulder; it is the world's tallest freestanding structure, reaching a height of 553 metres. Riding past the CBC Radio Broadcasting Building and the Metro Convention Centre, you can see the uniquely-shaped Roy Thomson Hall in the distance on your left. Cross York Street and go past Union Station. (Further down York Street, the all-new Air Canada Centre, home of the Toronto Maple Leafs, is on the right.) At Bay Street, the Royal York Hotel will be on the left while Hummingbird Centre, formerly known as the O'Keefe Centre for the Performing Arts is on the right. As you ride through the intersection at Victoria Street, look to your left for the Hockey Hall of Fame. Built in 1885, it was originally the Bank of Montreal and is a fine example of rococo architecture. Further down on Front Street West, you will notice a long wedge-shaped building. This striking building, known as the "Flat Iron", was owned by Toronto's Godderham Family, who were big in the beer industry. On the bottom floor is a local bar called "Down Under", from where you can take an elevator ride to the top of the "Flat Iron," if you ask.

At Church Street, signal and turn [L]. As you cycle north, you will quickly discover how it got its name. The first church you come across is the historic St. James Cathedral. Built in 1853, it was the fourth Anglican church built on this site. Further up

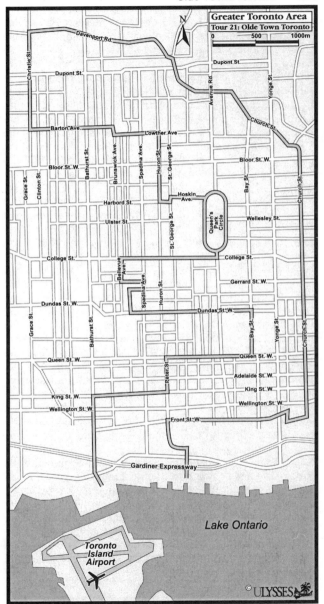

the street, at Queen Street East, is the Metropolitan United Church of Canada. Today, many of Toronto's homeless have taken to camping on its grounds.

Turn [L] onto Shuter Street and ride past St. Michaels Catholic Cathedral and Hospital. Directly ahead is the world-famous four-level Toronto Eaton Centre. Cycle past Massey Hall, cross Victoria Street and make a [L] turn onto Yonge Street. Before turning, look for the Pantages Theatre, permanent home to the "Phantom of the Opera," which is just a few metres down the street on the right. Ride past the Elgin Theatre, turn [R] onto Queen Street and then make another [R] onto James Street.

Follow James Street past the historic offices of the Salvation Army. Continue straight through the elbow in the road and follow the cobblestone walkway into an open-air courtyard. Here, tucked away in the shadow of the towering Eaton Centre, is the church of the Holy Trinity, built in 1847.

Swing [L] towards the clock tower, then bear [R] and then exit onto Dundas Street West via the Marriott Hotel walkway. Turn [R], but be careful as you cross a number of street car tracks. Once you have crossed Yonge Street, continue cycling to Church Street. Turn [L] and ride past Ryerson University to the big blue leaf at Maple Leaf Gardens. Cross Carlton Street and continue to follow Church Street across Bloor Street. Church Street swings left, crossing Yonge Street and becoming Davenport Road; it even picks up a cycling lane in the process. Several kilometres along the road, cycle across Dupont Street and get into the left-hand turn lane. About halfway up the hill, turn [L] and continue riding along Davenport Road.

Past Spadina Avenue and the staircase that leads up into the gardens at Casa Loma, turn [R] onto Kendall Avenue. It is an uphill ride to the front doors of Casa Loma. At the top of the hill on your right is the 1866 castle, former home of banker James Austin. Directly ahead is historic Spadina House. Casa Loma perfectly exemplifies the elegance and opulence of the Edwardian era. This mansion is a great place to explore; its secret passages and underground tunnels are only part of its overall appeal.

As Kendall Avenue swings to the left past Spadina House, it turns into upper Spadina Avenue. At the next street, turn [L] and ride to the [T] intersection. Turn [L] once more and follow Walmer Street past the Casa Loma stables; here, make a [R] turn back onto Kendall Avenue. Riding downhill, turn [R] at the Davenport Road stop lights and coast past George Brown City College. Continue to follow the road as it crosses Bathurst Street and goes past an old TTC building. Three streets later, turn [L] at the Christie Street stop lights.

Upon reaching Willowvale Park, make a [L] turn onto Barton Avenue and ride through this very quiet residential area. There are a number of four-way stops along Barton Avenue, so remember to yield the right of way. Crossing Bathurst Street, proceed to the [T] intersection at Brunswick Street. Turn [R] and then [L], riding around a small park to join Lowther Avenue. Cycling along the annex, ride past the Walmer Road Baptist Church and cross Spadina Road, turning [R] onto Huron Street. This area is highlighted by some very striking architecture, including St. Thomas Anglican Church, the John P. Robarts Library and Varsity Stadium. As you ride across Bloor Street, further down to the left is Canada's largest museum of fine art and archeology. The Royal Ontario Museum is also world-famous for its large collection of dinosaurs and Egyptian mummies.

Turn [L] at Harbord Street, where a cycling lane will appear as you ride past the Catholic mission. Continue along the road, which is now called Hoskin Avenue and lined with the majestic buildings of the University of Toronto. At Queen's Park, swing [R] and then immediately get into the left-hand lane. Ride one complete loop of the Queens Park promenade. As you pass the Parliament Buildings, immediately after Hoskins Avenue, move into the right-hand lane. Bear [R] to get onto University Avenue. At the College Street stop lights, turn [R] and pedal across Spadina Avenue. Notice the interesting clock tower at fire station No. 8 as you prepare for a [L] turn. Crossing several street car tracks, turn [L] and follow Bellevue Avenue to a [L] turn onto Nassau Street. Riding towards Spadina Avenue once again, the lively sounds of Kensington Market will fill the air. Turn [R] onto Spadina Avenue and make another [R] onto St. Andrews Street, which take you into the heart of the market. Fresh produce is always available here and Kensington Market is a good place to find all the essentials for a wonderful picnic lunch. Turning [R] onto Kensington Street, ride through the rest of this European-style bazaar to Dundas Street West.

Turn [L] and cross Spadina Avenue into Chinatown, which is one of the largest communities of its kind in North America. Past the Art Gallery of Ontario, the 1817 Georgian-style residence known as The Grange will be to your right, and at McCaul Street, St. Patrick's Chinese Church is on your left. Known as the Grange Shopping District, this area offers many unique shopping opportunities. Continue riding east, cycle across University Avenue and then turn [R] onto Bay Street.

At Queen Street, turn [R] and travel west past Toronto's City Hall, Nathan Phillips Square and Osgoode Hall. A short distance ahead, high above the ground, is the CityTV truck, spinning its wheels. At St. Patricks Street, turn [L] and cycle to a [L] turn onto Nelson Street, which takes you into the heart of the Toronto Insurance District. Turn [R] onto Simcoe Street and cycle to another [R] turn onto Pearl Street. Following this quiet little back alley, pass the interesting mural on Old Eds Warehouse before turning [L] onto John Street. Glance to the left as you cross King Street West and look for the Princess of Wales Theatre.

At Wellington Street turn [R]; the Sky Dome and CN Tower are now quite near. Ride across Blue Jays Way and bear right at Clarence Square. Make a [L] turn onto Spadina Avenue and then quickly turn [R] onto the continuation of Wellington Street. Spadina can be very busy and it might be easier to walk your bicycle across the road.

At Bathurst Street, signal a [L] turn and ride over the Front Street bridge to Fort York. The first fort, built in 1783, was destroyed by American solders in 1813. It was quickly rebuilt but saw little use in the years after the War of 1812. At the Fleet Street stop lights, continue straight along Bathurst and swing [L] onto the Queens Quay at Canada Malting. Joining a cycling lane, ride to the stop lights at lower Spadina Avenue. Turn [R] and pedal towards and under the Gardiner Expressway, cycling up a slight grade to a [R] turn onto Brimner

Avenue. At the next street, Navy Court, turn [L] and ride back to the Toronto SkyDome.

OFF-ROAD CYCLING

Public Trails

Caledon

Caledon Rail Trail (35 km)
Surface: Original Railbed/hardpacked
Beginning: Terra Cotta and Palgrave
Contact: Supervisor of Parks-Operations and Development, Town of Caledon, P.O. Box 1000, 200 Church Street, Caledon East, Ontario L0N 1E0, ☎(905) 584-2273.

Newmarket Area

Beaver River Wetland Trail (19 km)
Surface: Original Railbed
Beginning: Blackwater and Woodville
Contact: Manager of Policy and Planning, Lake Simcoe Region, Conservation Authority, 120 Bayview Parkway, Box 282, Newmarket, Ontario L3Y 4X1, ☎(905) 895-1281.

Richmond Hill/Markham Area

Sutton Zephyr Rail Trail (14 km)
Surface: Original Railbed
Beginning: East of Guillimbury, east of Hwy 48 and Holburn Rd goes to Caterin Road in Georginia

Waterfront Trail
Toronto to Trenton (not complete; always under development, a new guide book will be made available in 1999)

Contact: Lake Ontario Waterfront Trail, 207 Queen's Quay West, Suite 580, Toronto, Ontario M5J 1A7, ☎(416) 314-8572.

Resort and Conservation Trails

Newmarket/Bradford Area
Scanlon Creek Conservation Area (13 km of trail): Lake Simcoe Region Conservation Authority, P.O. Box 282, Newmarket, Ontario L3Y 4X1, ☎(905) 895-1281.

CENTRAL ONTARIO

Central Ontario is the province's heartland. Beginning along the north shore of busy Lake Ontario, it follows the Trent-Severn waterway to the Kawartha Lakes, including the highlands of Victoria and the unique liftlocks of the city of Peterborough. As one continues north, over 600 beautiful little lakes are scattered through the hills, cliffs and forests where the resort town and cycling trails of Haliburton are also found.

THE TOURS

22. Peterborough: The Heart of the Kawarthas

With the youthful attitude of a university town and an ideal location on the Kawartha Lakes, Peterborough is the hub for a variety of exciting activities. The highlights of this tour include a very special zoo along the Otonabee River, the world's highest hydraulic lift lock and cycling one of several recreational greenways within the city limits.

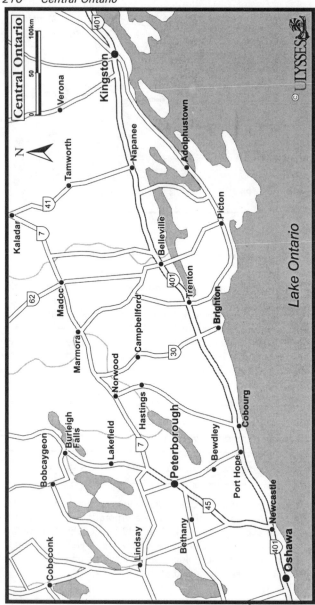

Central Ontario

Tour 22: Peterborough: The heart of the Kawarthas

● ATTRACTIONS

1. Riverside Park
2. Centennial Fountain
3. Rotary Park
4. Nicholl's Oval Park
5. Old Marina Railway Bridge
6. Trent University
7. Riverview Park and Zoo
8. Cemetery
9. Artspace
10. Quaker Oats

Return Distance: 32 km
No. of recommended legs: 1
Level of Difficulty: 🚴
Surface: Asphalt and some reconditioned railbed

Villages/Towns/Cities: Peterborough

Local Highlights: Hutchison House, Hydraulic Lift Lock, Trans Canada Trail, Art Gallery of Peterborough, Centennial Fountain, Kawartha Downs, Otonabee Region Conservation Authority, Peterborough Centennial Museum and Archives, Peterborough Petes Hockey, Riverview Park and Zoo, Showplace Peterborough, Trent University, The Canoe Museum, Lang

Practical Information

Population:
Peterborough: 68,500

 Tourist Information

Greater Peterborough Chamber of Commerce, 175 George St North, Peterborough, Ontario, K9J 3G6, (705) 748-9771, w w w . c i t y . p e t e r b o r o u g h . o n . c a ww.county.peterborough.on.ca

 Bicycle Shops

Cycle 2000 & One, 175 Simcoe St, K9H 2H6, (705) 749-3364; Cyclepath, 165 Charlotte St, K9J 2J7, (705) 742- 7720; Fontain Sport and Cycle, 384 Queen St, K9H 3J6, (705) 742-0511; Manfred's Bike and Hike, 248 Wolseley, K9H 4Z6, (705) 745-8210; Spokes N Pedals, 464 Aylmer St North, K9H 3W2, (705) 745-7343

 Special Sights and Events

Annual Summer Festival of Lights, Havelock Country Jamboree & Trade Show, Scottish Tea, Snofest, Canada Day, Lakefield Larry, Maplefest, Breakfast with the Birds, Summer Theatre, Rock 'N Rail Historical Festival, Scottish Halloween, Hogmanay

 Accommodations

Hotel/ Motel/ B&B/Camping

Off-Road Cycling

Yes, several in the area. Refer to "Off-Road Cycling" at the end of this chapter.

 Market Days

Every Saturday, Morrow Park.

Pioneer Village, 4th Line Theatre, Whetung, Petroglyphs Provincial Park, Stony Lake Cruises, Warsaw Caves

Recommended Bicycles: Hybrid/Mountain/Touring

Tour Suggestions: Because some of this tour runs along multi-use recreational pathways, remember to yield to pedestrians. It's also a good ride for children because of the off-road pathways and the Rivervew Zoo.

How to Get There: A number of routes go to Peterborough: Hwy 7 from the east, Hwys 115 and 28 from the south, Hwy 7 from the west and Hwy 28 from the north. Directions to this tour's starting point at Riverside Park (not to be confused with the Riverview Park and Zoo): go east on Hunter St. crossing over the Otonabee River turning [R] on Burnham St. Go past the Lions Club building and make a [R] turn onto Dale St., and follow the road into the park. To the left is the parking lot, to the right are the Quaker Oats Tennis Courts. This is a quiet little park, tucked out of the way, making it an ideal location to safely park a vehicle.

In the 1800s the local natives called present-day **Peterborough** *Nogojiwanong*, "the place at the end of the rapids." When Adam Scott, the area's first settler, arrived in 1821 to build a mill, it wasn't long before a settlement quickly grew. The area was known as Indian Plains, then Scott's Plains, Scott Mills and Scott's Landing. For a time, it was even called Robinson Settlement, when the British government settled 2,000 starving

Irishmen in the area. When the post office opened in 1829, it was renamed as Peterborough in honour of Peter Robinson.

Itinerary: Cycle to the corner of Burnham and Hunter St, turn [R] onto Hunter St and ride into downtown East City Ashburnham. Riding through a fairly dense commercial core, cross Mark St and pass the Mark St United Church. Just past the church on the left, are two cement cairns marking the entrance to the Rotary Greenway. Signal and turn [L] onto this reconditioned Canadian National Spur Line which was originally 15 km long and ran along the banks of the Otonabee River from Sherbrooke St to the hamlet of Lakefield.

As you cycle through a residential section of town, the trail comes out into a large open area. Once the site of the former railway yard, this space is now the Rotary Park. On your right are a hill and Nicholl's Oval Park. On your left take some time to explore the many paths leading down to the river. Along the river are a series of dams that tame the rushing waters of the Otonabee as it drops more than 1000 feet in less than 10 miles, creating a local supply of hydro electric power. Just before crossing Parkhill Rd and rejoining the trail, to your left on the other side of the river is Inverlea Park, which is the site of the city's first house.

Several kilometres into the ride, the pathway passes a group of condominiums. It was here in 1862 that the four-storey Auburn Woollen Mills were built. Using the power of the Dickson and Ashburnham lumber raceways, and only the finest wool, the mill created a world-renowned tweed. At the condominiums, look for the paths that lead to an old railway foot bridge linking the east and west shores of the Otonabee River. A little further upstream is a good spot to view Hilliard's Dam. After crossing Armour St and Television Rd, the pathway comes to a [T] intersection at Nassau Mills Rd.

Turn [L] on Nassau Mills Rd, then up and over the Trent Canal. Here the canal joins the Otonabee River. As the road bends back towards the canal, look to the left to see the railway swing bridge. A closer look at the 1890s bridge and bridge master's house across the canal can be had by turning [L] at the green rowing club building and following the canal back to the bridge.

Cycling towards the Trent University science building, just before going under the walkway, look right for a set of stairs and an elevator. Make use of this access point to the walkway. Riding over the river, follow the cement pathway as it weaves its way through the campus, finally exiting onto West Park Drive. Most people picture a university as an age-old institution. This is not the case with Trent University, as it was not granted university status until 1963. Leaving the campus grounds, turn [R] onto Nassau Mills Rd and [L] onto the pathway at Water St.

Pedalling for approximately 1 km, go past the local golf course and turn [L] into Riverview Park and Zoo. This is a well-planned, community zoo and is a great place to explore. Particularly interesting is the old pump house at the far end of zoo. Known as the Monkey house for obvious reasons, it was built in 1893 as Peterborough's second Pump House, assisting Pump House No. 1 in providing water to a rapidly expanding population. At that same end of the park, the trail resumes and passes the Riverview Railway and an old Sabre jet fighter. The trail gradually becomes narrower and narrower and finally ends at the Marina Blvd Streetlights. Cross Water St to join Marina Blvd, then pass the Northcrest Arena and Community Centre. At the [T] intersection of Hilliard St, turn [L] and enjoy a wide bicycle lane until making a [R] turn onto Dumble Avenue. Cycling to Barnardo Avenue, make a [L] turn followed by a [R] turn at the flower triangle onto Wolseley St. Now you are in an older residential area of town. Cross Chemong Rd and turn [L] onto Fairbairn St. At Parkhill Avenue, the entrance to Jackson Park is on your right. Upon entering the park, the trail immediately descends to a picturesque little pond with a covered bridge at one end. With tires now rolling over crushed gravel, follow the pathway until it reaches a [T] intersection and the park's trail map. Turning [R] will follow Jackson Creek Kiwanis Rail Trail, which is part of the Trans Canada Trail. This is a beautiful ride that goes on for kilometres. Equally pleasant are some of the park's off-road trails.

To continue the ride, at the trail junction turn [L] and follow the railbed as the map directs, bearing gradually to the right under

Parkhill Rd, past a red brick house and across Bonaccord St. The trail exits onto McDonnell St and Park St N. Turn [R] onto Park St N by following a unique little cutoff and then make a [L] turn onto Hunter St. These next few directions are confusing but simply put, follow the box around. At the Reid and Hunter stop sign, turn [R] and then [L] passing St. Peter in Chains Church. Change to the left-hand lane, turn [L] and then [R], rejoining Hunter St. Cycle back towards the Otonabee River, to the George Street Royal Bank. It is impossible not to notice the murals painted on nearby buildings. Immediately after passing the Quaker Oats building, Hunter St crosses the river via the world's longest, unreinforced concrete bridge, going past Burnham St. Cycling back through downtown East Ashburnham, the road begins to climb before descending to the Peterborough lift lock tower and visitor's centre.

Impressive-looking Lock 21 of the Trent-Severn Waterway is said to be the world's highest hydraulic lift. It is used to carry pleasure craft and water 20 metres straight up as demonstrated by a working model in the visitor's centre, or better yet, wait to see the real thing. The waterway meanders across Central Ontario for nearly 386 km. Beginning at the Bay of Quinte, a boater would have to travel through a combination of 36 conventional locks, pass through 2 flight locks, ride up 2 hydraulic lift locks and be carried along by a marine railway before reaching Georgian Bay.

Cycle under the lift locks and turn [R] onto Ashburnham Drive, following the Trent Canal over a set of railway tracks, past an abandoned railway swing bridge, to a [R] turn onto Maria St. (There is a trail that begins at the Lock 21 Visitor's Centre. The trail follows the canal's north bank to Maria St.) Left of a grated swing bridge is a set of conventional locks allowing access to Little Lake. At Rogers Cove, turn into the parking lot and head for the water. The Centennial Fountain, the highest jet fountain in Canada, should be spurting water 76 metres (250 feet) into the air. Cycling along Maria can be a technical ride, especially when crossing over a set of very rough railway tracks before turning [R] onto Burnham St. To complete the figure eight, turn [L] onto Dale Avenue and return to Riverside Park.

23. Victoria County Adventure:
Peterborough, Fenelon Falls and Lindsay

Starting in Peterborough, follow a portion of the Trans-Canada Trail onto the rural roads of Victoria County. The first leg of the journey zigzags through the Kawartha hills, visits the oldest lock on the Trent-Severn Waterway and concludes at Fenelon Falls, the "Jewel of the Kawarthas." The second leg begins along a former CN rail line and leads into the pretty town of Lindsay. Here it joins some exhilarating country roads, climbing to several spectacular views of the countryside before returning to the city of Peterborough.

Return Distance: 155 km (76 km, 79 km)
No. of recommended legs: 2
Level of Difficulty: 🚲 🚲 🚲
Surface: Asphalt, crushed gravel rail trail,
some jeep road

Villages/Towns/Cities: Peterborough, Fee's Landing, Bobcaygeon, Fenelon Falls, Cameron, Lindsay, Fox's Corners, Downeyville, Fowlers Corners

Local Highlights: Oldest Lock on the Trent-Severn Waterway, Fenelon Falls Historical Rail Station, Kawartha Settlers Village, Mayboro Lodge, Victoria County Museum, Rhymes and Times Doll Museum, Highland Cinema and Museum, Emily Provincial Park, Fenelon Falls and Lock 34

Recommended Bicycles: Hybrid/Mountain/Touring

Tour Suggestions: The first day covers more distance than the second, but will prove to be an easier ride as it does not encounter as many long climbs.

How to Get There: There are a number of routes to Peterborough: Hwy 7 from the east, Hwys 115 and 28 from the south, Hwy 7 from the west and Hwy 28 from the north.

Begin the tour at Jackson Park, which is located at the junction of Parkhill Rd and Fairbairn St. On any cycling trip, time always seems to fly by too quickly. Perhaps we can thank or blame one-time Peterborough resident Sir Sandford Fleming for this, because he invented Standard Time in 1884. It also seems appropriate that this trip begins in a recreational corridor: the city of Peterborough has always been involved in the recreational pursuits of its community, in particular the game of hockey. Many famous NHL stars like Steve Yzerman, Steve Larmer and Bob Gainey played for the Peterborough Petes hockey team, one of the OHL's most successful franchises.

Itinerary: Leg 1 (Peterborough to Fenelon Falls, 76 km). Cycling past the shoreline of the Jackson Park Pond, follow the crushed gravel trail to a [T] intersection. Here a number of paths branch off in different directions to destinations outlined on the trail map. Swing [R] and follow the Jackson Creek Kiwanis Trail through forest, open meadows and wetland. After crossing Ackison Rd, the rail trail has not been reconditioned and the ride is somewhat rough. The trail passes a transformer station and a radio broadcast tower, then exits onto Lilly Lake Rd, 2nd Line. At this point, turn [L] onto the road and follow it across Hwy 7A.

Word has it that, if you don't mind heights, it is possible to continue along the railbed joining our intended route at Victoria Rd 10, just after it crosses Hwy 7.

Cross Hwy 7A and go past a unique-looking fenced-in stone home. The road starts to rise and fall after crossing Orange Corners Rd. For the next two kilometres, this roller coaster road changes from asphalt into a well-oiled gravel surface. Notice the gravel pit and sand hill in the distance on the right. Upon reaching the blacktop of Victoria Rd 10, turn [R] and begin a long gradual climb past Doughty Aggregates and a trio of communication towers, coasting to the lights at Hwy 7.

After Hwy 7, the railbed joins Victoria Rd 10. Prepare for and make a [L] turn onto Victoria Rd 14/10, just after passing Emily Provincial Park. Once past Pigeon Lake, ride through the marina town of **Fee's Landing** and turn [R], leaving Victoria Rd 14 for Victoria Rd 10, Centerline 10. Cycling along a moderately level road at Victoria Rd 17, turn [R] and enjoy the ride along this winding road as it makes its way back to the lake. Just after

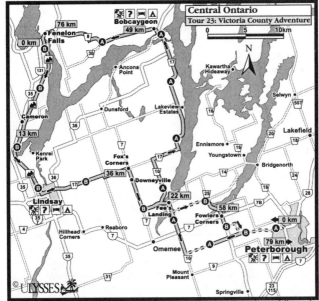

running through a large wetland area, the road ends at Victoria Rd 36. Keep right and cycle into the community of Bobcaygeon, crossing Little Bob and Big Bob Channels. At Victoria Rd 8, turn [L] and continue toward Fenelon Falls.

At this point in the trip, **Bobcaygeon** makes an excellent midday stop. Once on Cty Rd 8, take the next street left, at the fire hall and cycle into downtown Bobcaygeon. The town's name comes from the Indian word, Bob-ca-je-won-unk, meaning "shallow rapids." The area around the oldest lock of the Trent-Severn Waterway, built in 1833, makes an ideal spot to stretch your tired muscles.

Rejoining Victoria Rd 8, which has recently been widened, the road snakes through the countryside, going past several notable buildings, including Twin Bears Farms and Providence Church. At the junction of Victoria Rds 25, 8 and 121, swing [L] onto Victoria Rd 121. Cycle past the Westwood Hockey Stick Company into Fenelon Falls.

Practical Information

Population:
Peterborough: 68,500
Bobcaygeon: 2,500
Fenelon Falls: 1,800
Lindsay: 17,000

? Tourist Information

✦ **Peterborough:** Greater Peterborough Chamber of Commerce, 175 George St North, Peterborough, K9J 3G6, (705) 748-9771, www.city.peterborough.on.ca, www.county.peterborough.on.ca, www.kawartha.net
✦ **Bobcaygeon:** Bobcaygeon and Area Chamber of Commerce, 123 East St S., Box 388, Bobcaygeon, K 0 M   1 A 0 ,   (7 0 5)   7 3 8 - 2 2 0 2 , www.kawartha.net/~bobcom/bobcham.htm;   Victoria County Tourism, 26 Francis St, Box 9000 Lindsay, K9V 5R8, (705) 324-9411 ext. 233, www.victourism.org
✦ **Fenelon Falls:** Fenelon Falls, North Kawartha District Chamber of Commerce, 103 Lindsay St, Box 28 Fenelon F a l l s ,   K 0 M   1 N 0 ,   (7 0 5)   8 8 7 - 3 4 0 9 , www.kawartha.net/~fencom/fenelon.htm
✦ **Lindsay:** Lindsay and District Chamber of Commerce, 4 Victoria Avenue North, Lindsay, K9V 4E5, (705)   324-2393,   www.peterboro.net/~lpl/, www.kawartha.net/~bobcom/victoria.htm

🚲 Bicycle Shops

✦ **Peterborough:** Cycle 2000 & One, 175 Simcoe St, Peterborough, K9H 2H6, (705) 749-3364; Cyclepath, 165 Charlotte St, Peterborough, Ontario, K9J 2J7, (705) 74 2-7720;   Fontain Sport and Cycle, 384 Queen St, Peterborough, K9H 3J6, (705) 742-0511; Manfred's Bike and Hike, 248 Wolsely, Peterborough, K9H 4Z6, (705) 745-8210;   Spokes N Pedals Ltd, 464 Aylmer St North, Peterborough, Ontario, K9H 3W2, (705) 745-7343

✦ **Fenelon Falls:** Spokes for Folks, Lock 34, Fenelon Falls, K0M 1N0, (705) 738-1996
✦ **Lindsay:** Mike Gorman Sports and Cycle Lindsay, 8 Lindsay St South, Lindsay, K9V 2I6, (705) 328-3823

 Special Sights and Events

✦ **Peterborough:** Annual Summer Festival of Lights, Havelock Country Jamboree & Trade Show, Scottish Tea, Snofest, Canada Day, Lakefield Larry, Maplefest, Breakfast with the Birds, Summer Theatre, Rock 'N Rail Historical Festival, Scottish Halloween, Hogmanay
✦ **Bobcaygeon:** Kawartha Settlers' Village Settlers Days, Annual Fiddle & Step Dance Contest, Pigeon Lake Yacht Club Regatta, Fall Fair, Canada Day, Arts and Craft Show
✦ **Fenelon Falls:** Arts & Crafts Show, Fenelon Agricultural Fair, Kawartha Arts Festival, Lions Club Annual Car and Truck Show, Lobsterfest, Steam Show, Windmill Picnic Park, The Twenty-First Century hydro electric project
✦ **Lindsay:** Historical Society Craft and Quilt Show, Lindsay River Festival, Easter in the Park, Blooms of Summer House Tour, Lindsay Central Exhibition

 Accommodations

✦ **Peterborough:** Hotel/ Motel/ B&B/Camping
✦ **Bobcaygeon:** Inns/Cottages/Motels/Camping
✦ **Fenelon Falls:** Motel/Inns/Cottages/Camping
✦ **Lindsay:** Motel/Inns/Camping

 Off-Road Cycling:

✦ **Peterborough and Lindsay:** Yes, several in the area. Refer to "Off-Road Cycling" at the end of this chapter.

 Market Days:

✦ **Peterborough:** Every Saturday, Morrow Park

Fenelon Falls is an exciting little place to visit. Coming into town from the north, make a right turn onto Frances St at the lights and go past the Bank of Montreal. At the end of the street are Garnet Graham Park and a nice swimming area on the shores of Cameron Lake. To the left of the park is a trail that leads past an old railway swing bridge and historic Maryboro Lodge Museum, the former home of James Wallis, the founder of the village. The town was originally named Cameron's Falls, but when the post office opened in 1838 it was changed to honour a respected Sulpician missionary. Follow the canal through the downtown core, and to the spectacular 7-metre (23 feet) falls and Lock 34.

Itinerary: Leg 2 (Fenelon Falls to Peterborough, 79 km). A short distance after the falls on Hwy 121, look for the renovated red train station, now a tourist information booth, on the left. The Victoria Recreation Transportation Corridor can be joined just behind the train station. Heading south out of town, it passes by a senior's complex, through a light industrial area and finally leaves the town at the Fenelon Water Control Pollution Centre. The trail is in reasonably good condition and cyclists can easily ride two abreast for most of the way. For most of the ride, Hwy 121/35 can be seen to the right. Some caution is recommended, even though all road crossings are signed and/or have orange gates. Two wetland areas make the ride very special. At the first wetland the trail narrows, bulrushes tower high above, and the grass completely covers the railbed, silencing all tire noise, and allowing the natural sounds of the marsh to be appreciated.

The Victoria Rail Trail crosses Long Branch Rd at the village of **Cameron**, passing two old houses built during the early stages of the railroad. Though it is hard to imagine now, Cameron once had a busy two-story train station which was home to the section foreman, a cattle yard and a siding for additional cars.

Look for Osprey nests as the rail trail travels through the Ken Reid Conservation Area on the west shore of Sturgeon Lake. If you look under the bridge, you can see its original piers. When looking skyward, the large white-winged "birds" circling high above are actually gliders from a nearby airport. As you near Lindsay, the surface condition of the rail trail improves. Caution is recommended when crossing a small wooden bridge over a drainage ditch just before the first trailor park. The rail trail passes between the remains of a 1911 train trestle as it enters the city of **Lindsay**. After crossing William St N and Eglinton St, the trail exits onto Victoria Ave N near the Calvary Pentecostal Church. Turn [L] and follow Victoria Ave N, past the Victoria Park Armoury, turning [L] onto Kent St and into downtown Lindsay.

This enchanting city with its wide main street was named in memory of the town's first surveyor's assistant, who was accidentally shot in the leg in 1825 and subsequently died from his wounds. Lindsay has had its fair share of colourful people and interesting events. Character actress Marie Dressler made her debut at the Lindsay Opera House at the age of five, and Ernest Thompson Seton, who grew up nearby, went on to produce 40 books on North American Wildlife. In 1958 the first bullfight in Canada was staged here, with matadors armed only with wooden swords. Back in 1872, Pearl Hart, the only woman ever to rob a stagecoach, was born in Lindsay. A ride around the downtown core will reveal much about the city's heritage through its architecture and the location of its only bicycle store. Visit the Chamber of Commerce located across from the armoury and pick up a walking tour brochure, to make the ride around Lindsay even more satisfying.

Following Kent St to the [T] intersection at the old Academy Theatre, turn [L] onto Lindsay St S, Hwy7B/35B and follow the road as it descends over Lock 33 turning [R] onto Queen St, Hwy 36B. Cross over Hwy 36 N, and continue along Victoria Rd 17, Pigeon Lake Rd past the blue Lindsay water tower and the old Century Drive-In. At the stop sign, turn [R] onto Victoria Rd 7, ride through the hamlet of **Downeyville**, then make a [L] turn onto Victoria Rd 14, also called Peace Rd. This is an appealing, undulating road that winds through the countryside, past a green shingled house at McBrian Farms and the Victoria County Forest.

Travelling on this familiar road, cross Pigeon Lake and turn [R] onto Victoria Rd 10. Ride past Emily Provincial Park and turn [L] at the next road, Valley Rd. The next six kilometres will require some effort as the climbs are numerous and the road surface is now mostly hard-packed gravel. The ride is fairly easy and you have a view of a picturesque valley with wood and stone fences at the top of each hill. Cross Bethel Rd and continue cycling to another stop sign at Victoria Rd 26. Across the road are the St. James Emily Anglican Church and a commemorative cairn. Turn [R] onto Victoria Rd 26 and ride over the southern end of Chemong Lake, crossing Hwy 7 onto Hwy 7A at **Fowlers Corners**. Turn [L] onto the next road, Stockdale Rd, and follow it around a sharp right hand bend. At this point the road narrows and its surface is a hard-packed gravel that is somewhat rutted. Enjoy the spectacular view before the road descends into a valley and exits onto Lily Lake Rd. Turning [R] onto the paved surface of Lily Lake Rd, follow it to another [R] turn onto Ackinson Rd. Turn [L] onto the railbed and return to Jackson Park. You might want to rejoin the railbed at Lily Lake Rd. Even though it's a little rough, it does eliminate the hills.

---

24. Kawartha Cycling and Spelunking Adventure: Peterborough, Lakefield and the Otonabee River

---

Just a short ride east of Peterborough, in the Indian River Valley, are the interesting little hamlet of Warsaw and a unique geological formation. A day in the area will pass quickly when hiking 13 kilometres of trail and exploring the dark nooks and crannies of the Warsaw Caves. The highlight of the outing is cycling along the shores of the Otonabee River and back into the city of Peterborough.

Return Distance: 65 km
No. of recommended legs: 1
Level of Difficulty: 🚲
Surface: Asphalt

Villages/Towns/Cities: Peterborough

Local Highlights: Hutchison House, Hydraulic Lift Lock, Trans-Canada Trail, Art Gallery of Peterborough, Centennial Fountain, Kawartha Downs, Otonabee Region Conservation Authority, Peterborough Centennial Museum and Archives, Peterborough Petes Hockey, Riverview Park and Zoo, Showplace Peterborough, Trent University, The Canoe

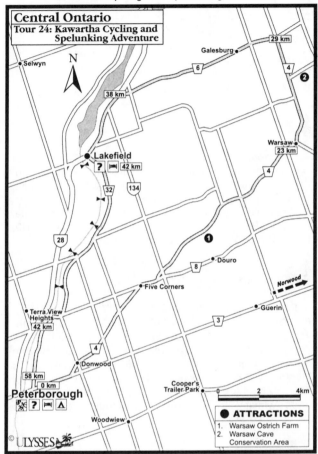

Museum, Lang Pioneer Village, 4th Line Theatre, Whetung, Petroglyphs Provincial Park, Stony Lake Cruises, Warsaw Caves, Langs Pioneer Village, Stoney Lake Navigation Company

Recommended Bicycles: Touring/Hybrid/Mountain

Tour Suggestions: Bring an extra change of clothing if you plan to go spelunking at the Warsaw Caves, as the rocks are not kind to cycling lycra.

Practical Information

Population:
Peterborough: 68,500
Lakefield: 2,600

 Tourist Information

✦ **Peterborough:** Greater Peterborough Chamber of Commerce, 175 George Street North, Peterborough, K9J 3G6, (705) 748-9771, www.city.peterborough.on.ca, www.county.peterborough.on.ca
✦ **Lakefield:** Kawartha Lakes Chamber of Commerce, Eastern Region, Box 537, Lakefield, K0L 2H0, (705) 652-6963, www.lakefield-district.com

 Bicycle Shops

✦ **Peterborough:** Cycle 2000 & One, 175 Simcoe Street, Peterborough, K9H 2H6, (705) 749-3364; Cyclepath, 165 Charlotte Street, Peterborough, K9J 2J7, (705) 742-7720; Fontain Sport and Cycle, 384 Queen Street, Peterborough, K9H 3J6, (705) 742-0511; Manfred's Bike and Hike, 248 Wolseley, Peterborough, K9H 4Z6, (705) 745-8210; Spokes N Pedals Ltd, 464 Aylmer Street North, Peterborough, K9H 3W2, (705) 745-7343

 Special Sights and Events

✦ **Peterborough:** Annual Summer Festival of Lights, Havelock Country Jamboree & Trade Show, Scottish Tea, Snofest, Canada Day, Lakefield Larry, Maplefest, Breakfast with the Birds, Summer Theatre, Rock 'N Rail Historical Festival, Scottish Halloween, Hogmanay
✦ **Lakefield:** Great Canadian Wine & Cheese Show, Lakefield Fair, Lakefield Larry Groundhog Day,

Victoria Days, Festival of Horses, Annual Rose Show, Annual Fair, Wednesday Hikes at Warsaw Caves

 Accommodations:

✦ **Peterborough:** Hotel/ Motel/ B&B/Hostel/Camping
✦ **Lakefield:** Inn/Resort/B&B

 Off-Road Cycling:

✦ **Peterborough:** Yes, several in the area. Refer to "Off-Road Cycling" at the end of this chapter.

 Market Days:

✦ **Peterborough:** Every Saturday, Morrow Park

How to Get There: There are a number of routes to Peterborough: Hwy 7 from the east, Hwys 115 and 28 from the south, Hwy 7 from the west and Hwy 28 from the north.

Cycling the backroads of Douro County can be an thrilling experience, especially in early morning or in the twilight hours of the day. This is when the area's abundant wildlife makes their presence known. Don't be surprised if a coyote lopes swiftly alongside you or a deer suddenly jumps out of a ditch.

Itinerary: To get to this tour's starting point at Riverside Park (not to be confused with the Riverview Park and Zoo), go east on Hunter St, cross the Otonabee River and turn [R] on Burnham St. Go past the Lions Club building and make a [R] turn onto Dale St following the road into the park. To the left is the parking lot, to the right are the Quaker Oats Tennis Courts. This is a quiet little park, tucked out of the way, making it an ideal location to safely park a vehicle. Cycle to the corner of Burnham and Hunter Sts, turn [R] onto Hunter St and ride into downtown East City Ashburnham. Riding through a fairly dense commercial core, cross Mark St and travel past the Mark Street United Church. Just past the church on the left are two cement cairns marking the entrance to the Rotary Greenway. Signal and turn [L] onto this reconditioned Canadian National Spur Line.

As the trail exits onto Parkhill Rd/Peterborough Rd 4 at a set of traffic lights, turn [L] and climb past the sports field at Nicholl's Oval Park Park. A short distance after the Warsaw Road Bridge is Television Rd and the community of Donwood. Land here is difficult to farm, and fields are planted haphazardly on any available flat ground. Just a short distance past the local taxidermy, look for the Warsaw Ostrich Farm. After going under a large hydro corridor, the road begins to climb before descending into the village of Warsaw. First settled in 1834, Warsaw was first known as Dummer's Mills and then renamed Choate's Mills in 1839 after the local mill owner's cousin. On the long winding downhill ride into town, Peterborough St goes past a couple of interesting old stone homes before it swings to the left. Turn [R] onto Mill St and coast to the [T] intersection at the bottom of the hill.

Before making a [L] turn onto Water St, spend some time riding around the village's back streets. This can be an interesting diversion before descending into the darkness of the Warsaw Caves. Follow Water St/Peterborough Rd 4 as it climbs past Quarry Lake to Warsaw Caves Rd. Turn [R] and follow the signs as directed to the Warsaw Cave Conservation Area. There is a small admission charge into the park, but it's well worth it.

When finished spelunking and exploring the "kettles", return to Peterborough Rd 4 and follow it north to Peterborough Rd 6. Turn [L] and cycle through the hamlet of Galesburg to another [T] intersection at Hwy 28. Make another [L] turn and ride Hwy 28 into the town of **Lakefield**. Hwy 28 becomes Queen St, as you get closer to the downtown core. Just before crossing the Otonabee River, turn [L] onto Water St, River Rd, Peterborough Rd 32. Lakefield was first called Nelson's Falls after John Nelson who settled in the area in 1819. It is a charming community that has preserved much of its past. A ride around this Irish town will reveal many interesting buildings and much about the town's early years along the rapids.

Today, Lakefield is best remembered as the place where novelist and children's book author, Margaret Lawrence, did most of her writing, and for its Preparatory Boys School, whose pupils have included His Royal Highness, Prince Andrew.

The ride on Peterborough Rd 32 from Lakefield to Peterborough is one of prettiest in the province. Cycling at river level approximately one kilometre out of town, you will pass a little picnic area and Sawyer Creek Lock 25 along River Rd. Flowing slowly, the river has widened considerably, becoming a continuous mirror that perfectly reflects the ever-changing surroundings. At Douro Lock 24, the road follows the river shorline to the left and then right, swinging once more as it approaches the Otonabee Lock 23 rest area. Upon reaching Trent University, continue following the river as it passes under the University's connecting walkway. Cycle past the old railway swing bridge and the green rowing club building, cross the river and make a [L] turn onto the Rotary Club Trail. Follow the trail past several road crossings before it returns to East City Ashburnham and Riverside Park.

25. Port Hope to Cobourg and Back (including Portions of the Waterfront Trail)

Explore the heritage port towns along the shores of Lake Ontario to get a taste of life long ago as it travelled that long and winding road towards present day. Today the road includes part of the Waterfront Trail System which is being developed along the north shore of Lake Ontario, from Hamilton to Brockville. Along the way, the two towns encountered still have an attachment to their romantic past and, with a steady hand on the tiller they have been substantially committed to making the waters and beaches of Lake Ontario cleaner and more inviting.

Return Distance: 46 km
No. of recommended legs: 1
Level of Difficulty: 🚲🚲
Surface: Mainly asphalt,
some reconditioned railbed

Villages/Towns/Cities: Port Hope, Cobourg

Local Highlights: ✦ **Port Hope:** Historic downtown Port Hope, Ganaraska Trail and Forest, Capital Theatre - Canada's only Operating Atmospheric Theatre, Canadian Fire Fighter's Museum, St. Marks Church, Dorothy's House Museum
✦ **Cobourg:** Cobourg Marina, Art Gallery of Northumberland, Victoria Hall, Dressler House, Victoria Park Beach, Waterfront walking trail, Rotary Floral Clock, Barnum House Museum in Grafton

Recommended Bicycles: Touring/Hybrid/Mountain

Tour Suggestions: Very nice summer's evening ride or, if starting out in the morning, pack a lunch for a picnic at Cobourg's Victoria Park Beach

How to Get There: From the east or west take Hwy 401 to Hwy 2, exit 461. A good starting place is the free parking lot, at the mouth of the Ganaraska River. Follow Hwy 2/Toronto St, and turn left onto Ridout St which changes to Walton St when it enters the downtown core. Turn [R] at Mill St, cross Hwy 2/Peter St, and go past the local senior citizens hall and the Canadian Fire Fighter's Museum to the free parking along the river.

It is easy to understand why the site of present-day Port Hope was once home to a Cayuga Indian village called Ganaraski or Cochingomink. At the mouth of the Ganaraska River fishing and hunting were good, and by early 1788 the area, then called Pemetaccutiang, was being surveyed for a settlement which became known as Smith's Creek. By 1817 the town was also referred to as Toronto, but to avoid confusion with the new name for the town of York, it was renamed Port Hope after the Lieutenant Governor of Quebec.

Itinerary: On the way to the lake and the Port Hope Marina, just before turning onto Madison St, take note of the East Beach rest area and rest rooms. It's a nice ride out to the end of the pier with a panoramic view of the city on the way back.

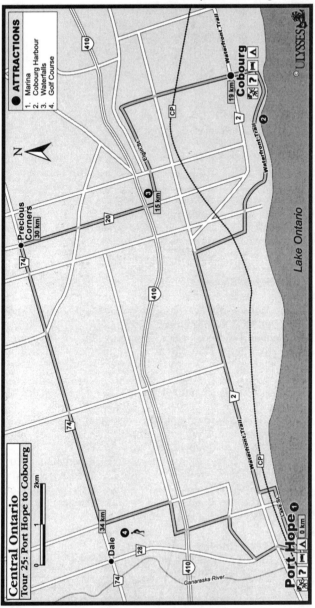

Practical Information

Population:
Port Hope: 11,505
Cobourg: 15,079

 Tourist Information

✦ **Port Hope:** The Port Hope and District Chamber of Commerce, 58 Queen St, Port Hope, L 1 A 3 Z 9, (9 0 5) 8 8 5 - 5 5 1 9, www.town.porthope.on.ca/p_hope/index.htm
✦ **Cobourg:** Cobourg Chamber of Commerce, 212 King St West, Cobourg, K9A 2N1, (905) 372-5831, www.town.cobourg.on.ca

 Bicycle Shops

✦ **Port Hope:** Proform Cycle and Accessories, RR 4, Hwy 2, Cobourg, K9A 4J7, (905) 885-4857
✦ **Cobourg:** Sommerville's, 84 King St W, Cobourg, K9A 2M4, (905) 372-7031

 Special Sights and Events

✦ **Port Hope:** Architectural Conservancy of Ontario, Down the Garden Path, Port Hope Annual Fall Fair, Float your Fanny Down the Granny River Race
✦ **Cobourg:** Copen Annual Stamp Exhibition, Great North American Land Yacht Regatta Car Show, Cobourg Highland Games, three different theatre groups including outdoor summer theatre, Cobourg Film Festival, Fall Fantasy Quilt Show

 Accommodations
✦ **Port Hope and Cobourg:** Hotel/Motel-Inns/B&B/Camping

 **Off-Road Cycling**

✦ **Port Hope and Cobourg:** Yes, refer to the "Off-Road Trails" at the end of this chapter.

 **Market Days**

✦ **Cobourg:** Seasonal, Saturday mornings May to December

Immediately after turning [L] onto Madison, the road begins to curve to the left and climb. Turn [R] onto Caldwell St and join the Port Hope Waterfront Trail at the end of the road. The trail becomes a gravel pathway and a refreshing ride along the lake, starting with a quick downhill to lake level. This portion of the trail was opened on June 3, 1998, and judging by appearances has been well used. Head east along Lake Ontario's north shore, keep riding past the Esco Limited offices and plant, but be careful when crossing the two wooden log bridges.

The trail continues to follow the lake shore and eventually ends at the Gage River parking lot. At this point, take a few moments to explore the single track along the river, which eventually comes to a dead end at the CNR railway tracks, then follow Lake St out of the parking lot. Travel west through the Port Hope Water Treatment Facility and continue along Lake St until arriving at the first of two Esco Limited buildings.

A few metres before Esco Limited's large manufacturing facility, on your right, is a long gated lane that leads to the back of the plant. If the gate is open, proceed up the lane and look for an opening to the right at the end. Cross over the CNR tracks via an old walkway. Turn [R] onto Hwy 2 and follow the Waterfront Trail into Cobourg.

If the gate is closed, continue following Lake St past the Esco Limited manufacturing plant and turn [R] at the Esco Limited office building onto Hope St South. At the stop lights turn [R] onto Hwy 2 and follow the Waterfront Trail into Cobourg.

A great deal of planning went into redeveloping Hwy 2/ Cty Rd 2 by incorporating a generous cycling lane, the Waterfront Trail, into the highway. Leaving the city of Port Hope behind, Hwy 2 passes a small business mall which is home to the local bicycle shop. A short distance after a large conglomeration of gas pipes owned by Perth Hydro is the Cumberland Pistol and Revolver Club and the tasty fresh produce of the Burnham Family Farm Market.

Before Cobourg's Northumberland Mall, turn [R] onto Rogers Rd and follow it to the left as it becomes Carlisle St. At the [T] intersection of Burnham St, turn [R] and follow it past St. Michael's Cemetery, bearing right at the Heath St [Y] junction. Continue along Burnham, past the Burnham Public School, then cross over and under a number of railway tracks. As you cross King St W, a pocket of fresh lake air streams up Burnham from Monk's Cove, a small park at the end of Burnham St that overlooks the lake.

Turn [L] onto Monk St and take a few moments to enjoy the beautiful displays of the Northumberland Community Gardens. Monk changes into Tremaine Terrace as it bends to the right. On your left is the entrance to the Peace Park. Turn [L] to cross Cobourg Creek into the park, and follow the trail as it gracefully bends to the right, exiting onto Clyde St. Continue along Clyde St and cross Ontario St onto Sydenham St. At Durham St turn [R] and travel towards the lake. The decrepit abandoned stone building on your left was an 1812 army barrack. Go through a narrow entrance at the end of Durham St, then follow a rocky trail to your left into the marina. At the Cobourg Yacht Club, the surface of the trail turns into interlocking brick. Bicycle rentals are available for boaters who moor at the harbour.

The ride along the promenade of Cobourg's Harbour is picturesque and very enjoyable. In 1829 the first of many piers was built here and welcomed hundreds of ships each year until the decline of lake shipping in 1859. The harbour was also home to the America's Cup Challenger, the Countess of Dufferin and the Steamship Cobourg car and freight ferry. As the harbour pathway exits into a parking lot, take note of the red coast-guard rescue ship on the right and the entrance to the Victoria Park Boardwalk on the left. The Victoria Beach shoreline is clean and inviting, shade is provided by the many century-old trees and the view is dramatic. Rest areas, play areas, entertainment and camping are all located along the boardwalk.(Cycling is not permitted on the boardwalk).

Leave the boardwalk at the children's play area and take sometime to explore this European-style settlement. Walking tour brochures are available at the tourist office. Founded in the latter part of the 1790s, the settlement has gone through a number of name changes, beginning with Buckville, then Amherst and finally Hamilton after the township. The locals even nicknamed it "Hardscrabble" before agreeing on its present designation which commemorated the marriage of Princess Charlotte to Prince Leopold of Saxe-Coburg, Germany. The extra 'o' in the name has been attributed to an error made by the local clerk. The magnificent town hall is one of 70 heritage sites in the downtown core. Victoria Hall is one of Canada's most elegant buildings and was built because the locals mistakenly thought Cobourg would be chosen as the capital of Upper Canada, back in 1856.

Rejoin the boardwalk and slip onto the saddle again at Bay St. Turn [R] at the [T] intersection and follow D'Arcy St across King St E/Hwy 2. Cycle several kilometres to the Elgin St stop sign and turn [L]. Follow the truck bypass as it crosses Division St/Cty. Rd 45, cycle past a number of fast food outlets and the Union Cemetery and turn [R] onto Ontario St/Cty Rd 20. Travelling north on Ontario St, the road climbs past the Old Mill Restaurant and the Cobourg Creek Country Club, and crosses over Hwy 401 to a relaxing downhill descent.

Enjoy a small cycling lane as you ride along this Hamilton Township rural road towards Precious Corners. One of the township's original hamlets, it was named after Joseph Precious and his family who arrived in 1829. After turning [L] at the [T] intersection onto Cty. Rd 74/ Dale Rd, look for the last vestige of the early settlement, an abandoned cemetery with only eight gravestones.

A short distance ahead of Northumberland Rd 18 is the Dale Rd School, a long downhill and then a stiff climb to the Bethesda United Church of Canada. At Theatre Rd, turn [L] and cycle past the local golf course to Telephone Rd. Turn [L] and follow the road as it parallels Hwy 401 crossing over Gage Creek, turning [L] onto Hamilton Drive at the top of the hill.

Immediately after crossing Hwy 401, turn [R] onto Croft St and go past Viceroy Homes to a [L] turn onto Rose Glen Rd. After Wladyka Park, turn [R] onto Ward St and climb a small hill to the ivy-covered Trinity College. Continue along Ward St, turn [L] onto Mill St and [R] onto Walton St. This area immediately surrounding downtown Port Hope along the Ganaraska River has been designated as a Heritage Conservation District. This is a fine example of a formal main street, because most of the buildings in this area were built in a 30-year period between the 1840s and the 1870s.

Before returning to the Marina parking lot and the blue waters of Lake Ontario, you will have noticed one of two significant landmarks. One that should not be missed because of its size, is the Port Hope stone railway viaduct. Massive in size yet graceful in design, its stone arches in 1856 were part of the longest section of continuous railway in Canada, linking Toronto and Montreal. The second landmark is the limestone Victorian Grand Trunk Railway Station, just west and south of the viaduct on Hayward St.

---

26. Kent Portage: The Oldest Road in Ontario

Cycle back to the past along the Bay of Quinte and several historic routes, including Ontario's oldest road.

Return Distance: 35 km
No. of recommended legs: 1
Level of Difficulty: ☜☜
Surface: Asphalt

Villages/ Towns/Cities: Trenton, Carrying Place

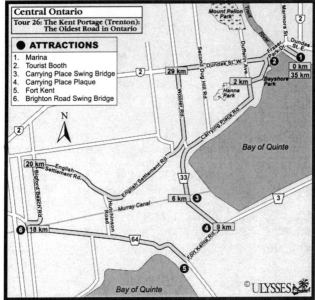

Central Ontario

Tour 26: The Kent Portage (Trenton):
The Oldest Road in Ontario

● **ATTRACTIONS**
1. Marina
2. Tourist Booth
3. Carrying Place Swing Bridge
4. Carrying Place Plaque
5. Fort Kent
6. Brighton Road Swing Bridge

Local Highlights: RCAF Memorial Museum, Fort Kente, CFB Trenton Air Force Base, Murray Canal Swing Bridge, Trenton Greenbelt Waterfront Trail, Lock One Interpretation Centre, Bay of Quinte, Mount Pelion Canon

Recommended Bicycles: Touring/Hybrid/Mountain

Tour Suggestions: A very nice evening country ride with frequent appearances of local wildlife at dusk.

How to Get There: The tour starts in the City of Trenton at the Trenton Marina. Get off Hwy 401 at exit 525 and make a [L] turn onto Dundas St W. Cross the Trent River and turn right onto Ontario St and follow it to the marina parking lot.

In the mid-1800s, the Trent River was one of two major trade routes in Ontario. Two different communities, Annwood and Trenton, developed on both sides of the river at the Bay of Quinte. They eventually merged in 1829, and the town was known as River Trent, Port Trent, then Trent Port until 1853 when the formal name of Trenton was adopted. Government

Practical Information

Population:
Trenton: 16,500

 Tourist Information

Trenton Chamber of Commerce, 97 Front St, Trenton, K 8 V   4 N 6 ,   (6 1 3)   3 9 2 - 7 6 3 5 , www.quinte.on.ca/trenton/index.html / Prince Edward County Chamber of Tourism & Commerce, Box 50, 116 Main St, Picton, K0K 2T0, (613) 476-2421, www.pec.on.ca / The Bay of Quinte Tourist Council, PO Box 726, Belleville, K8N 5B3 (613) 962-4597, www.quinte.on.ca

 Bicycle Shops

Reilly's Sports Excellence, 20 Dundas St W, Trenton K8V 3P2 (613) 392-9161

 Special Sights and Events

Opening of the Trent Severn System, Canada Day, Concerts in the Park, Trenton St Heat Cruizers Car Show, Quinte International Air Show, Scottish/Irish Festival, Trenton Summer Festival, Fort Kente Portage Festival, Festival Trenton, Wellers Bay Bass Derby, Amazing Loyalist Country Adventure, Classic Country Music Reunion

 Accommodations
Hotel/Motel/B&B/Camping

 Off-Road Cycling

Yes, see the "Off-Road Trails" at the end of this chapter.

influence has long been felt in the area; since 1919 in fact, when a film plant was built in the hopes that Trenton would become the movie capital of Canada. Today, the Canadian Air Force Training Base is located here and it is common to see drab olive green miliary aircraft flying overhead.

Itinerary: Exit onto Ontario St from the Robert Patrick Trenton Marina, and turn [L] onto Dundas St W/Hwy 2. Cross the bridge and turn [L] at the lights onto Albert St. The local tourist information booth is directly ahead. Following the road as it bends to the right, turn [L] onto Creswell Drive. Bayshore Park and the Bay of Quinte should be on the left. Turn [L] at Dufferin Ave/Cty Rd 33 and follow this former loyalist path towards **Carrying Place**.

A cycling lane appears just after rounding a left bend in the road. Sometimes road designations can be confusing, since this road goes by a lot of different names: Carry Place Rd, Queens Hwy 33, The Loyalist Parkway and Cty Rd 33.

Catching occasional glimpses of the Bay of Quinte on the left, watch for a unique road name on the right, Second Dug Hill Rd. Don't you wonder how it was named. As you cycle through a wetland area on Cty Rd 33, traffic may be backing up as it nears the Murray Canal Swing Bridge. The canal itself is over eight kilometres long, creating a safe, short and fast water transportation link between Lake Ontario and the Bay of Quinte. Spend a few moments at the information rest area on the far side of the bridge. There is always water traffic and it's fascinating to watch the swing bridge in action.

Continuing along Cty Rd 33, the old Carrying Place Cemetery on your right warrants some scrutiny. As you approach the flashing light, look for the Carrying Place plaque on your right before turning [R] onto Northumberland Rd 64. After St John's Anglican Church, built in 1824, the next several kilometres will be spent riding on the oldest road/pathway in Ontario, the Kente Portage. A splendid view of Weller Bay is just ahead after crossing Northumberland 64 onto a gravel surface. To your left is the replica of the 1813 Fort Kente built by Capt. Coleman's Dragoons. This is not the fort's original position; it was actually built on the opposite side of the road. If the grass has not been trimmed, watch out for poison ivy.

Retracing your steps, turn [R] onto Cty Rd 64, better known to locals as the Gardenville Rd. Since this road is fairly flat, good time can be made to another Murray Canal crossing, the Brighton Road Swing Bridge. A short distance away, on the other side of the bridge, make a [R] turn at the variety store onto Bigford Rd and follow it past the Mount Carmel Cemetery. At English Settlement Rd, turn [R] and pass a number of flower wagon displays and the final resting place of Gilligan's S.S. Minnow.

At the [T] intersection of Wooler Rd, turn [L] and travel towards Hwy 2, passing a large apple orchard on your right. Turn [R] onto Hwy 2 and make your way into Trenton. As you approach the downtown core, a tower and several church spires stand high above the horizon like beacons welcoming the cyclist home. A little time spent exploring the downtown core before returning to the marina parking lot will yield much information about this gateway to the Trent Severn Waterway.

---

27. Lake on the Mountain Adventure: Picton and Prince Edward County

---

The locals say that the soil is deep and rich in Prince Edward County, and this certainly holds true in more ways than one. Starting in Picton, our route travels along the peaceful back roads of Prince Edward County, following the shores of Prince Edward Bay to a friendly welcome from the folks at the Rose House Museum. As the road rounds Pleasant Point, take a few moments to appreciate the beauty of Prinyer's Cove before ascending to Lake on the Mountain and a stunning view of the Picton Bay area.

Return Distance: 60 km
No. of recommended legs: 1
Level of Difficulty: 🚲🚲
Surface: Asphalt

Villages/Towns/Cities: Picton, Waupoos, Glenora

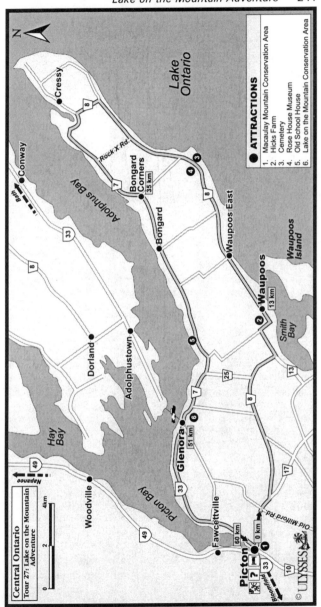

Central Ontario
Tour 27: Lake on the Mountain Adventure

● ATTRACTIONS
1. Macaulay Mountain Conservation Area
2. Hicks Farm
3. Cemetery
4. Rose House Museum
5. Old School House
6. Lake on the Mountain Conservation Area

Practical Information

Population:
Picton: 4,400

 Tourist Information

Prince Edward County Chamber of Commerce, PO Box 893, 116 Main St, Picton, Ontario K0K 2T0, (613) 476-2421, www.pec.on.ca; The Bay of Quinte Tourist Council, PO Box 726, Belleville, Ontario, K8N 5B3, (613) 962-4597, www.infolinkwsd.com/quinte

 Bicycle Shops

Annie's Pedal & Prop, 210 Main St, Picton, Ontario, K0K 2T0; Bloomfield Bicycle Co., 225 Main St, Bloomfield, Ontario, K0K 1G0, (613) 393-1060

 Special Sights and Events

Jet Rally, Prince Edward Horse and Pony Show, Art on the Fence, United Empire Loyalist Day, Antique Fair, Bloomfield Flag & Flower Festival, Art in the Country, Canada Day, Ghosts of the Past, Picton Fair, Annual Model Train Show, Prince Edward County Pumpkinfest, Lantern Tour of Historic Picton, Quinte Summer Music Festival

 Accommodations

Motel/Resort/Inn/B&B/Camping

Local Highlights: Macaulay Heritage Park, Mariners' Park Museum, Prince Edward County Courthouse, Rose House Museum & North Marysburgh Museum, Sandbanks Provincial Park, Lake on the Mountain, The Exotarium, Regent Theatre

Recommended Bicycles: Touring/Hybrid/Mountain

Tour Suggestions: pack a picnic lunch and enjoy a day of leisurely cycling fun.

How to Get There: A number of routes to Quinte County, Picton are available: Hwy 401 from the east and west, and Hwys 7, 30, 14 and 62 from the north and south. The closest international border crossing is near Alexandria Bay in New York; follow the 401 west from there.

Back in 1786, Picton must have been at the centre of a heated controversy. It grew from the merger of two settlements that developed at the head of Picton Bay. The original and financially successful town of Hallowell was a thriving community when Revered William Macaulay established another settlement on a nearby 500 acres (203 ha) of land. He named the property after Gen. Sir Thomas Picton, a major-general in the Napoleonic Wars. Through his position in the community as pastor of St. Mary Magdalene Church he succeeded in uniting the two communities in 1837. Picton has managed to preserve its past through many of its heritage sites and stories of long ago. One such tale involves Sir John A. Macdonald, Canada's first Prime Minister and a Father of Confederation, and his rather outrageous escapades as a youth in the town of Picton.

Itinerary: Start from the convenient Mary St municipal parking lot, which is one block east of the Loyalist Parkway/ Main St at the [T] intersection of Elizabeth and Mary Sts. Exit the parking lot by turning [R] and follow Mary St as it turns into York St. Past the intricate stone work of the original country courthouse and gaol, which now contains the County of Prince Edward Archives, York St ends at Church St. Directly in front is the Macaulay Heritage Park. Turning [L] onto Church St, you will pass the Macaulay homestead and St. Mary Magdalene Church. Built in 1825, the church now serves as the county museum. Notice the old cemetery on your right when reaching the stop sign at Union St. Make a right turn onto Union and ascend Prince Edward County Rd 8, going past Macaulay Mountain Conservation Area, Birdhouse City and an old Shooting Star P86 fighter jet.

As the road twists and turns its way through the county's rolling landscape, you may notice that some of the homes just past Old Milford Rd are flying a Loyalist Flag. The flag was created to mark the union of these two thrones in 1606 and is a combination of Great Britain's Saint George flag and the white and blue flag of Scotland. This new flag was called the Union Flag and it was under this flag that the United Empire Loyalists entered Prince Edward County in 1776. Today, the flag is better known as the "Union Jack" or the British flag and for the better part of four hundred years it has flown without interruption in the commonwealth.

A short distance ahead of the township of North Marysburgh sign is the unique Traveller's Tales book shop. Enjoy the sweet aroma of cedar and the occasional climb as you cycle along Cty. Rd 8, going past Cty. Rd 25 before arriving at Prince Edward County Rd 13. Continue following Cty Rd 8 to the left as it quickly descends past a windmill. It then bends sharply to the right, and begins to climb as it swings back to the left. Just around the bend, the unique crest of the Duke of Marysburgh Pub comes into view. Occasionally catching glimpses of Smiths Bay and Lake Ontario on your right, the road passes the North Marysburgh Community Hall and Willow Water B&B on the left. As the sign says, Willow Water offers all saddle sore cyclists a place to rest for a few moments and the chance to enjoy some fresh cool water.

Back on the road again, the grapes that grow in this part of the county have a robust taste. Just ahead on the left is St. John's Anglican Church and the turnoff for County Cider Estate Winery. When looking at the map, **Waupoos**, an native name meaning "rabbit," looks like a small community. In reality, it is a very large hamlet. Beginning at the junction of Cty. Rd 8 and 13, it finally ends at Rock X Rd. Cycling past the 200-year-old Hicks Farm, a red building appears on the left in the distance. Simple in design, the Rose House Museum is home to a collection of historic artifacts which tell many stories of struggle and success in the township of Marysburgh. To the left of the large silo, opposite the museum, is a road that descends to the oldest cemetery in Prince Edward County. This was once the Rose Family cemetery, and it preserves the legacy of one of the island's most respected families.

The road now moves away from the lake, passing the Vahonneh Area girl guide camp as it begins to climb at Wavey Rd, finally levelling out at Rock X Rd. Be prepared for a rapid descent and keep an eye on the road, as the view of Lake Ontario can be quite distracting. Following Cty Rd 8 as it continues to arc left, now at lake level, the view at Prinyer's Cove will elicit some oohs and ahs.

At this point, Cty Rd 8 changes into Cty. Rd 7, and off in the distance two tall smoke stacks peek above the horizon in contrast to Cressy United Church, just a short distance ahead. Wisteria vines cover the hydro wires and are quite a sight when they bloom. Cycling uphill past a red-roofed art gallery, this is the first of five fairly good climbs before reaching Lake on the Mountain. Just after the third hill, Cty. Rd 7 goes past an old school house on the right. This was the county's No. 3 school house, probably built around 1875. The next five kilometres go through some pretty bleak-looking farm land before ascending through a rock cut to the waters of Lake on the Mountain.

At the top of the hill to the right is a stunning view of Picton Bay, Adolphustown and the Loyalist Parkway. Below, the Glenora Car Ferry shuttles cars across the bay all day long. To the left is the tranquil lake that defies the laws of nature and is the subject of many myths and legends, Lake of the Mountain.

Going past the old Lake of the Mountain Inn, Cty. Rd 7 descends immediately to a [T] intersection at Hwy 33. A right turn leads to the Glenora Ferry which sails across Adolphus Reach to the continuation of the Loyalist Parkway. Turn [L] and follow Hwy 33 past the MacFarland Conservation Area back into Picton. The road descends as you pass the harbour and then begins to climb towards the downtown core. Keeping left at the [Y] intersection, be cautious as you follow Hwy 33/Main St into the city's busy downtown area. At Elizabeth St, turn [R] and return to the Mary St parking lot.

28. Lighthouse and Lookouts

No matter where you ride in Prince Edward County, your excursion is bound to be satisfying. Starting in the hamlet of Milford, you quickly leave its many enticing boutiques behind and ride past the Mariners' Memorial Museum. The highlight of this trip that ends at the Point Traverse Lighthouse is a stop at Little Bluffs Lookout. Here you will be rewarded with an inspiring view of Prince Edward Bay and the hamlet of Waupoos.

Return Distance: 56 km
No. of recommended legs: 1
Level of Difficulty: 🚲 🚲
Surface: Asphalt, several kilometres of loose gravel

Villages/Towns/Cities: Picton, Milford, South Bay, Point Traverse, Salmon Point, Cherry Valley, Bloomfield

Local Highlights: Macaulay Heritage Park, Mariners' Park Museum, Prince Edward County Courthouse, Rose House Museum & North Marysburgh Museum, Sandbanks Provincial Park, Lake on the Mountain, Exotarium, Regent Theatre, Black River Cheese Company, Hicks General Store, Scott's Mills Conservation Area, Bird watching at Pt. Traverse, Quinte Educational Museum

Recommended Bicycles: Mountain/Hybrid

Tour Suggestions: pack a picnic lunch to enjoy at the Point Traverse lighthouse or on the beach at Sandbanks Provincial Park.

How to Get There: A number of routes to Quinte County, Picton are available: Hwy 401 from the east and west, Hwy 7, 30, 14 and 62 from the north. From the south, the closest international border crossing is near Alexandria Bay in New York, from which you follow Hwy 401 west.

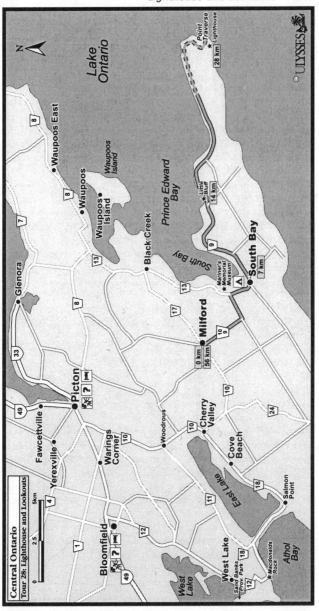

Central Ontario
Tour 28: Lighthouse and Lookouts

© ULYSSES

Practical Information

Population:
Picton: 4,400
Bloomfield: 606

 Tourist Information

Prince Edward County Chamber of Commerce, PO Box 893,
116 Main St, Picton, K0K 2T0, (613) 476-2421,
w w w . p e c . o n . c a / p i c t o n / i n d e x . h t m l,
w w w . p e c . o n . c a / m i l f o r d / i n d e x . h t m l,
w w w . p e c . o n . c a / b l o o m f i e l d / i n d e x . h t m l,
www.pec.on.ca/other/sandbnks.html, www.pec.on.ca/
Bay of Quinte Tourist Council, PO Box 726, Belleville,
K8N 5B3, (613) 962-4597, www.infolinkwsd.com/quinte

 Bicycle Shops

✦ **Picton:** Annie's Pedal & Prop, 210 Main St, Picton,
K0K 2T0
✦ **Bloomfield:** Bloomfield Bicycle Co., 225 Main St,
Bloomfield, K0K 1G0, (613) 393-1060

 Special Sights and Events

Jet Rally, Prince Edward Horse and Pony Show, Art on the
Fence, United Empire Loyalist Day, Antique Fair, Bloomfield
Flag & Flower Festival, Art in the Country, Canada Day,
Ghosts of the Past, Picton Fair, Annual Model Train Show,
Prince Edward County Pumpkinfest, Lantern Tour of Historic
Picton, Quinte Summer Music Festival, Milford Fair,
Mariners' Service

 Accommodations
Motel/Resort/Inn/B&B/Camping

Market

Yes, seasonal

 **Off-Road Cycling**

Yes, see "Off-Road Cycling" at the back of this section

Located in an out of the way spot, the pretty little village of **Milford** has developed into a thriving community along the shores a quiet mill pond. The village's original mill, built by the Clapp family is still standing. Opened in 1810, the mill, now known as Scott's Mill, continues to operate, serving the community as a tourist attraction and craft store. Today, Milford is a cyclist's haven, making it a good place to start a day of cycling in Prince Edward County.

Itinerary: Starting from the Milford Town Hall, located a short distance from the town centre on Prince Edward Rd 10, exit the parking lot by turning [R] and following Cty Rd 10. Cycle past the fire hall, where the road descends and then climbs back up to the predominately level roads of the South Bay area. At the first [T] intersection, turn [R] onto Prince Edward Rd 13. False Duck Island lighthouse marks the location of the Mariners' Memorial Museum, which has some Titanic artifacts and old maps of Prince Edward County that date back to the early 1800s.

Immediately after you turn onto Cty Rd 13, hidden to the left behind some trees will be the South Bay Cemetery, circa 1820; some of its stones bear interesting inscriptions. As Cty Rd 13 descends towards the waters of Lake Ontario, curving around the small hills, taking the path of least resistance, there should be several "Watch for Snakes Crossing the Road" signs posted. These reptiles seem to be the greatest users of this country road.

Just before the halfway point of the tour, Cty Rd 13 passes the greenhouses of the South Bay Cactus Farm and the corrals of the South Bay Ostrich Ranch. A few kilometres past the "iron bed of flowers" (an advertisement for a local B&B), don't miss visiting Little Bluffs Conservation Park, which is a good place to stop on the return route. Just ride up the long gravel road and continue along one of the jeep trails to an awe-inspiring view.

Prince Edward County is one of the oldest settled areas in the province and has many old barns and homes that have been left in a sad state of disrepair. Arriving at the Babylon Rd [T] intersection, turn [L] and follow the road as it bends sharply to the right. At Gravelly Rd, the surface becomes loose gravel for the next ten kilometres. It will be much easier to ride if you cycle on the grass at the edge of the road as you pass School House No.16 and the red Union Church. The beautiful blue sparkling waters of **South Bay** and the sweet-smelling cedar forest of the Prince Edward National Wildlife Preserve's highlight the rest of your trip to the Point Traverse lighthouse. At **Point Traverse** are a rangers station, the old lighthouse, a boat dock and a number of cottages. Swinging to the right, follow the road around the harbour to the lighthouse and the rocky shores of Lake Ontario. A new battery-operated beacon has replaced the old lighthouse guiding mariners by beaming out an identifying sequence of flashes.

Retrace your route to return to Milford. Alternatively, continue straight when you reach Babylon Rd (gravel), instead of bearing to the right and following Cty Rd 13. Follow Babylon Rd to a [T] intersection, turn [R] and cycle to a [L] turn onto Cty Rd 13, retracing your original route back into Milford.

---

29. Athol Bay, Sandbanks and Sand Dunes

Beginning in the relaxing resort town of Picton, follow the undulating roads of western Prince Edward County to the shores of Lake Ontario and Sandbanks Provincial Park. Here you can enjoy the park's white sandy beaches and its many hiking trails. If you are feeling adventurous, a ride on the sand dunes is definitely an experience to remember! The tour

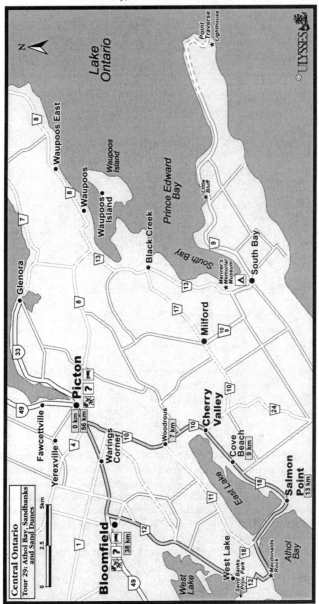

concludes with a visit to the Bloomfield Bicycle Co. and a ride along the Loyalist Parkway.

Return Distance: 50 km
No. of recommended legs: 1
Level of Difficulty: 🚲 🚲
Surface: Asphalt

Villages/Towns/Cities: Picton, Milford, South Bay, Point Traverse, Salmon Point, Cherry Valley, Bloomfield

Local Highlights: Macaulay Heritage Park, Mariners' Park Museum, Prince Edward County Courthouse, Rose House Museum & North Marysburgh Museum, Sandbanks Provincial Park, Lake on the Mountain, Exotarium, Regent Theatre, Black River Cheese Company, Hicks General Store, Scott's Mills Conservation Area, Bird watching at Pt. Traverse, Quinte Educational Museum

Recommended Bicycles: Touring/Hybrid/Mountain

Tour Suggestions: pack a picnic lunch to enjoy at the Point Traverse lighthouse or on the beach at Sandbanks Provincial Park.

How to get there: A number of routes to Quinte County, Picton are available: Hwy 401 from the east and west, Hwy 7, 30, 14 and 62 from the north. From the south, the closest international border crossing is near Alexandria Bay in New York, from which you follow Hwy 401 west.

Picton is a Loyalist town whose origins date back to the American Revolution, when people of all nationalities settled in the Bay of Quinte region. It is the county's largest city and home to the Bay of Quinte's deep harbour and the oldest fair in the province. Because of its location along the Loyalist Parkway, its streets spread out like the branches of a tree. Some of these roads veer off each other at difficult angles, making turns onto and off of them somewhat confusing.

Itinerary: Start from the Mary St municipal parking lot, found one block east of the Loyalist Parkway/Main St, at the

[T] intersection of Elizabeth and Mary Sts. Leave the parking lot by turning [L] onto Mary St and cycle past the large United Church at the end of the street. Built in 1898, this particular site has seen three different churches, including the present one. As you round the bend, Mary becomes Chapel St. Just before the lights at Main St, turn [L] onto Ferguson St. After passing the Glenwood Cemetery and the Letitia Youmans historical plaque, the road changes into Grove St. Turn [L] at Ontario St, then make a [R] turn onto South St. At Spring St, turn [L] and then make a [R] onto Albert St, cycling to a [T] intersection at Lake St, Prince Edward Rd 10.

There is no cycling lane on this busy country road, but drivers for the most part respect cyclists and generally wait until the road ahead is clear before passing. The road climbs a small hill, enters the community of **Cherry Valley** and then descends past the local convenience store. Continue straight, past the turnoff for Cty Rd 10, and follow Prince Edward Rd 18 along the south shore of East Lake.

Gradually climbing once it leaves Cherry Valley, Cty Rd 18 passes the Woodland Echos silo, a junkyard of old farm equipment and a very old church that was built in 1860 and has been converted into an interesting Bed & Breakfast. Here, Cty Rd 18 widens becoming a more comfortable road to ride. Every now and then, delightful views of East Lake appear before you descend slowly to lake level and cross a dense wetland area with hundreds of water lilies. Just after passing through Outlet and crossing the East Lake Bridge, Cty Rd 18 arrives at Cty Rd 12, the turnoff for Sandbanks Provincial Park.

Turn [L] and follow Cty Rd 12 into the park. A very busy spot in the summer, this area has textbook examples of a bay mouth sandbar and a coastal sand dune system. Wild-looking dunes tower 25 metres (six stories) above you! Continue along Cty Rd 12, and bypass the lineup at the park by swinging right and following the road along the shores of East Lake Sector. On a busy weekend, park rangers line the road preventing people from sneaking into the park. For a short time, enjoy the cool, stimulating breezes off Lake Ontario. They don't last for very long, however; Cty Rd 12 bends to the right just after passing Macdonald Rock, leaving the water behind. At the

Lakeshore Lodge Rd four-way stop, make a [R] turn and pedal through a very dense woodlot. Once clear of the forest, the welcoming beaches of the West Lake will appear to your left, many enticing boutiques line the road on both sides. About 10 kilometres past the turnoff for Cty Rd 18 is the community of **Bloomfield**. First called Bull's Mills after the man who had 12 milling operations in town, in 1830 it was renamed Bloomfield after a veteran of the War of 1812 who was a local skipper and operated ships on the Bay of Quinte. Bloomfield has a main street that seems to go on forever and is bordered by some of the province's oldest maple and oak trees.

Entering Bloomfield on Cty Rd 12, which becomes Stanley St in town. The road climbs to a [R] turn onto Hwy 33. Cycling along the Loyalist Parkway through downtown Bloomfield, be sure to stop at the best attraction in town, the Bloomfield Bicycle Company; the staff at this unique shop always have a friendly smile and warm handshake for fellow cyclists. They will also direct you to some of the county's best off-road cycling. From here, the road climbs again. Follow Hwy 33 past a working windmill to the historic West Lake Boarding School, which was the first seminary in Canada for the Society of Friends and is a fine example of Loyalist neoclassical architecture. The cycling lane along the Loyalist parkway is wide enough for two cyclists to ride side by side, but it ends at Picton. At the Walton Street stop lights, turn [R] and follow Chapel and Mary Street to the Mary Street parking lot.

OFF-ROAD CYCLING

Public Trails

Bancroft

Hasting City Heritage Trail (156 km)
Surface: Original Railbed
Beginning: Glen Ross to Lake St. Peterborough
Contact: Hastings Heritage Trail Association, P.O. Box 1517, Bancroft, Ontario K0L 1C0, ☎(613) 332-1513.

Minden

Haliburton Country Trails (24 km)
Surface: Original Railbed, loose surface
Beginning: Victoria/Haliburton Border to the Town of Haliburton
Contact: Tours, Strategy Streeting Committee, P.O. Box 147, Minden, Ontario K0M 2K0, ☎(705) 286-6016.

Lindsay

Victoria Recreation Transportation Corridor (55 km)
Surface: Original Railbed
Beginning: Lindsay to Kinmount
Contact: Victoria County, 26 Francis St. Box 9000, Lindsay, Ontario K9V 5R8, ☎(705) 324-9411.

Peterborough

Jackson Creek Kiwanis Trail (4 km)
Surface: Loose surface
Beginning: Jackson Park and Ackison Rd
Contact: Otonabee Region Conservation Authority, 380 Armour Rd, Suite 200, Peterborough, Ontario K9H 7L7, ☎(705) 745-5791.

Rotary Greenway Trail (5.6 km)
Surface: Loose surface/Asphalt
Beginning: Hunter St E and Armour Rd at Trent University
Contact: Rotary Trail Committee, Rotary Club of Peterborough, 252½ Charlotte St, Peterborough, Ontario K9J 2V1, ☎(705) 748-8825 or (705) 748-1767.

Miller Creek Wetland (1 km)
Surface: Loose surface
Beginning: Bridgenorth on East Communication Rd
Contact: Otonabee Region Conservation Authority, 380 Armour Rd, Suite 200, Peterborough, Ontario K9H 7L7, ☎(705) 745-5791.

Resort and Conservation Trails

Haliburton Forest (300 km of trail): RR 1, Haliburton, Ontario, K0M 1S0, ☎(705) 754-2198.

Bancroft Area
Silent Lake Provincial Park (20 km of trail): Ministry of Natural Resources, P.O. Box 500, Bancroft, Ontario K0L 1C0, ☎(613) 332-3940 or Silent Lake ☎(613) 339-2807

Haliburton/Minden Area
Sir Sam's Inn-Eagle Lake (26 km of trail): Haliburton Highlands Chamber of Commerce, Box 147, Minden, Ontario K0M 2K0, ☎(800) 461-7677 or Sir Sam's Inn ☎(705) 754-2497.

Peterborough/Woodview Area
Petroglyphs Park (13 km of trail): Ministry of Natural Resources, P.O. Box 500, Bancroft, Ontario K0L 1C0, ☎(613) 332-3940 or Park Office ☎(705) 877-2552.

Sandbanks Provincial Park
RR 1, Picton, Ontario, K0K 2T0, ☎(613) 393-3319.

EASTERN ONTARIO

Eastern Ontario is rich in natural wonders. In the south, enjoy the allure of the St. Lawrence River, the cool clean waters of Lake Ontario and the area's unique attraction, the 1000 Islands. To the north along the meandering Rideau River, take in the rolling hills and the spectacular scenery of the Ottawa Valley, home to Canada's capital, Ottawa. Savour the pageantry, history and impressive natural beauty along the Ottawa River and the Ontario-Quebec border.

THE TOURS

30. Limestone and Black Powder:
Discovering Kingston

Cycling around the streets of Kingston is one of the more enjoyable experiences you can have in this province. It is a great way to become acquainted with its past, its culture and the excitement of its daily hustle and bustle.

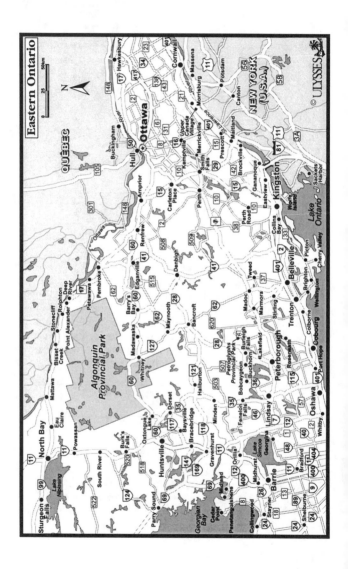

Eastern Ontario

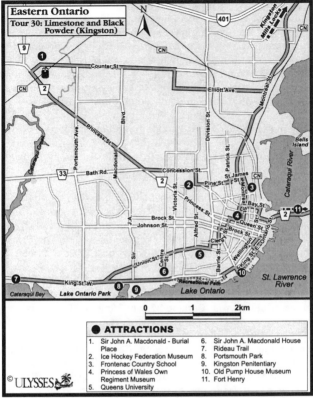

Eastern Ontario

Tour 30: Limestone and Black Powder (Kingston)

● ATTRACTIONS

1. Sir John A. Macdonald - Burial Place
2. Ice Hockey Federation Museum
3. Frontenac Country School
4. Princess of Wales Own Regiment Museum
5. Queens University
6. Sir John A. Macdonald House
7. Rideau Trail
8. Portsmouth Park
9. Kingston Penitentiary
10. Old Pump House Museum
11. Fort Henry

©ULYSSES

Return Distance: 26 km
No. of recommended legs: 1
Level of Difficulty: 🚲
Surface: Asphalt

Villages/ Towns/Cities: Kingston

Local Highlights: Agnes Etherington Art Centre, Bellevue House, Canadian Forces Communications and Electronics Museum, City Hall, Correctional Services of Canada Museum, Fairfield House and Park, Fort Frederick and the Royal Military College Museum, Fort Henry, Kingston Archaeological Centre, Kingston Mills Lock Station, Marine Museum of the Great Lakes, Military Communications and Electronics Museum, Miller

Museum of Geology and Mineralogy, Princes of Wales Own Regiment Museum, Pump House Steam Museum, St. George's Cathedral, Union Gallery, St Lawrence Cruises, Confederation Tour Trolley, International Ice Hockey Museum, Frontenac County Schools Museum, Murney Tower Museum, Queens University, Brock Street Shopping District, St. Lawrence River, Kingston Mills, Little Cataraqui Creek Conservation Area

Recommended Bicycles: Touring/Hybrid/Mountain

Tour Suggestions: This is a trip that will take a complete day so plan for a picnic lunch along the waterfront.

How to Get There: Kingston is halfway between Montreal and Toronto, in southwestern Ontario on the north shore of Lake Ontario. From Hwy 401, take exit 617, one of four exits to the downtown core. A good starting place is the Via Rail Station located south of Hwy 401, west of Division Street on Counter St.

In the late 1600s, present-day Kingston was known to the local native population as "Cataraqui", which means "Rocks standing in water". In 1671 the French built Fort Frontenac which later played a pivotal role in the Seven Years War for control of French interests in North America. Called King's Town by the first homesteaders, it did not take long for the name to be shortened to its present form. A number of influential people hailed from this city: Canada's first prime minister, Sir John A. MacDonald; Molly Brant, who played an important role in communications between the Iroquois and British in the 1800s, and Ontario's third premier and lieutenant-governor, Sir Oliver Mowat. Kingston was also home to the first school and the first daily newspaper in Upper Canada.

Itinerary: The best way to become familiar with a heritage city like Kingston is to visit as many of the historical sights and attractions as you can. Leaving the Via Rail Station parking lot, turn left onto Counter St and cycle towards Cty Rd 2. At the James Street Funeral Home, turn [R] onto Purdy Mill Rd. Follow the road up a slight grade turning [R] at the next road and then [L] into the Cataraqui Creek Cemetery. This is a very old cemetery with some famous names; it could take a few hours

Practical Information

Population:
Kingston: 56,697

 Tourist Information

Greater Kingston Tourist Information Office, 209 Wellington St, Kingston, Ontario, K7K 2Y6, (613) 548-4453; Visitor Welcome Centre, 209 Ontario St, Kingston, Ontairo, K7L 2Z1, (613) 548-4415, www.kingstonarea.on.ca

 Bicycle Shops

Frontenac Cycle, 397 Princess St, Kingston, Ontario, K7L 1B4, (613) 542-4455; J & J Cycle Shop, 675 Bath Rd, Kingston, Ontario, K7M 4X2, (613) 389-6777; Cyclepath, 339 Princess St, Kingston, Ontario K7L 1B7, (613) 542-3616; La Salle Sports, 574 Princess St, Kingston, Ontario K7L 1C9, (613) 544-4252; Milne Harvey, 315 Bagot St, K7K 3B6, (613) 546-1397; Source for Sports, 121 Princess St, Kingston, Ontario, K7L 1A8, (613) 542-2892; Re-Cyclesport & Fitness, 368 Main St, Bath, Ontario, K0H 1G0, (613) 352-1170

 Special Sights and Events

Kingston Summer Festival, Fall Fair, Rideau Valley Art Festival, 100 Great Canadians Auction, Riverfest, Grand Theatre Summer Festival, Fireworks Extravaganza over Boldt Castle, Kingston Busker Rendezvous, French Festival, Loyalist Days, All Folks Festival, 1000 Island Playhouse, Fort Henry seasonal events, Limestone City Blues and Jazz Fest, Maple Madness, Fanfayr, Kingston Haunted Walks

Accommodations

Hotel/Motel/B&B/Camping

Off-Road Cycling

Yes, see the "Off-Road" section at the end of this chapter.

Market Days

Kingston Historic open-air farmers market and indoor market at the Horn of Plenty

to explore. Follow the signs to the burial place of Sir John Alexander MacDonald, the first Prime Minister of Canada.

Retrace your steps by making a [R] turn onto Counter St and then [L] onto Cty Rd. 2. Move into the right lane before crossing the CNR railway tracks and descending into the small modern retail area of the city. Cty. Rd. 2 becomes Princess St just after crossing Portsmouth. Just past the third set of lights, at Sir John A. MacDonald Blvd, move into the left lane.

Turn [L] onto Concession St which is a multi-lane one-way street. The Kingston water tower is directly in front of you, to the east. After the immense Kingston Memorial Centre, make a [R] turn at the lights onto Alfred St. Cycle to the corner of York St; to the right is the International Ice Hockey Federation Museum which highlights the contributions of Canadian hockey players to the NHL through displays of personal memorabilia.

Following Alfred St north towards Concession St, turn [R] onto Pine St. Cross at the Division St lights to enter a colourful area of old Kingston where the houses are so close together you could reach out of your bedroom window and shake your neighbour's hand. At the [T] intersection of Patrick St, turn [L] and then [R] onto James St. Cross Montreal St and turn

[R] on Baggot St. A short distance ahead on the left is the Frontenac Country Schools Museum, a living archive of restored educational items from the early 1900s.

Continue past the museum school and turn [R] onto John St, then make a [L] turn back onto Montreal St. At Ordnance St, turn right and go around the block to take in the spectacular architecture and masonry of the 1861 Providence Manor. Rejoin Montreal St and cross Ordnance St; Artillery Park should be on your left. A few feet ahead on the right is the Princess of Wales Own Regiment, a stoic-looking castle-type mansion (museum) that highlights the achievements of the PWOR and its predecessors. The museum also has displays about Canadian citizens who served their country in war and in peace.

After St. Paul's Anglican Church, turn [R] onto Queen St and then [L] onto Clergy St. Before crossing Princess St you will pass two very impressive buildings, St. Andrew's Presbyterian Church and Queen St United Church. On the left corner of Brock St is historic Elizabeth Cottage, and further down the street is the Kingston Hospital. Turn [R] onto Brock St, go past St. Mary's Catholic Church and make a [L] turn onto Barrie St.

Cycle by the Angus Heatherton Art Centre and another very old church, Chalmer's United, and make a [R] turn onto Clergy St W. At Division St turn [L] and cycle into the heart of Queen's University. The large rock and mineral displays of the Miller Museum of Geology are located at this [T] intersection, in Miller Hall. Make a [R] turn onto Union St and try to imagine that along a good part of this street, in the Queens University Archives, are over 5.5 kilometres of manuscripts, photographs, architectural drawings, sound and video tapes all relating to the university and the City of Kingston.

Continue along Union St, passing the arena, library and registrar's office, one of the older buildings on the campus. At Centre St turn [L] and cycle to the home of Canada's first Prime Minister, Bellevue House National Historic Park Site.

Return to Union St and follow it west. On the left is the back entrance to the St Mary's of the Lake Hospital and on the right is the Donald Gordon Centre, a regional correctional staff college. When Union St meets Front Rd/King St W, keep to your right, following Front Rd uphill past the Church of the Good Thief.

The road descends quickly once you cross Portsmouth St. Go past St Lawrence College and the local golf course. At the bottom of the hill is the Little Cataraqui Marsh. Turn [R] into the Rideau hiking trail parking lot. The Rideau Trail begins in this marshy area on the shores of Lake Ontario and follows the route taken by many pioneers from Kingston to Ottawa in the late 1800s. The 300 kilometres trail passes through Westport, Perth, Smith Falls and Bells Corners, ending at Richmond Landing in Ottawa. The trail parking lot makes a very nice spot for a break and the trail into this very quiet woodland setting is even rideable for a short distance.

Exiting the Rideau Trail parking lot, turn [L] onto Front Rd/King St W and travel east towards downtown Kingston. At the top of the hill is the Lake Ontario Campground and a Government of Ontario Psychiatric Hospital. Following the rolling shoreline of Lake Ontario, King St W passes through the historic village of Portsmouth and climbs past the ominous walls of Canada's oldest reformatory prison, the Kingston Penitentiary. Spend some time exploring Portsmouth which was settled in 1835; its back streets make for an interesting diversion.

A cycling lane and some very striking architecture appear just after the penitentiary. On the right are the Correctional Services Regional Headquarters and on the left is an excellent view of St. Mary's of the Lake Hospital. Just after descending past the Water Purification Plant, join the Kingston waterfront trail on the [R] for a pleasant ride along the shores of Lake Ontario. It's impossible to miss the two rectangular-shaped marble rocks, where 3,000 men crossed from Garden Island into battle, capturing Fort Frontenac from the French on August 27, 1758.

You have quite a view of the lake as the asphalt path swings towards the water. The huge round tower just past the hospital is the 1846 Moore Murney Tower Museum. Used for defense, it is considered one of the finest Martello towers in North

America. Today this museum houses three floors of military and local artifacts. Continue along the lakeshore path, going past the band stand and exiting onto Emily St, bearing to the left to rejoin King St East.

Turning [R] onto King St E, make a [R] turn onto West St and follow it as it turns into Ontario St. At the bottom of the hill is the Old Pump House Museum. Home to monster engines and model trains, it also offers an easy access point to Kingston's waterfront. Interesting-looking old steamers can be seen along the path behind the pump house to the Marine Museum of the Great Lakes. It was here, at Mississauga Point, that Loyalists travelling from Montreal landed in 1784, establishing a camp which eventually grew into the City of Kingston.

Take the time to explore along the channel and inside the marine museum which contains the original engines and pumps that successfully served Kingston and the Great Lakes shipping industry for almost 68 years. Visit the Alexander Henry, an old ice breaker which has been converted into a B&B. Rejoin Ontario St and cycle towards the downtown core. Just past the Canadian Pacific steam engine, the *Spirit of Sir John A*, are the tourist information booth and Confederation Park.

Pass Kingston City Hall and turn [L] onto Brock St to do a circle tour of this area. The Kingston Custom House and St. George's Cathedral are only a few of the highlights. After exploring the downtown core, locate Johnston St and follow it back to Ontario St. Travel along Ontario St towards the Lasalle Causeway. The gang plank for the 50-car Wolfe Island Ferry is at Barrack St to your right.

After bending sharply to the right, Ontario St crosses the Cataraqui River via the La Salle Causeway. When crossing this grated bridge, do not look down. Rather, look to the front as bicycles tend to bounce around on this type of grated surface. Proceed to the lights and turn [R] onto Duty St. To the right is the entrance to the Royal Military College and to the left is a long climb to Fort Henry and a remarkable view of Kingston's skyline.

Fort Henry at one time held a major strategic position in Upper Canada. It was originally built quickly during the War of 1812 and, as a result, had to be torn down and rebuilt in the mid-1830s. Since then, this 126-room fort has become home to an enormous amount of British and Canadian military history. A great deal of dedication has gone into preserving the furnishings, the appearance and the operation of the fort so that it closely conforms to the time when it was occupied by British soldiers. After briefly stepping back in time, pick up your speed on the downhill descent to the Fort Henry stockade.

At Hwy 2, a [R] turn will take you past the Barriefield Rock Garden Project and Hwy 15. The road levels out just before reaching the Kingston Canadian Forces Base. One kilometre further along Hwy 2 is the Communications Museum and Kingston's Vimy Barracks. At this point, unless you plan to ride the waterfront trail to the MacLachlan Woodworking Museum or Gananoque, retrace your steps to the La Salle Causeway.

Once across the La Salle Causeway and back in the city, keep to your right. Follow the road to the north as it turns into Place d'Armes. Make a [R] turn onto Wellington St and round it to Rideau St. Turn [R] onto Rideau St, cycle past Rideau Park and turn [R] again onto Montreal St. An interesting side trip at this point would be to turn [R] at Belle Park Drive and follow the road through Cataraqui Park and cross over to Belle Island.

Return to Montreal St, continue north and turn [L] onto an undulating Elliott Ave. After crossing Division St, Elliott Ave becomes Leroy Grant Drive as it descends to Counter St. Turn [L] onto Counter street, and go past the Kingston PUC building. After crossing Sir John A MacDonald Blvd, the road descends past Bill Hatchet Park and crosses the CNR tracks to the Via Rail Station parking.

Optional Kingston Mills Tour (36 km): Before returning to the Via Rail Station, why not visit a very picturesque spot just north of the city? The Kingston Mills Lock Station is the first lock on the Rideau as it winds its way north to Ottawa. It is a very spectacular place with the wild-looking rock formations of the Canadian Shield forming a system of four natural adjoining locks. Also on site is the Lockmaster Anglin's House, now a tourist information booth, and the restored 1830 military blockhouse. Continue along Montreal St, now the Battersea Rd/Hwy 11, and cross Hwy 401. Make a [R] turn onto Kingston Mills Rd/Frontenac 21 and ride along this scenic road to the locks. To return to the Via Rail Station, retrace your steps to Battersea Rd and turn [L] and then [R] onto the next road, McAdoos Lane. Cycle through a light industrial area and make a [L] onto the Old Perth Rd/Division St. Cross Hwy 401, turn [R] at the lights and follow Counter St to the Via Rail Station.

---

31. The Rideau Canal and the 1000 Islands Parkway: Kingston, Ottawa and Brockville

---

Experience one of Ontario's most beautiful and interesting bicycling excursions where the serenity of the Rideau Canal's many blue lakes and the ingenuity of its lock system can be viewed. You will quickly become mesmerized with the Ottawa River and the mirrored images along the St Lawrence Seaway. Following the Old Perth Rd, experience the route taken by wagons of yesteryear as they passed through the villages of Westport and Perth. Join a recreational trail along the Ottawa River and cycle into the heart of the nation's capital. On the return journey, visit the jewel of the Rideau, Merrickville, indulge in fresh chocolate at Smiths Falls and try to find Canada's oldest railway tunnel in Brockville. Finally, after arriving at the Thousand Islands National Park, cycle along the St. Lawrence River into the Town of Gananoque and follow the waterfront trail back into Kingston.

Return Distance: 444 km (86 km, 98 km,
82 km, 68 km, 65 km, 45 km)
No. of recommended legs: 6
Level of Difficulty: 🚲 🚲 🚲
Surface: Asphalt

Villages/Towns/Cities: Kingston, Westport, Perth, Franktown, Richmond, Ottawa, Kemptville, Merrickville, Smiths Falls, Brockville, Mallorytown Landing, Gananoque

Local Highlights: See the related tour information at the end of this tour.

Recommended Bicycles: Touring/Hybrid/Mountain

Tour Suggestions: A number of this tour's legs require a solid cycling effort, with five or more hours riding for each leg. Allow yourself an extra day or two in Ottawa so that you can explore the nation's capital. Please refer to the Ottawa itineraries (Tours 32 and 34) also found in this section of the book.

How to Get There: Kingston is halfway between Montreal and Toronto, in southwestern Ontario on the north shore of Lake Ontario. Take Hwy 401 to exit 617, one of four exits to the downtown core. A good starting place is the Via Rail Station located south of Hwy 401, west of Division St on Counter St.

Sparkling like a diamond necklace, the blue lakes of the Rideau Canal invite you to experience the thrill of cycling along their 202 kilometres of shorline and canals. Built over six years by thousands of Irish Immigrants and French Canadians as a supply route from Ottawa to Kingston, it became a secure way to transport goods during the War of 1812. The canal was a major transportation route until the arrival of the railways. Today it still sees a great deal of traffic, but more for leisure than for business.

Itinerary: Leg 1 (Kingston to Perth, 86 km). Beginning our journey in the historic City of **Kingston**, located at the mouth of the Rideau Canal, leave the Via Rail parking lot by turning [L] onto Counter St. Cycle past the burial place of Sir John A. MacDonald, make a [R] turn onto Hwy 2 and follow it to Sydenham Rd. Turning [R] onto Sydenham Rd/Frontenac Rd 9, you will cycle past a number of cemeteries.

Cross Hwy 401, then turn [R] onto Burbrook Rd at the flashing light. Follow this strip to the [T] intersection at Frontenac 10. Turn [L] onto Old Perth Rd and prepare for a long gradual climb. Follow the road through the villages of Glenburnie, Bucks Corners and, a short distance past Inverary, enjoy the marvellous view of Loughborough Lake as Frontenac 10 crosses its placid waters.

Cautiously proceed through the flashing light at Frontenac 5, then pass Perth Rd Public School and the fiery red granite rock

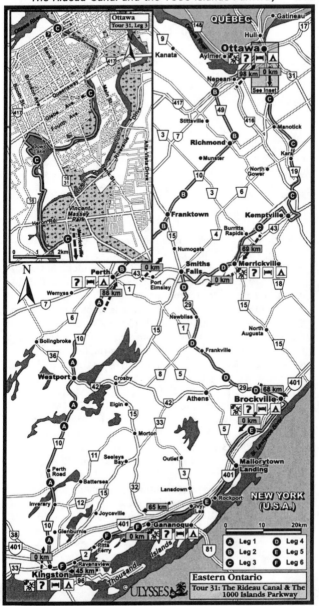

Eastern Ontario
Tour 31: The Rideau Canal & The
1000 Islands Parkway

Practical Information

For Kingston see Tour 30. Limestone and Black Powder: Discovering Kingston

Population:
Perth: 6,000
Ottawa: 316,000 (Capital Region: 1,000,000)
Merrickville: 995
Brockville: 21,600
Gananoque: 5,200

 Tourist Information

✦ **Perth:** Perth Chamber of Commerce, 34 Herriott St, Perth, Ontario, K7H 1T2, (613) 267-3200
✦ **Ottawa:** Ottawa Tourism and Convention Authority, 130 Albert St, Suite 1800 Ottawa, Ontario, K1P 5G4, (613) 237-5150, www.tourottawa.org
✦ **The Rideau Canal:** Rideau Canal, 34a Beckwith St South, Smiths Falls, Ontario, K7A 2A8, (613) 283-5170
Most lock stations have washrooms, first aid and picnic facilities. Overnight camping is always nearby.
✦ **Merrickville:** Merrickville Chamber of Commerce, PO Box 571, Merrickville, Ontario, K0G 1N0, (613) 269-2229, www3.sympatico.ca/merrickville/WELCOME.HTM
✦ **Brockville:** Chamber of Commerce at the Blockhouse Island, 1 King St West, PO Box 1341, Brockville, Ontario, (613) 342-6553,www.brockville.com
✦ **Gananoque:** 1000 Islands Gananoque Chamber of Commerce, 2 King St East, Gananoque, Ontario K7G 1E6, (613) 382-3250, www.gananoque.com/gananoque.html, St. Lawrence Islands National Park - Parks Canada, 2 County Rd 5, RR 3, Mallorytown, Ontario, K0E 1R0, (613) 923-5261

Westar Sports, 501 Hazeldean Rd, Kanata, Ontario, K2L 1V6, (613) 836-6996; World Class Cycles, 1501 Carling Ave, K1Z 7M1, Ottawa, Ontario, (613) 728-7960

✦ **Merrickville:** Bridgeman Sports, 24 Beckwith St South, Smiths Falls, Ontario, K7A 2A8, (613) 283-1339

✦ **Brockville:** Jones Dave Sport Shop, 65 King St West, Brockville, Ontario, K6V 3P8, (613) 345-5574 Q J Johnny, 198 King St West, Brockville, Ontario, K6V 3R5, (613) 342-5543; Racers Edge Pro Shop, 6 Delhi, Brockville, Ontario, K6V 4H3, (613) 345-2133; Senior R Services, 148 King St West, Brockville, Ontario K6V 3R4, (613) 342-8644

✦ **Gananoque:** T. I. Cycle, 590 Stone St, Gananoque, Ontario, K7G 1Z2, (613) 382-5144

 Special Sights and Events

✦ **Kingston:** Kingston Summer Festival, Fall Fair, Rideau Valley Art Festival, 100 Great Canadians Auction, Riverfest, Grand Theatre Summer Festival, Kingston Busker Rendezvous, French Festival, Loyalist Days, All Folks Festival, Fort Henry seasonal events, Limestone City Blues and Jazz Fest, Maple Madness, Fanfayr, Kingston Haunted Walks

✦ **Perth:** Festival of Maples, Strawberry Social, Canada Day, Stewart Park Festival, Annual Art Show, Glorious Garlic Festival, Horse Around, Annual Glen Tay Block Race, Perth Autumn Studio Tour, Art in the Garden, Outdoor Summer Theatre, Perth Fair, Murphy's Point Provincial Park, Inge-Va, Purdon Conservation Area, Duel Park, Canada's oldest department store, Matheson House, Hands-on-garden, Perth Wildlife Reserve

✦ **Ottawa:** Winterlude, Tulip Festival, National Capital Race, Reflections of Canada, National Capital Air Show, Canada Dance Festival, Sound and Light Show, Festival Canada, Sparks St Busker Festival, Ottawa Chamber Music Festival, International Jazz Festival, Bluesfest, Changing of the Guard Railway Museum, Smiths Falls Heritage House Museum

✦ **Merrickville:** Lombardy Fair, Heritage House Arts Show, Settlers Days, Historical Industrial Ruins, Blockhouse Museum, Merrickville Lock Station, Smiths Falls Historic Rideau Canal Museum, Canada's Oldest Yacht, Hershey Chocolate Factory

✦ **Brockville:** Artists Studio Tours, Brockville Antique Show, Great Balloon Rodeo, Symphony of Lights, Brockville Ghost Walks/Fulford Mansion, Loyalist Days/Fort Wellington, Canada Day Celebrations/Fort Wellington, 1000 Islands Poker Run, Riverfest, Brockville Museum, Brockville Railway Tunnel, Lemoine Point Conservation Area, County Courthouse and Jail, Fulford Place

✦ **Gananoque:** Celebrate Our Heritage, Festival of the Islands, The Great Gananoque Chili Cook-Off, 1000 Island Boat Cruises, Gananoque Museum, Landon Bay Gardens, Historic 1000 Islands Village Foundation, House of Haunts, 1000 Island Skydeck, 1000 Islands Wild Kingdom, Boldt Castle

 Accommodations

✦ **Kingston and Ottawa:** Hotel/Motel/B&B/Camping
✦ **Perth:** Resort/Inns/Motel/B&B/Camping
✦ **Merrickville:** Inns/B&B/Camping
✦ **Brockville and Gananoque:** Hotel/Motel/B&B/Camping

 Off-Road Cycling

✦ **Kingston and Ottawa:** Yes, see the "Off-Road Trails" at the end of this chapter.

 Market Days

✦ **Kingston:** Kingston Historic, open air, farmers market and indoor market at the Horn of Plenty
✦ **Perth:** Every Saturday May to October
✦ **Ottawa:** Daily

that towers high above the road. Ride through the village of Perth Rd (not the same as Perth, which is a little further). Frontenac 10 continues to undulate, climbing steeply at times but always twisting and turning its way around the lakes of the Rideau Canal. Keep an eye out for an old goat shed high on a hill to your left just before Bedford Mills. Once in Leeds and Grenville County after crossing Newboro Lake, the road begins to descend to a [T] intersection at Upper Rideau Lake, one of 33 lakes within 24 kilometres.

Turn [L] onto Hwy 42 and enter the town of Westport, originally known as Manhard's Mills. At the large red public school, turn [R] onto Cty Rd 10. As the road descends through town it crosses a small fish sanctuary before going straight up Foley's Mountain. Once at the top of the hill, take a break (you will need it) and enjoy a beautiful view. The entrance to the Foley Mountain Conservation Area is on the right. The kilometres continue to build as the road passes Pike Lake into the county of Lanark, finally arriving in the peaceful town of **Perth**. At the junction of Frontenac 10 and 1, turn [L] at the lights and follow Gore St E into downtown Perth.

Settled in 1815 by 700 Scottish immigrants, this exciting old town on the River Tay was named after Perthshire, Scotland. The town is famous for making a 22,000-pound cheese for the 1892 Chicago World's Fair. Don't miss visiting the Matheson House and the site of the last fatal duel in Canada, which was fought between two law students in present-day Duel Park. Here, you may get a chance to hear Canada's oldest town band practising nearby, filling the air with music.

Itinerary: Leg 2 (Perth to Ottawa, 98 km). Beginning in the town of Perth at the corner of North St/ Lanark Rd. 10 and Gore St E, make a [R] turn off Gore St onto North St. Lanark 10 passes the historic St. Andrew's Presbyterian Church and crosses a set of railway tracks; the ride for the next several kilometres is very dull. After passing through the small hamlets of Richardson and Gillies Corners, turn [L] onto Hwy 15. Travel north through the village of Franktown and make a [R] turn onto Richmond Rd. After riding past a Christmas Tree Farm and through the town of Prospect, cross Dwyer Hill Rd/Carlton Rd 3. Watch for golf balls coming across the road from the River Bend Golf Course on the Jock River. After the turnoff for Munster, the road expands into four lanes as it enters **Richmond**, an early 1800s military settlement.

At Lanark Rd 49 turn [L] onto Eagleson Rd and cycle towards Kanata. Row upon row of townhouses fill the skyline, finally giving way to a myriad of retail stores. Eagleson Rd, now four lanes, passes the Robertson Rail Trail and the Old Quarry Trails parking lot before crossing Hazeldean Drive. A bicycle lane appears on the road just before it crosses Hwy 417. Be careful after passing through the stop-lights at Campeau Drive, as cars join Eagleson Rd on your right.

Turn [R] onto the next road, Corkstown Rd, and join the paved bicycle path on your left. The path begins as a pretty ride through a meadow, crossing a creek several times. At the first [T] intersection, keep right as you pass under a set of railway tracks, and at the second [T] bear right again. After crossing Water Creek, the path changes to a hard-packed calcium and then into hard-packed sand, similar to a jeep road. Continue to follow the trail as it goes through a set of gates, bearing left as it follows Moodie Drive. The large glass dome on the left belongs to Nortel. Watch for cars as the bicycle path crosses a number of driveways.

When the trail exits onto Carling Ave, cross the street and join the recreational path on the north side. It is not far to Dick Bell Park and Marina, which has a great view of the Ottawa River. Too bad that cycling along the shoreline in this park is out of the question, since "no cycling" signs are posted here. Washrooms and a place to rest are available a short distance past the marina at Andrew Haydon Park. There is another good rest spot further along, just past the large silver-dome arena. Make a [L] turn following the path which leads to Lakeside Gardens and the Ottawa River.

When the main trail reaches Britannia St, it splits into an upper and lower path. Keep to the lower trail as it offers several entrances to Mud Lake. Coming back along the river, the trail turns sharply to the [R] and then [L] (no bicycles straight ahead) as it goes under the Ottawa River Parkway. Moving away from the river at the Woodroffe Rd, take a moment and cross the parkway to the Kitchissippi Lookout.

The trail eventually goes back under the parkway at Ile Bate Island and runs parallel to the Ottawa River for the next several kilometres. The path follows the shoreline of the oldest Trans-Canada thruway, and passes large cement bunker cairns that stand stoically on guard all along the river. These cairns, or *Inukshuks*, were traditionally built by the Inuit as landmarks. In the Arctic they are placed in long rows to drive caribou towards waiting hunters. These particular cairns are primarily the work of one man who cemented these figures together during the year, and makes for some interesting conversation.

As you ride past the Lemeus Island Water Purification Plant and under a CN railway bridge, the Ottawa Skyline appears on the horizon. The trail exits onto Fleet St just behind the municipal campground, Le Breton. Turn [R] and cross a walkway in front of an old waterworks building, bearing to the left once across. Continue following the trail, and keep right while going past the Trans Canada Trail Pavilion. Ride under the Wellington St Bridge and through a segmented tunnel, turn [L] and then [R] following the trail along the river. This is a confusing section. If you get up to the Old Mill Restaurant, just retrace your steps to the pavilion and remember to go under the bridge.

The view from this vantage point along the Ottawa River takes your breath away. The sight of the Parliament Buildings that seem to merge with the granite cliffs of the Ottawa River is simply stunning. This leg ends at the Ottawa River Locks, which have eight levels and located between the Chateau Laurier and Parliament Hill. Continue following the canal as it climbs upwards, going under Rideau St and exiting in downtown **Ottawa** at the National Arts Centre. Days could be spent exploring this city and its surrounding countryside. Take full advantage of everything Ottawa has to offer: an exciting nightlife, numerous museums and great cycling everywhere you look! See the Tour 32: "Ottawa Explorer".

Itinerary: Leg 3 (Ottawa to Merrickville, 69 km). Starting from the Hog's Back Falls parking lot (refer to Tour 40 for directions), turning [L] onto Hog's Back Rd followed by a [R] turn onto Riverside Drive. No cycling path is provided on this multi-lane road, so avoid rush hour traffic. Go past Uplands Rd and then Hunt Club Rd; on the left is CFB Ottawa. Here, the road narrows to two lanes, just opposite the airport. Going through Cedardale along Ottawa Carlton 19, watch for cattle crossing the road just before Gloucester Glen. At times the canal comes very close to the road, which makes you wonder if it ever floods.

At the [T] intersection of Leeds and Grenville 43, turn [R] towards **Kemptville**. At the stop-lights make another [R] onto Leeds-Grenville 44. Follow the road and turn [L] before the canal onto River Rd, Leeds-Grenville 23. At the [T] intersection turn [R] and continue following River Rd, going past the Burritts Rapids Rd. If you can spare the time, there are plenty of side trips and interesting places to see and visit along this route. Some highlights are the hamlets of Burritts Rapids, Nicholsons and Clowes Locks, the Oddessy Cow Palace and an old cemetery just before the [T] intersection at Leeds-Grenville 43. Turn [R] onto Leeds-Grenville 43 and cycle into the amazing little village of **Merrickville**, which is there to be explored and enjoyed. This lovely restored village has seen its share of firsts: the first house in Ottawa was built with wood from the town's original mill, the first nursery and seed farm in Ontario was just a few minutes east of the village, and in 1908 Canada's first Boy Scout troop was started here.

Itinerary: Leg 4 (Merrickville to Brockville, 68 km). Continue following Leeds-Grenville 43 by turning [R] onto Mill St and ride over the the swing bridge across the Rideau Canal. At the flashing lights, make a [L] turn onto Leeds-Grenville 43, West Broadway St. The canal is now on your left for the first time during this trip. Once you arrive in Lanark County, a cycling lane appears and makes for a comfortable ride into **Smiths Falls**. Turn [R] onto Hershey Drive and take the time to tour the world famous chocolate maker. From Hershey Chocolates, turn [L] onto Lorne St and then [R] onto Queen St. At the lights turn [L] onto Chambers St and make another [L] at the [T] intersection onto Beckwith St, or Brockville St. Passing the Rideau Canal Museum and Old Stys Lock, follow Hwy 29 by way of a very wide cycling lane, available all the way into Brockville. Located in the village of Frankville is the historical house of female suffragette Louise C. McKinny, remembered as the first woman in the British Empire to gain a parliamentary seat. When a tall church steeple comes into view, the community of Addison is just ahead and a few kilometres further down the road is the Johnson Wildlife Centre. At Tincap, proceed through the lights and cross Hwy 401 into the captivating city of **Brockville**. First known as Buell's Bay, it went through several other name changes including Snarlington before being named after a war hero, General Sir Isaac Brock. One of the oldest cities in the province, it is the only one in Ontario to have a New England-type town square. It is also home to the oldest railway tunnel in Canada, which runs under the city to the waterfront, and a well-preserved Victorian downtown.

Itinerary: Leg 5 (Brockville to Gananoque, 65 km). From Hwy 401 continue along Cty Rd 29/William St towards downtown Brockville. Turn [R] onto King St/Hwy 2. Travelling west along King St past Rotary Park and Fulford Park, the King's Hwy adopts its new name, Leeds-Grenville 2. At the city limits, just past Lawrence Park, the road picks up an additional two lanes for a short distance. After crossing Jones Creek, look for the lighthouse on the rocks. Much of the exposed escarpment in this area has been enhanced by local landowners with moss and colourful flowers. Continue past the first Leeds-Grenville Rd 5 on the right. Look for a red house and turn [L] onto the second Leeds-Grenville Rd 5. Follow the old Mallorytown Rd over Hwy 401 to the [T] intersection at Old River Rd and the "River of a Thousand Dreams."

Turn [R] onto the 1000 Islands Parkway and cycle into the heart of the St. Lawrence National Park. On the right is the bike path. While the bike path is a nice alternative, the view from the road is still better. The parkway does its best to follow the St. Lawrence River but from time to time it moves away, following the natural lay of the land. The islands are home to many eye-catching cottages and you must remind yourself to keep your eyes on the road. Just past the Turtle Crossing sign, the road passes through the peaceful hamlet of Rockport before climbing past Horse Thiefs Bay Rd. At the Hill Island Bridge, the bike path joins the parkway, but resumes on the other side.

There is another splendid view on the left, just over the Landon Bay parallel bridges. At Jackstraw Lane, the bicycle path joins the parkway. Follow the road to the right as it rejoins Leeds-Grenville Rd 2/Hwy 2. Turn [L] and go under the welcoming railway bridge into the town of **Gananoque**. To complete this leg, cycle along King St E to the Town Hall and Museum at the Gananoque River. A true tourist haven, Gananoque has some appealing features: live theatre, boat cruises, clean beaches, a rich history and a number of significant historical buildings.

Itinerary: Leg 6 (Gananoque to Kingston, 45 km). From the Town Hall and the Museum, cross the Gananoque River keeping to the right, and follow King St W, which becomes Leeds-Grenville 2 on the far side of town. After passing through the welcoming pillars, join the Waterfront Trail with its very wide cycling lane. The road passes the first of two access points for the Howe Island Ferry.

Optional side trip: Howe Island makes for an excellent side trip, at a minimal cost. Turn left and make the crossing to the island. Following its south shore to the Pitts Ferry crossing. When you return to the mainland, turn [L] onto Hwy 2 and continue towards Kingston. Turning [R] would take you to the MacLaughlin Woodworking Museum.

At Dear Ridge Drive, the road crosses an imaginary line into the County of Frontenac. A few kilometres ahead is a pretty little wetland and the MacLaughlin Woodworking Museum. The museum is a worthwhile stop, not only for its washrooms and a water cooler, but for its interesting collection of ancient woodworking tools that were once used by early pioneers. Leave the museum and cycle up a two-kilometre grade, past the second turnoff for the Howe Island Ferry, Pitts Rd. The road finally levels out just before Hillview Rd and the large sheep operation on the left.

At the St Lawrence Golf and Country Club, enjoy a quick descent to Treasure Island. After the Adoma Community Centre, you will cycle past hundreds of lily pads floating in Abby Dawn Creek before enjoying the last major climb on Frontenac 2. The City of Kingston quite close when you pass Vimy Barracks and the Museum of Communications.

After a nice downhill ride, cross the La Salle Causeway back into the city, keeping to the right once over the bridge. Follow the road to the north as it turns into Place d'Armes. Make a [R] turn onto Wellington St and follow it around to Rideau St. Turn [R] onto Rideau St, cycle past Rideau Park and turn [R] again onto Montreal St.

Turn left onto undulating Elliott Ave. After crossing Division St, Elliott Ave becomes Leroy Grant Drive as it descends to Counter St. Turn [L] onto Counter St, and pass the Kingston PUC building. After crossing Sir John A MacDonald Blvd, the road descends past Bill Hatchet Park and crosses the CNR tracks to the Via Rail Station parking lot.

---

32. Ottawa Explorer: A Full Day in Under Two Hours

A great ride for the first time cyclist visiting the city. You quickly get caught up in the community's hustle and bustle. Cycling along the streets of the nation's capital is perhaps the best way to become familiar with the city's general layout, its history, its culture and natural beauty.

Return Distance: 28 km
No. of recommended legs: 1
Level of Difficulty: 🚲🚲
Surface: Asphalt city streets

Villages/Towns/Cities: Ottawa

Local Highlights: Bicycling Magazines Rated Top 10 Bicycle Shop in Hull, Quebec, Champlain Lookout, Meech Lake, Pink Lake, Mackenzie King Estate, Parliament Hill, By Ward Market, Canadian Museum of Civilization, Rideau Canal, Sparks St Mall, National Gallery of Canada, Casino de Hull, Canadian War Museum, Notre Dame Basilica, Agriculture Museum, Canadian Museum of Contemporary Photography, Canadian Museum of Nature, Currency Museum of the Bank of Canada, National Archives, National Aviation Museum, National Museum of Science and Technology, Royal Canadian Mint, Laurier House,

Gatineau Park, Symphony of Sound, Rideau Hall, Rockcliffe, Supreme Court of Canada, Changing of the Guard

Recommended Bicycles: Touring/Hybrid/Mountain

Tour Suggestions: A quick, noon hour workout, or a leisurely after dinner ride. It can even be expanded into a full day of sightseeing.

How to Get There: A number of routes lead to Ottawa: Hwy 417 from the east, Hwys 416, 16 and 31 from the south, Hwy 7 from the west, Hwy 17 from the northwest and Hwy 148 (Quebec) from the northeast.

Several centuries ago, the present day site of Ottawa was known as Collins' Landing and then as Bellow's Landing. In 1827, a full survey was carried out and the area was renamed Bytown. Another change was made in 1855 and the town was renamed Outaouak (changed to Ottawa), after an Algonquin Indian site which held an important position on the nearby Ottawa River. At first, just before Confederation, it wasn't considered a viable site for the nation's capital. By 1857, it had been discussed for some time as to whether the capital should be in Toronto, Montreal, Kingston or Quebec. Fortunately for Ottawa, our forefathers passed the buck and let Queen Victoria make the decision. For a number of different reasons, she decided on Ottawa and by 1866 the Parliament Buildings were built and in use. Today, the city has a very clean, well-ordered, tidy look about it. It has preserved the past, yet continually moves forward to meet and adapt to the constant demands of its local citizens and the nation. The city thus has numerous green areas; more than a hundred kilometres of shared recreational pathways, the world's longest skating rink and numerous annual cultural events.

Itinerary: Start on Parliament Hill, beside the 1967 Centennial Flame, which was built to commemorate the 100th year of Confederation. The building directly in front is called the Centre Block and is home to the House of Commons and the Senate. The other two buildings, the East and West Block, are used for the administration. A ride around Centre Block reveals the Ottawa Locks and a number of interesting commemorative

statues. Directly behind Parliament Hill, along the river, is an area known as "Cat Hill"; a haven to many a wild cat, racoon and squirrel. If you are in the right spot at the right time, you may see the kind soul with food in hand who comes out to feed the animals each day.

Leave Parliament Hill by making a [R] turn onto Wellington St and go past the Confederation Building. At Bank St, as you ride past the Bank of Canada, look carefully for the glitter of gold, as this is where the world's largest single gold depository is stored. A little further on are St. Andrew's Church and the Supreme Court of Canada. The National Library and Archives are located on Lyons St.

Keep left as Wellington St passes through the lights at the Portage Bridge. Make a [L] turn onto Commissioner St or go further down the road to Booth St. Turn [L] onto Slater St, then

Practical Information

Population:
Ottawa: 316,000 (Capital Region: 1,000,000)

 Tourist Information

Ottawa Tourism and Convention Authority, 130 Albert St, Suite 1800 Ottawa, Ontario, K1P 5G4, (613) 237-5150, www.tourottawa.org

 Bicycle Shops

Award Cycle and Sports, 2280 Carling Ave, K2B 7G1, (613) 596-6665; Bicycle Mobility, (613) 722-4352; Chain Reaction Bike Shop, 750 Gladstone Ave, K1R 6X5, (613) 234-2453; Cycle Bertrand, 136 Eddy Rue, J8X 2W8, (613) 771-6858; Cycle Power, 1568 Merivale Rd, K2G 3J9, (613) 226-3647; Fosters Sports Centre, 305 Bank St, K2P 1X7, (613) 236-9611; Freewheel Cycle and Sports, 1890 Bromley Rd, K2A 1C1, (613) 728-7750; Fresh Air Experience, 1291 Wellington St, K1Y 3A8, (613) 729-3002; Full Cycle, 1073 Bank St, K1S 3W9, (613) 730-2856; Full Cycle, 409 St. Laurent Blvd., K1K 2Z8, (613) 741-2442; Full Tilt Cycles, 1469 Richmond Rd, K2B 2R9, (613) 726-0132; McCrank's Cycles, 889 Bank St, K1S 3W4, (613) 563-2200; Neusy's Bicycle Repair Shop, 276 Somerset East, K1N 6V8, (613) 233-6750; Pecco's, 78 Murray St, K1N 5M6, (613) 562-9602; Poison Spider Bicycles, 179 Rideau St, K1N 5X8, (613) 562-1344; Rebec and Kroes Cycle and Sports, 1695 Bank St, K1V 7Z3, (613) 521-3791; The Bike Stop, 225 Preston St, K1R 7R1, (613) 569-1058; Tommy And Lefebvre, 464 Bank St, K2P 1Z3, (613) 236-9731

Westar Sports, 501 Hazeldean Rd, Kanata, Ontario, K2L 1V6, (613) 836-6996; World Class Cycles, 1501 Carling Ave, K1Z 7M1, Ottawa, Ontario, (613) 728-7960

 Special Sights and Events

Winterlude, Tulip Festival, National Capital Race, Reflections of Canada, National Capital Air Show, Canada Dance Festival, Sound and Light Show, Festival Canada, Sparks Street Busker Festival, Ottawa Chamber Music Festival, International Jazz Festival, Bluesfest, Changing of the Guard

 Accommodations

Hotel/Motel/B&B/Camping

 Off-Road Cycling

Yes, see "Off-Road" section at the end of this chapter.

 Market Days

Daily

make another [L] turn onto Bronson St. Cycle uphill and turn [R] onto Queen St. Go around the block that passes in front of the 1932 Christ Church Cathedral and its impressive green spires. Upon returning to Queen, turn [L] and proceed to O' Connor St, cycling past the Delta and Citadel hotels. At the lights, turn [R] onto O'Connor.

Follow this one way street past Export Canada and the historic Chalmer's United Church. Cross MacLeod St and go past the three-storied Canadian Museum of Nature. Turn [L] onto Argyle St and make another [L] onto Metcalfe St. Now you are behind the museum, which houses numerous exhibits on prehistoric Canada and creatively designed displays featuring Canadian mammals and birds. At MacLeod St, turn [L] and then quickly turn [R], rejoining Metcalfe St.

Metcalfe St is another one-way road. At Laurier Ave, turn [R], and go past the National Capital Commission. At the corner of Elgin St is the impressive First Baptist Church. Further down on the right, the older building with turrets was the first teachers' college in Canada. In front of it to the left is Confederation Park.

Because there is no left turn onto Elgin St, walk your bicycle across the street, remount, then follow Elgin St uphill to Queen St. Get into the left-hand lane, and turn [L] at the lights onto Queen St. Ride to Metcalfe, turn [R], and go past the Sparks St Mall Shopping Centre. At Wellington St, turn [R] and pass the Parliament Buildings and information centre. Wellington St becomes Rideau St after it crosses the Rideau Canal. Turn [L] at the lights onto the one-way Sussex Drive, and go past the National Department of Revenue. At York St, turn right into the By Ward Market area. Slow down as this area of town is a bustling, open-air market. Since it began in the 1840s, it has always been a centre of activity and today is surrounded by streets, houses, cafes, restaurants and boutiques.

The aroma of fresh baked goods fills the air when turning [L] onto By Ward St, which is followed by another [L] turn onto Clarence St. At Sussex Drive turn [R] and cross St. Patrick St. The large glass building on your left is the National Gallery of Canada which houses a collection of more than 45,000 works of art including a Canadian art history display. On the right is the elegant Notre Dame Basilica. Built in 1841, it is the oldest church in the city and a quick peek inside reveals a beautiful choir stall and many intriguing artifacts. Just ahead is a highly visible military tank that guards the front doors of the Canadian War Museum as well as another nearby building. This second building is the Royal Canadian Mint. At one time the mint struck common Canadian coins, but today it only produces silver, gold and platinum collector's pieces.

Once past the Macdonald-Cartier Bridge, Earnscliffe is on the left. This is the present-day home of the British High Commission. As Sussex Drive crosses Green Island and the Rideau River, Ottawa City Hall is on the right. On the left are two waterfalls that are so close together that the water forms a curtain as it falls into the Ottawa River. When translated into French, "curtain" becomes "rideau" thus explaining how the Rideau River was named.

Over the next kilometre you pass some impressive homes. The Prime Minister's residence is just past the falls on the left. To the right, at John St, is the region's first school building. A short distance ahead, around a bend in the road, is Rideau Hall, 1 Sussex Drive. Built in 1838, this Regency-style home was specifically built for the Governor General, Canada's representative of the Queen of England. Today, five rooms in the home and the property's attractive gardens are open for public viewing. Take some time to ride the streets around Rideau Hall. They make for an interesting excursion, passing by many beautiful homes and embassies.

Across from Rideau Hall, a visit to Rockcliffe Park affords a beautiful panorama that encompasses the City of Hull and the Ottawa River. A short distance past Rideau Hall, Sussex Drive becomes Rockcliffe Drive. Continue along the road (bike path on the right) as it follows the river. When it begins to descend, look for a [Y] junction to the right. Keep right and join Acacia Ave and prepare yourself for a pleasant surprise. Opulent older homes abound, all of which look as though they've just had a makeover. Many of these homes are embassies and have incorporated the unique characteristics of their own countries into their design. The streets in this neighbourhood are definitely worth exploring!

Continuing along Acacia Ave, at the Beechwood Ave [T] intersection, turn [R] and continue past the Community St Church to Vanier Parkway. Once across the Rideau River, Beechwood Ave changes into St. Partrick St, passes the Notre Dame Basilica and crosses Sussex Drive.

Turn [L] onto Mackenzie Ave. This one-way street passes the Connaught Building, the Canadian Museum of Contemporary

Photography and the one building that dominates all others on the Ave, the unmistakable Chateau Laurier. This is the city's premier hotel, built for the Canadian Pacific Railway in 1912. Its first guest was Sir Wilfred Laurier, a railroad promoter elected Prime Minister of Canada in 1896.

Turn [R] onto Wellington St, cross the Rideau Canal and the Ottawa Locks, and return to Parliament Hill. In the twilight hours of summer, the highlight of this ride will be the "Reflections of Canada, A Symphony of Sound" presentation. This is a sound and light show that inspires a sense of unity through the stimulating narration of letters, journals and everyday conversations, all set to music and accompanied by giant image projections plus a light show on the Parliament towers.

---

33. Gatineau Hills Legwarmer

The Gatineau Hills are an Ottawa attraction that should not be missed. This is a challenging ride along roads and recreational trails that wind their way steadily upwards through the forest to an inspiring view of the Ottawa Valley.

Return Distance: 68 km
No. of recommended legs: 1
Level of Difficulty: 🚲 🚲 🚲 🚲
Surface: Asphalt, road and recreational pathways

Villages/Towns/Cities: Ottawa, Hull

Local Highlights: Bicycling Magazine's Top 10 Rated Bicycle Shop, Cycle Bertrand, in Hull, Quebec, Champlain Lookout, Meech Lake, Pink Lake, Mackenzie King Estate, Parliament Hill, By-Ward Market, Canadian Museum of Civilization, Rideau Canal, Sparks St Mall, National Gallery of Canada, Casino de Hull, Canadian War Museum, Notre Dame Basilica, Agriculture Museum, Canadian Museum of Contemporary Photography, Canadian Museum of Nature, Currency Museum of the Bank of Canada, National Archives, National Aviation Museum, National Museum of Science and Technology, Royal Canadian Mint,

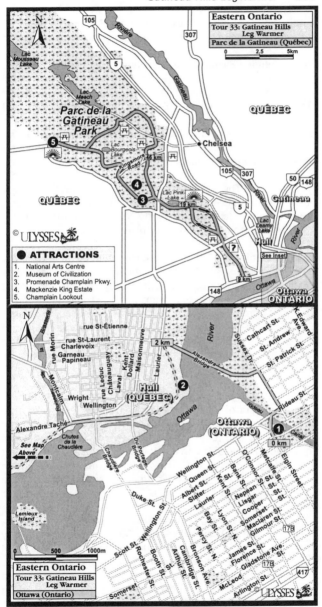

Eastern Ontario
Tour 33: Gatineau Hills
Leg Warmer
Parc de la Gatineau (Québec)

● **ATTRACTIONS**

1. National Arts Centre
2. Museum of Civilization
3. Promenade Champlain Pkwy.
4. Mackenzie King Estate
5. Champlain Lookout

Eastern Ontario
Tour 33: Gatineau Hills
Leg Warmer
Ottawa (Ontario)

Laurier House, Gatineau Park, Symphony of Sound, Rideau Hall, Rockcliffe, Supreme Court of Canada, Changing of the Guard

Recommended Bicycles: Touring/Hybrid/Mountain

Tour Suggestions: Motorized vehicles are not permitted in Gatineau Park on "Bike Day" Sundays during the summer. Look for the "Tourist Information on Wheels," a bike squad of tourist agents on specially built bicycles, as you near the Canadian Museum of Civilization. Bring lots of bottled water as there are only a few water fountains in the Gatineau hills.

How to Get There: A number of routes lead to Ottawa: Hwy 417 from the east, Hwys 416, 16 and 31 from the south, Hwy 7 from the west, Hwy 17 from the northwest and Hwy 148 (Quebec) from the northeast.

The concept for the Gatineau Park was initiated in 1913 by the Holt Commission. By 1934 the Federal Woodlands Preservation League had convinced the federal government to acquire 10,000 acres of land in the Gatineau Hills. Today the National Capital Commission is responsible for approximately 36,000 acres within the park. They have developed hundreds of kilometres of hiking trails, maintain 35 kilometres of winding panoramic roads and have designated 90 kilometres of trail for off-road cycling.

Itinerary: Beginning at the entrance of the National Arts Centre, at the junction of Queen and Elgin St, make a [R] turn onto Elgin and follow it as it merges with Rideau St. Turn [L] onto Sussex Drive and [L] again onto St. Patrick St. After passing the National Gallery of Canada, join the bicycle path on the left just before crossing the Ottawa River into **Hull**. After the bridge, turn [L] onto the Voyageurs Path and follow it toward the Museum of Civilization.

This path goes part way around the museum and then descends to the Ottawa River. The Museum is architecturally impressive and a visit inside details the contributions of Canada's native peoples, her early settlers and other cultures. At the [T] intersection keep right, cross a wooden bridge, and go past a series of water pipes and under a bridge, following the trail as it climbs to a [T] intersection. Turn [R] and follow the trail as it exits onto Rue Maisonneuve at the Portage Bridge. Take this road and turn [L] at the lights onto Laurier which turns into Blvd Alexandre Taché. Cross Eddy, which was named after the famous American, Ezra Butler Eddy. Eddy played an important role in the development of the area through his connections with the logging industry. His name is still a household word associated with matches, clothes pins and the pulp and paper industry. At the Montcalm traffic lights, rejoin the bicycle path on the left.

The trail passes some rigid-looking wolves and a bronzed boat frame, and crosses a set of railway tracks before going up a slight grade. Keep [R] at the [T] intersection and exit onto the road at the University of Hull. Turn [R] onto Belleau and cross Alexandre Taché, joining the trail on your left.

To take advantage of the park's best vantages, stay on the road as it ascends to the Champlain Lookout. Once past the welcome centre, the road immediately begins to rise and crosses Rue St-Raymond. There are a few downhill rests, but these are always followed by even higher climbs. The Pink Lake Lookout is up past the entrance to Hickory Trails, at the top of the Gatineau Hills' fourth heart-pumping climb.

After Pink Lake, the road rapidly rises and falls. Turn [L] onto the Champlain Parkway. Ride past the set of stairs which are the back entrance of the Mackenzie-King Estate. The road continues to be a leg burner as it passes through several areas of bogged-out forest. The grade of the road becomes even more vertical after Bourgeois Lake and Fortune Ave Parkway. Climbing past two more outlooks, Huron and Etienne-Brulé, the road finally ends at the Champlain Lookout with an incredible view of the Ottawa Valley.

Once you catch your breath, prepare for a blazing downhill ride back to Fortune Ave Parkway. Watch for white-tailed deer coming out of the forest on the right. Turn [R] and follow Fortune Parkway as it descends and curves to the left before crossing Meech Lake Rd for the first time. After re-crossing Meech Lake Rd, you will see the access points for the mountain bike trails. Upon entering a large open area, note that the parking lot on the left is a convenient place to leave your car if you want to ride the mountain bike trails another day.

Before you continue along the parkway and go under Kingsmere Rd, an optional highlight at this point (one hour minimum) would be to keep right, follow Kingsmere Rd and visit the gardens and picturesque ruins of Mooreside, the summer home of Canada's tenth prime minister, William Lyon Mackenzie King.

Ride past the turnoff for the Champlain Parkway, and the Pink Lake lookout. At the bottom of the next valley, look to your left for the well-marked recreational trail access point. Turn [L] onto the trail and immediately climb up a steep little hill. Rises on this trail are always followed by wicked downhills and there are plenty of thrills in store on these very narrow paths through the woods. On this part of the ride, the path will come to a number of [T] intersections. Always turn right, and eventually the trail will climb one last time before it exits back out onto the parkway. After passing the welcome booth, rejoin the pathway and follow it back to Alexandre Taché. Turn [L] onto the road and follow Taché past Montcalm, then turn [R] onto Maisonneuve. Then cross the Ottawa River via the Portage Bridge, turn [R] onto Wellington St and turn [L] into the parking lot of the Old Mill Restaurant. Keep to the right and ride under Wellington St through a segmented tunnel. Turn [L] then [R], and follow the trail along the river past the Ottawa locks before returning to the National Arts Centre.

---

34. To Hog's Back Falls and Back: Ottawa's Rideau Canal Recreational Trail

---

With only a few hours to spare, this tour is a nice way to spend a warm summer's evening or a Sunday afternoon. Following the Rideau Canal from Parliament Hill to a crossing at Hog's Back Falls, the loop is completed via a lesser travelled path along the Rideau River past Rideau Falls back to the National Arts Centre.

Return Distance: 30 km
No. of recommended legs: 1

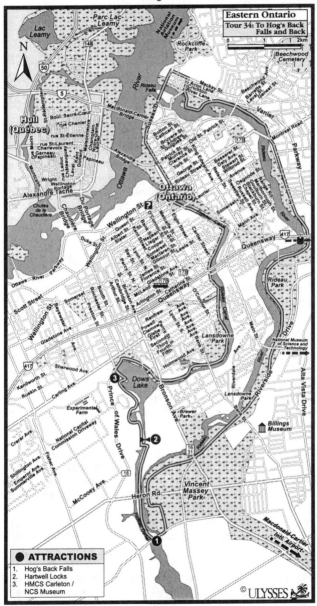

Eastern Ontario

Tour 34: To Hog's Back Falls and Back

0   1   2km

● **ATTRACTIONS**

1. Hog's Back Falls
2. Hartwell Locks
3. HMCS Carleton / NCS Museum

© ULYSSES

Level of Difficulty: 🚲
Surface: Asphalt and 1.5 km of
crushed gravel trail

Villages/Towns/Cities: Ottawa

Local Highlights: Parliament Hill, By Ward Market, Canadian Museum of Civilization, Rideau Canal, Sparks St Mall, National Gallery of Canada, Casino de Hull, Canadian War Museum, Notre Dame Basilica, Agriculture Museum, Canadian Museum of Contemporary Photography, Canadian Museum of Nature, Currency Museum of the Bank of Canada, National Archives, National Aviation Museum, National Museum of Science and Technology, Royal Canadian Mint, Laurier House, Gatineau Park, Symphony of Sound, Rideau Hall, Rockcliffe, Supreme Court of Canada

Recommended Bicycles: Touring/Hybrid/Mountain

Tour Suggestions: An excellent ride for the whole family or the first time cyclist. It is also a great tension reliever after a long day on the road or a hard day at the office.

How to Get There: Ottawa is fairly easy to find. From the north, take Hwy 17; from the east take Hwy 417; from the south follow Hwy 416, 16 and 31, and from the west take Hwy 17. Once in the nation's capital, join the Rideau Canal pathway behind the National Arts Centre, which starts at the junction of Queen Elizabeth Driveway and Albert/Slater St by the MacKenzie King Bridge.

Ottawa is probably the only city in Canada where some companies pay their employees to bicycle to work. The Rideau Canal was built for less than four million dollars including the construction of its 47 locks. Today, it serves as a pathway for boaters and its banks provide a safe transportation system for many different types of vehicles. In the winter, the canal becomes the world's longest skating rink, stretching for over 7.8 kilometres.

Itinerary: The canal pathway at Queen Elizabeth Driveway and Slater St is high above the canal but there are plenty of stairs decending to the water. Eventually the pathway and the canal meet and follow Queen Elizabeth Driveway for quite a distance. The pathway goes under Hwy 417 and the Pretoria Bridge while running alongside Lansdowne Park, then climbs away from the canal for a short distance, rejoining it at the man-made Dows Lake. At the bottom end of the lake is a very busy marina/restaurant, and trail directions at this point are not very well marked.

Keep to the canal on the left and follow what looks like a bike path around the lake. The trail changes to crushed gravel after passing in front of the HMCS Carlton/NCS Museum. Cross a little bridge and follow the pathway to the Hartwells Locks. Lift your bicycle and cross the locks, rejoining the bicycle path at the bottom of the stairs on the other side. Continuing south, go past a golden-roofed mosque under Base Line Rd and Colonel By Drive, to the 450-million-year-old landscape of Hog's Back Falls. An amazing sight! Lock up your bicycle before heading for the best lookouts at the bottom of the rapids. Cross the falls by way of a set of stairs or return to the road rejoining the trail on the east side of the Rideau River. Take the time to look around or relax at the snack bar.

Behind the snack bar the trail exits into the Hog's Back Falls parking lot and then begins again in the northeast corner of the lot. The trail now follows the shoreline of the Rideau River. Descending from the parking lot past the golden mosque, the land is less developed, more remote and in some ways more visually pleasing. Cycle under Heron Rd through Vincent Massey Park, a well-equipped rest area, and enjoy another downhill ride to the Bronson Ave underpass. The riverside of the Rideau is much more interesting, more rugged and has more climbs. Parallelling Riverside Drive, the trail goes past the Ottawa Memorial Hospital through a secluded wooded area then under Hwy 417, the Queensway. Just before the Queensway, notice the dead-end path on the other side of the river which can be accessed by the old railway bridge on your left. Just past the Queensway, the path comes back down along the river to a set of rapids.

Rejoin the path on the other side of Montreal Rd and cycle through Kingsview Park. Follow the river and go under the

St. Patrick St Bridge. The trail turns into gravel by the little playground and tennis courts, but quickly changes back into asphalt at the white Minte Bridges at Union St. Cross Union St; the triangular shaped building on the left is Ottawa City Hall. The bicycle path follows Stanley Ave and ends at Sussex Drive. The Rideau Falls are directly ahead. Cross Sussex Drive and have a look at the falls. While you're there, you can also visit the Canada and World Interpretation Centre.

Follow the walkway over the falls to a finished park area and lookout which is a memorial to the Royal Regiment of Canadian Artillery. Continue across a second walkway, pass the Central Heating and Cooling Plant of the NRC and exit back out onto Sussex Drive. Once past the National Research Council building, you come to the Canadian War Museum and the National Gallery of Canada. Bear right onto the Alexandra Bridge Rd and then quickly turn [L] onto the one-way MacKenzie Ave. Do not continue along Sussex as it turns into a one-way street, going in the opposite direction. At the Chateau Laurier, turn [R] onto Rideau St and then [L] onto Elgin St and return to the National Arts Centre at the junction of Queen and Elgin St.

OFF-ROAD CYCLING

Public Trails

Lanark

K & P Trail Conservation Area (40 km)
Surface: Original Railbed
Beginning: Snow Rd (near Hwy 509) and Barryvale (off Hwy 501)
Contact: Community Relations, Mississippi Valley Conservation Authority, PO Box 268, Lanark, Ontario K0G 1K0, ☎(613) 259-2421.

Russel-Ottawa Area

New York Central Fitness Trail (8 km)
Surface: Asphalt
Beginning: Russel to Embrun
Contact: Township of Russell, 717 Rue Notre Dame, Embrun, Ontario K0A 1W1, ☎(613) 443-3066.

Resort Trails

Pembroke Area
Forest Lea Trails (11 km of trail)
Ministry of Natural Resources, Box 220, Riverside Drive, Pembroke, Ontario N4K 3E4, ☎(613) 732-3661, Riverside Park ☎(613) 735-2251.

Ottawa Area
Morris Island Conservation Area (13 km of trail)
Mississippi Valley Conservation Authority, PO Box 268, Lanark, Ontario N4K 3E4, ☎(613) 259-2421.

Perth/Lanark Area
Palmerston Canonto Conservation Area (6 km of trail)
Mississippi Valley Conservation Authority, PO Box 268, Lanark, Ontario N4K 3E4, ☎(613) 259-2421.

Pembroke/Petawawa Area
Petawawa Crown Game Preserve (Fish Hatchery) (6.6 km of trail)
Ministry of Natural Resources, Box 220, Riverside Drive, Pembroke, Ontario N4K 3E4, ☎(613) 732-3661.

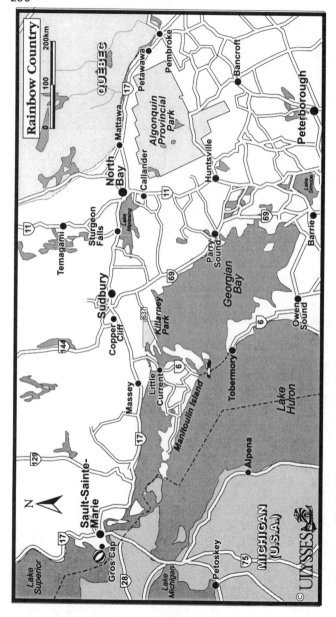

RAINBOW COUNTRY

Ontario's North extends from the nearly inaccessible, century old Algonquin Park over a land of unspoiled character and rugged beauty crossing hundreds of lakes, wetlands and rivers to the lands north of Superior.

THE TOURS

35. Sudbury: Nickel Capital of the World

A pleasant evening or early morning ride in the heart of the Sudbury basin. Beginning downtown, follow city streets as they wind their way up and down through Sudbury's rolling landscape. Towering reddish-grey rocks thrusting upwards out of a blackened moonscape surface are only eclipsed by the area's immense mining operations and its picturesque and inviting turquoise-blue lakes.

Return Distance: 25 km
No. of recommended legs: 1
Level of Difficulty: 🚲
Surface: Asphalt

Villages/Towns/Cities: Sudbury Region

Local Highlights: Downtown core, Science North, Cambrian College, Lake Laurentian Conservation Area, Laurentian University and Arboretum, Sudbury Neutrino Observatory, Ramsey Lake Trail

Recommended Bicycles: Touring/Hybrid/Mountain

Tour Suggestions: This is a quick way to get acquainted with the city in a couple of hours. If you are visiting for a day or two it can easily be expanded into a day-long outing

How to Get There: From the south take Hwy 400 north from Toronto to Hwy 69 N/Hwy 17 E. From the east follow Hwy 17 West. From the north, follow Hwy 144 South and from the West follow Hwy 17 East.

The Sudbury Region may owe its existence to the westward expansion of the Canadian Pacific Railway in 1833, but its continued survival is due to rich mineral deposits beneath the Sudbury basin. A gigantic meteorite collision is now known to have created the basin, and today this area is the largest single source of nickel in the western world. As the demand for nickel grew, the area developed in leaps and bounds and the environment was of secondary concern. Back in the early days of the mining industry, large piles of ore and wooden logs would be left to burn for days on end, producing a toxic smoke that killed vegetation and blackened rock. Today, through the efforts of the local population and responsible industry, Sudbury is again becoming green, slowly restoring the landscape to its original beauty.

Itinerary: Lock your car at the Sudbury arena, at the corner of Brady and Minto Sts. Facing south towards the arena a pretty little park is on your right and on your left the Bell Telephone Centre and the Civic Square. Between these two buildings is the thirteen-storey Provincial building which uses solar connectors to heat its hot water.

Cycling along Minto St, cross Brady and turn [L] onto Elgin St. Once past the train station and the Paris St overpass, Elgin St

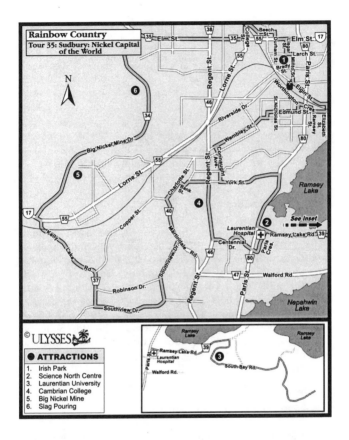

begins to climb. At the top of Elgin, get off the road and use the Elizabeth St walkway (on your right) to cross the railway tracks. Turn [R] onto Edmund St and [R] again onto Ramsey and continue following Ramsey as it turns into Worthington Crescent.

Turning [L] onto Medora St and at the [T] intersection, turn [R] and rejoin Edmund St. Smoke stacks should be visible in front and the road will begin to climb. Travelling through an older section of the city can be interesting. Take particular notice of

Practical Information

Population:
Sudbury: 93,000

 Tourist Information

Rainbow Country Travel Association, 2726 Whippoorwill Ave., Sudbury, Ontario P3G 1E9 (705) 522-0104, www.city.sudbury.on.ca, www.rainbowcountry.com

 Bicycle Shops

The Outside Store, 135 Cedar St, Sudbury, Ontario P3E 1A9, (705) 674-6003; Cameron Cycle and Services, 495 Notre Dame Ave, P3C 5K9, (705) 671-2052; Pinnacle Sports, 2037 Long Lake Rd, Sudbury, Ontario P3E 4M8, (705) 523-7400; The Bicycle Store, 37 Mont Adam, P3B 2H8, (705) 673-5168; DeMarco's Source for Sports, 25 Elgin St, Sudbury, Ontario, P3C 5B3, (705) 675-5677; Ethier Sports & Cycle, 444 Barry Downe Rd, Sudbury, Ontario, P3A 3T3, (705) 566-8999; Jim Taylor Cycle and Sports, 230 Elgin St, Sudbury, Ontario, P3E 3N6 (705) 675-8660

 Special Sights and Events

Canada Day Celebration, Dancing in the Park, Northern Lights Festival, Fringe Nord Theatre Festival, Blueberry Festival, Sudbury Gem & Mineral Show, Summer Celtic Fest, Canadian Garlic Festival, Cinefest, Cavalcade of Colours, Canadian National Powerboat Championships, Sudbury Snowflake Festival

Accommodations

Hotel/Motel/Bed&B/Camping

 Market Days

Farmer's Market, Shaughnessey St, Weekends, May to October

the long set of stairs at the corner of Nicholas and Edmund. Passing huge rocks in the moonlike landscape, be prepared to turn [R] onto Wembley St. Follow it past Wembley Public School, turn [L] onto Connaught Avenue.

After a leg-warming uphill climb, make a [L] turn onto York St. Turn [R] at the [T] intersection of York and Paris St. To the left is Sudbury's Centennial Project, the Bell Park Amphitheatre and a great view of Ramsey Lake and Science North. Be prepared to move into the left-hand lane as Paris St descends to the lights at Ramsey Lake Rd.

Turn [L] onto Ramsey Lake Rd. On your right is the Laurentian Hospital which is the base for Northern Ontario's helicopter ambulance service, and on your left is Science North, a hands-on science experience. Continue along Ramsey Lake Rd and look for the scenic lookout on the left. The lookout offers a spectacular view of the largest city-contained lakes in North America, which is only one of 36 lakes in the area that are over 10 acres in size. Further along are the bilingual campuses of Laurentian University. While in the area, make time to visit the impressive Thornloe Chapel or explore their unique arboretum.

Possible side-trip: continue along Ramsey Lake Rd, turn [R] onto South Bay Rd and follow it (passing the Lake Laurentian Conservation Area) for approximately five kilometres to a set of gates. Pass through the gates onto the newly renovated crushed gravel trail. "Phase One" of this multi-use trail system is underway. When it is completed, it will allow the you to go all the way around Ramsey Lake.

Retrace your steps to Science North on Ramsey Lake Rd, just before the street lights at Paris St, turn [L] onto Paris Crescent and pass between the two hospital towers. Note the interesting sculpture across the street before turning [R] onto Centennial Drive. Cross Paris St and go past a large baseball diamond, turning [R] onto Ramsey View Court. Signal [R] before turning onto Regent St and climbing uphill past Cambrian College. At the crest of the hill, move into the left-hand lane as it descends to York St. Turn [L] at the lights, following York St to Bank St to Charlotte St.

Turn [L] onto Charlotte St, and [L] again onto Martindale Rd. After a short climb, and a quick descent, make a [R] turn onto Southview Drive. Follow Southview to a three-way stop, turning [R] onto Kelly Lake Rd (note: if you continue along Southview Drive, you will encounter some of the interesting moonscape-type rock, namely Canadian Slick-Rock) which travels through a light industrial area to Hwy 17 (Lorne St, Regional Rd No. 55). Turn [L] onto Lorne St, following the ramp up to Big Nickel Mine Drive and to the Big Nickel Mine entrance. Sudbury's well-known landmark, the "Big Nickel," towers above as you explore the world of underground mining. Mail a letter from the only underground postal box in Canada by taking a tour that descends 20 metres into the ground.

Exit the Big Nickel Mine by turning [R] onto Big Nickel Mine Drive. As it snakes around present-day mining operations and through natural rock formations, take note of the parking area on your left. In the evening you can watch red-hot slag being poured here. Call ahead to confirm dates and time for slag pouring.

Turn right onto Elm St and follow it down to College St. Turn [L] onto College St, cross Pine St and after passing under the railway bridge turn [R] onto Frood Rd. Turn [L] onto Beech St, then turn [R] onto Durham St. At Elm St turn [L] and then turn [R] onto Lisgar St. Turn left at Larch St. The impressive grey St. Andrew's Place and the park where your journey began are nearby.

36. Riding for Gold at Wavy Lake

Plunge into the heart of Eden and experience the thrill of being alone in the wilderness. Gold rush cycling fever takes over as the exhilaration of not knowing what type of terrain you will encounter or what kind of beast will greet you around the next bend fills the air with tension.

Return Distance: 20 km
No. of recommended legs: 1
Difficulty: 🚲 🚲 🚲
Surface: Gravel, some jeep road and natural trail

Villages/Towns/Cities: Sudbury, Rheault

Local Highlights: Downtown core, Science North, Cambrian College, Lake Laurentian Conservation Area, Laurentian University and Arboretum, Sudbury Neutrino Observatory, Ramsey Lake Trail

Recommended Bicycles: Mountain/Hybrid

Tour Suggestions: DO NOT go on this wilderness ride alone, adopt the buddy system and take bug repellant!

How to Get There: To get to Sudbury from the south, take Hwy 400 N from Toronto to Hwy 69 N, then turn onto to Hwy 17 E. From the east, follow Hwy 17 W. From the north, follow Hwy 144 S; and from the West, follow Hwy 17 E.

Parking for Gold Mine Trail: follow Paris St (Regional Rd 80) south past Kelly Lake on your right, into the Town of Rheault. Continue to follow Regional Rd 80 as it changes into Tilton Lake Rd. At the [Y] junction, keep to your left and follow an undulating and winding road for the next two kilometres. There's plenty of dramatic black Canadian slick-rock to get your attention as the road changes from asphalt to hard packed gravel. At the second [Y] junction, keep to your right and follow Wavy Trail road downhill, keeping Wavy Creek on your left. Look for a gravel pit with two large stones blocking a gated entrance on your right. This is an excellent place to park your car for the next several hours.

Itinerary: From gravel pit entrance, turn [R] and follow Wavy Trail across Wavy Creek via Bailey's Bridge. There are some great views to your left and behind you. Once you have crossed over the bridge, turn [L] onto (next road) Lakes End Rd, and be prepared to get out of the saddle for a gravelly uphill climb to a long narrow road. Untamed, wild, and dark is the best way to describe the bush crowding in on this rough, undulating path to the gold mine trail.

Upon passing the sign for Uncle Tom's Cabin, keep an eye out for the trail entrance which is located to your left on top of the last hill, just before the road ends at the private entrance for Poulind Drive. As the trail entrance is not marked, a little bit of exploring may be required. Look for an area at the top of the hill where there is just enough room to park a car. This is the trail access point.

The trail crosses a narrow ditch and goes down a short steep stony grade that bends to the right joining a barely visible jeep road. The next few kilometres are a down-hill ride over grass, large loose baseball sized rocks, Canadian slick-rock and rutted tracks. The bush has grown in thickly on both sides of the trail creating a tunnel effect.

At the trail's only [T] intersection (look for the mine identification sign), turn [L] then pass by an old gate and follow the trail to an open area in the woods. There is a small portage at this point as you cross a meandering little stream. It becomes easier to navigate, as you rejoin the trail and follow it to a lake of tailings (white powder residue of a gold mine operation), which is the only lake that a cyclist can ride over without getting wet.

Once across the rubbery white lake, continue along the jeep trail and ride through a damp section of the trail, past some rather large ominous rock formations that may be home to who knows what. The remains of a long-forgotten mining operation are a little further along. Was gold found here? No one knows for sure, but it makes for a great ride. It looks authentic, but

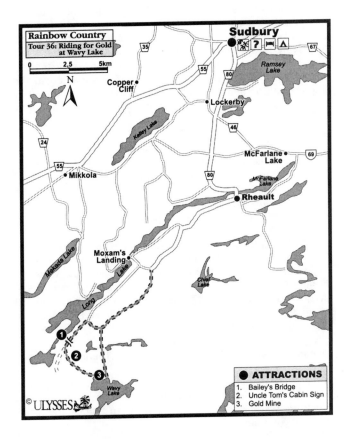

further investigation may prove otherwise. To complete the ride, retrace your path back to where you began.

37. Manitoulin Day Tripping: Lake Mindemoya, the Bridal Veil Falls and the Cup and Saucer Lookout

When you look at an Ontario road map, Manitoulin Island looks pretty small. Don't be fooled. Even if you spend several days cycling on this island, you would be hard pressed to see everything. Starting at Lake Mindemoya, this trip takes you clockwise around the lake to the eastern shore of Lake Kagawong. After passing the Bridal Veil Falls and historic Kagawong, it continues along one of the island's main logging roads, and through the West Bay Indian Reservation to the impressive Cup and Saucer lookout. The loop is completed by cycling along the western shores of Lake Manitou.

Return Distance: 90 km
No. of recommended legs: 1
Level of Difficulty: 🚲 🚲 🚲 🚲
Surface: Asphalt and gravel

Villages/Towns/Cities: Mindemoya, Monument Corner, Old Spring Bay, Bowser's Corner, Kagawong

Local Highlights: Bridal Veil Falls, Cup and Saucer Lookout, Ten Mile Point, High Falls, Providence Bay Beach, Mississagi Lighthouse Museum, Lake Mindemoya, Gore Bay Museum, Little Current-Howland Museum, McLean's Mountain, Assiginack Museum, S.S. Norisle and Heritage Park, Blue Jay Creek Fish Culture Station, Little School House and Museum, South Baymouth Fish Research Station

Recommended Bicycles: Hybrid/Mountain/(Touring)

Tour Suggestions: Accommodations should be booked well in advance as the island is a popular tourist destination. Do not drink the water out of Lake Manitou, even though the locals will tell you that it is safe.

How to Get There: From the south take Hwy 6 to the Tobermory Ferry; from the north follow Hwy 6 to Espanola and the Little Current swing bridge. The tour begins at the Mindemoya government boat dock. Travel north on Hwy 6 from South Baymouth, making a right turn onto Hwy 542. At the junction of Hwy 552, turn right and then left onto old Hwy 551, the first road after the local motel. At the lake, turn [L] and follow the road to the boat docks and the parking lot of the municipal park.

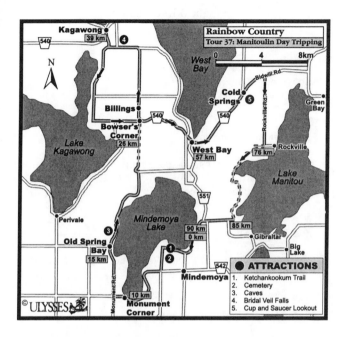

Located in the waters of Lake Huron, Manitoulin Island stretches 129 kilometres from east to west and varies from 4 to 48 kilometres in width. It is the world's largest freshwater island and has more than eight inland lakes. The name Manitoulin means "Spirit Island," and the Ojibwe, Odawa, and Potawatamie Indians believe that it is the home of the Great Spirit, or "Kitche Manitou."

Itinerary: Starting from the shores of Lake Mindemoya at the Carnarvon Park pavilion, make a [R] turn off the government boat dock onto the Ketchankookum Trail. Follow the road west as it swings away from the water and climbs past a local trailer park and the Mindemoya Cemetery. At the stop sign, turn [R] onto Lakeshore Rd. The local township sheds will be on the left. As you ride toward Cosey Cove Cottages, on a mix of asphalt and gravel, watch for pot holes in this old cedar-lined cottage road. Several kilometres ahead, the road curves back

Practical Information

Population:
Manitoulin Island: 11,000
Mindemoya: 388
Kagawong: 201
West Bay Reserve: 1000

 Tourist Information

Manitoulin Tourism Association Inc., PO Box 119, Little Current, Ontario, P0P 1K0, (705) 368-3021, www.Manitoulin-island.com

 Bicycle Shops

Gus' Bicycle Shop, 311 Old Webbwood Road, Espanola, Ontario, P0P 1C0, (705) 869-1346

 Special Sights and Events

Annual Wikwemikong Pow Wow, Three Fires Music Festival, Annual Manitoulin Island Arts Tour, Canada Day, Summerfest Weekend, Gore Bay Summer Theatre, Western Manitoulin's Folk's Fair

 Accommodations

Motel/Resort/Cottage/Camping

 Market Days

Seasonal farmer's market, Saturdays in Providence Bay.

towards the lake. The windy road along the shore of Manitoulin's third largest lake ends abruptly at the junction of Hwy 542/551. Turn [R] onto the highway and cycle to a small picnic area on the lake, which is 30 metres higher than Lake Huron. Lake Mindemoya's name comes from the natives' description of the lake's only island, located to the west of the rest area, which was said to resemble an old woman on her hands and knees.

Continuing west, the highway again swings away from the lake. At **Monument Corner**, also known as the Four Corners or Alexander's Corners, turn [R] onto Monument Rd. Take a few minutes to look at the 1921 statue of a soldier that honours local men who fought and died in the First World War. The statue originally stood in the middle of the intersection. Unfortunately, it was damaged by a motorist and its remains were relocated to the southwest side of the highway. Just after you join Monument Rd, it begins a gradual two-kilometre climb before it descends back along the lake into the summer community of Old Spring Bay, or Cavemount. When the island was bought for just $60.00 by the MacPherson family of Toronto in the 1880s, over 35 families had settled in this area. Take a few moments to refill your water bottles at the lakefront water pump, which provides safe, cool drinking water.

The ride along the bay is short, and your legs soon begin to warm up as you ride uphill to the Rock Garden Terrace Resort. The Mindemoya Lake Cave is located here and can be visited for a small fee. The 23-metre-deep cave was discovered by hunters looking for a fallen duck. The floor of the cave was strewn with 15 skeletons of Huron natives who were slaughtered by the Iroquois during the mid-1600s. Back on the road, cycle past the Carnarvon-Billings Line hiking trail to a [T] intersection. Turn [L] onto Jerusalem Hill Rd. At the top of the hill the road becomes gravel. The next six kilometres will be spent riding along a narrow, old logging road. As you cycle through second growth forest and past flat dolomite rock, you can still pick out some hardwood trees that were left behind after the last logging operation. Don't be surprised if you encounter fallen trees blocking the road.

At West Bay Rd (Hwy 540), turn [L] and coast downhill to **Bowser's Corners**, making a [L] turn onto Billings Concession 0 Rd. The easy ride to Lake Kagawong (the island's second largest lake), is followed by a stretch along the lake through rich agricultural land. At Hwy 540, turn [L] and ride past the local variety store to Bridal Veil Falls Park on the right side of the road. Stairs lead down to the bottom of the falls. The more adventurous can walk behind the veil of water that falls 20 metres from the Kagawong River above.

From the falls, continue straight on the road following it into **Kagawong**, or "Kag" as it is often called. (If you turn [L] on the highway after the falls, you will get to Gore Bay). The village was originally called Mudge Bay, but the name was changed to Kagawong in 1876 when the first post office opened. A native name, it translates to "where mists rise from falling waters." A walk along the river back towards the falls reveals a reconditioned generating station. After having been out of operation for 31-years, the station once again supplies hydro to Manitoulin Island. Kagawong's Upper St and lower Main St have a number of excellent turn-of-the-century buildings. Along the bay is the old Manitoulin Pulp and Paper mill, which now serves as the town's community centre. Kagawong has two great lookouts on Maple Point Rd: to get to them, follow the bay road northwest for several kilometres. Cycle past an interesting piece of building art based on the story of Lady Godiva. After climbing up two hills, you will get a fantastic view of Mudge Bay and Capperton Island on your right. The second lookout is only a few more kilometres ahead and to the left.

The uphill climb out of Kagawong will get your heart pounding as you retrace your path back to the Bridal Veil Falls. Continue riding along Hwy 540, watching for the unique triangular fences and shingle-sided homes. A short distance after Billings School No. 2, is a stone memorial with a bell on top, commemorating the area's first school. The road turns sharply to the left as you pass familiar Bowser's Corner. Logging trucks groan as they ascend the 8-degree grade to the top of Jerusalem hill. Take a break if you need it, and then tackle the hill feeling refreshed. About halfway up the hill you enter the

West Bend Indian Reservation, the island's second-largest native settlement.

Limestone rock lines the road as you ride into West Bay. The community was settled by 31 natives in 1847. Mechecowetchenong, or "hill of fish harpoon" as it was known in the 1870s became a Roman Catholic settlement for natives who had converted to the religion. East of Hwy 551 is a new Roman Catholic Church, which is in the shape of a twelve-sided tipi, and tries to evoke the feeling of traditional native fire pits. Hwy 540 is a slightly winding road that is only 900 metres long. It has a grade that fluctuates between five and eight degrees, and steady pedalling will get you to the top in no time.

At the Cold Springs Outpost, turn [R] onto Bidwell Rd. The entrance to the Cup and Saucer Lookout is just a few metres ahead on the right. Leave your bike behind and remember to lock up before hiking to the lookout. The hiking trail has been in existence since 1962 and the hill is the highest spot (351 metres) on the island. The trail is about 2 kilometres long and riding a fully-loaded bicycle along it is not recommended. When you reach the cliffs, climb to the top for an incredible view of Green Bay and Lake Manitou. Follow the edge of the cliff west to take in the spectacular view of West Bay and Mudge Bay. The more adventurous (leave your lycra back at the bike) can work their way through the rock chimney, or along the narrow ledge gaining access to the "Adventure Trail" – at their own risk, of course! Descending from the highest cliff, continue to follow the sloping trail west along the bluffs; it eventually returns to the parking lot after several hours of hiking.

Turning [R] out of the parking lot, follow Bidwill Rd as it winds its way through a grassy wetland area. Turn [R] onto the Rockville Rd. Careful, though gravel trucks run up and down this road on a regular basis. Give them a wide berth, as gravel can fly from these trucks and hit innocent cyclists! Descending to a [T] intersection, turn [R] (turning [L] takes you to Rockville) and cycle past the Rockville Community Hall. Follow the gravel road as it swings to the left. Occasional glimpses of Lake Manitou appear to your left, and the locals will tell you that you can drink directly from the lake. They may be right, but all the same, it is better not to tempt fate. Turn [R] at the large barn, at Camp Mary Anne, and continue west. Just before reaching Hwy 551, the road changes back to asphalt. Turn [L] onto the highway and ride past the remains of the original highway, which ran much closer to Lake Mindemoya. At the Idyll Glen Resort campgrounds, turn [R] onto the Ketchankookum Trail. Follow the road back along the island's warmest lake, completing the trip at the municipal parking lot.

OFF-ROAD CYCLING

Public Trails

Algonquin Park

J.R. Both Rail Trail
Surface: Western Uplands Trail, New Lake Ski Trail, Booth Rock Trail
Beginning: Track and Tower Trail
Contact: Ministry of Natural Resources Information Centre, MacDonald Block, Room M1-73, 900 Bay St, Toronto, Ontario M7A 2C1, ☎(416) 314-1717 or Ontario Parks 416-314-2000, East Gate Information Office 705-633-5572.

Parry Sound

Seguin Trail (67 km)
Surface: Original Railbed/loose surface
Beginning: Hwy 69 (12 km south of Parry Sound) to Fern Glen Rd (6 km west of Hwy 11)
Contact: Trail Coordinator, OMNR, 7 Bay St, Parry Sound, Ontario P2A 1S4, ☎(705) 746-4201.

Resort Trails

Algonquin Park
Minnesing Mountain Bike Trail (32 km of trail): Ministry of Natural Resources Information Centre, MacDonald Block, Room M1-73, 900 Bay St, Toronto, Ontario M7A 2C1, ☎(416) 314-1717 or Ontario Parks 416-314-2000, East Gate Information Office-705-633-5572.

Sault Ste. Marie
Crystal Creek Conservation Area (39 km)
Fort Creek Conservation Area (8 km of trail)
Shores Ridges Conservation Area (4 km of trail)
Sault Ste. Marie Region Conservation Authority, Civic Centre, 99 Foster Drive, P6A 5X6, ☎(705) 759-5341.

Searchmont Resort, PO Box 1029, P6A 5N5, ☎(705) 781-2340.

Elliott Lake
Mississagi Provincial Park and Area (43 km of trail): Mississagi Provincial Park Superintendent, PO Box 150, 62 Queen Avenue, Blind River, P0R 1B0, ☎(705) 356-2234.

Timmins
Golden Springs Trail (18 km of trail)
Hersey Lake Conservation Area (9 km of trail)
Mattagami Region Conservation Authority, c/o Civic Centre, 133 Cedar St S, P4N 2G9, ☎(705) 264-5309.

Timmins/Porcupine Area
Bart Thomson Trail (15 km of trail): Mattagami Region Conservation Authority, c/o Civic Centre, 133 Cedar St S, Timmins, P4N 2G9, ☎(705) 264-5309.

Thunder Bay
Sleeping Giant Provincial Park (63 km of trail): Sleeping Giant Provincial park Superintendent, Pass Lake, P0T 2M0, ☎(807) 475-1531.

INDEX

Abbreviations 44
Accommodations 35
Airlines 35
Avonton 23
Banking 79
Bed and Breakfasts 20
Benmiller (Southwestern Ontario) 36
Bicycle 84
Bicycle Types 29
Big Bay (Georgian Lakelands) 44
Bloomfield (Central Ontario) 162
Bobcaygeon (Central Ontario) 254
Books 219
Brockville (Eastern Ontario) 49
Burgessville (Southwestern Ontario) 277
Bus 74
Bus Companies 25
Cambridge (Festival Country) 25
Cameron (Central Ontario) 127
Camping 222
Camping Equipment 36
Car 41
Carrying Place (Central Ontario) 23
Cataract (Festival Country) 239
Central Ontario 104
       Off-Road Cycling 209
Checklist 254
Cherry Valley (Central Ontario) 40
Children 253
Circle Check 42
Climate 45
Clothing 18
Cobourg (Central Ontario) 40
Conestogo (Festival Country) 234
Corunna (Southwestern Ontario) 115
Courier Companies 63
Currency 22
Cycling Associations 19
                                                              27

Cycling Laws 27
Cycling Tours 31
Dehydration 45
Dorchester (Southwestern Ontario) 89
Downeyville (Central Ontario) 223
Dundas (Festival Country) 105
Eastern Ontario 257
        Off-Road Cycling 294
Elmira (Festival Country) 112
Elora (Festival Country) 100
Emergencies 21
Equipment 29
Equipment Checklist 40
Erin (Festival Country) 104
Fauna 17
Fee's Landing (Central Ontario) 218
Fenelon Falls (Central Ontario) 222
Fergus (Festival Country) 102
Festival Country 97
        Off-Road Cycling 148
Flamborough (Festival Country) 111
Flora 17
Fowlers Corners (Central Ontario) 224
Gananoque (Eastern Ontario) 278
Geography 16
Georgian Lakelands 153
        Off-Road Cycling 190
Glen Meyer (Southwestern Ontario) 73
Glen Morris (Festival Country) 127
Goderich (Southwestern Ontario) 83
Greater Toronto Area 193
        Off-Road Cycling 207
Hamilton (Festival Country) 110
Hardware 40
Harmony (Southwestern Ontario) 77
Hawkesville (Festival Country) 117
Holidays 20
Hope Bay (Georgian Lakelands) 167
Hotels 36
Howdenvale (Georgian Lakelands) 170
Hull (Eastern Ontario) 288
Independent Cycling 31

Internet 47
Kemptville (Eastern Ontario) 276
Kingston (Eastern Ontario) 260, 268
Lakefield (Central Ontario) 228
Leamington (Southwestern Ontario) 54
Lindsay (Central Ontario) 223
Lion's Head (Georgian Lakelands) 167
London (Southwestern Ontario) 88
Long Point (Southwestern Ontario) 73
Maps of Ontario 49
Merrickville (Eastern Ontario) 276
Milford (Central Ontario) 249
Money 19
Mooretown (Southwestern Ontario) 63
Motels 36
Niagara Falls (Festival Country) 141
Niagara-on-the-Lake (Festival Country) 145, 147
Normandale (Southwestern Ontario) 72
Off-Road Cycling 34
Oil Springs (Southwestern Ontario) 60
Ontario Cycling Laws 27
Ontario Cycling Publications 47
Organized Group Tours 32
Orton (Festival Country) 104
Ottawa (Eastern Ontario) 275, 292
Oxford Centre (Southwestern Ontario) 69
Paris (Festival Country) 126
Pelee Island (Southwestern Ontario) 54
Perth (Eastern Ontario) 273
Peterborough (Central Ontario) 213
Petrolia (Southwestern Ontario) 60
Picton (Central Ontario) 243, 252
Plane 23
Point Traverse (Central Ontario) 250
Police 21
Port Dalhousie (Festival Country) 128
Port Dover (Southwestern Ontario) 71
Port Hope (Central Ontario) 230
Port Royal (Southwestern Ontario) 73
Port Ryerse (Southwestern Ontario) 71
Queenston (Festival Country) 140, 147
Radio Stations 19

Raibow Country 297
      Off-Road Cycling 312
Rail Trails 34
Reece's Corners (Southwestern Ontario) 59
Regions 18
Richmond (Eastern Ontario) 274
Road Signs 26
Sarnia (Southwestern Ontario) 58
Sauble Beach (Georgian Lakelands) 170
Sauble Falls (Georgian Lakelands) 170
Shallow Lake (Georgian Lakelands) 171
Simcoe (Southwestern Ontario) 70
Smiths Falls (Eastern Ontario) 276
South Bay (Central Ontario) 250
Southwestern Ontario 51
      Off-Road Cycling 93
St. Jacobs (Festival Country) 116
St. Marys (Southwestern Ontario) 78
Stratford (Southwestern Ontario) 77
Sudbury (Raibow Country) 298
Taxes 20
Theft 46
Thorold (Festival Country) 133
Tillsonburg (Southwestern Ontario) 73
Tobermory (Georgian Lakelands) 169
Toronto 193, 201
Tour Companies 32
Tour Preparation 38
Tour Training 38
Tourist Information 17
Tours 31, 43
Trails 34
Train 24
Trans Canada Trail 34
Transporting Your Bicycle 22
Travel Documents 21
Travelling to Ontario 21
Trenton (Central Ontario) 239
Turkey Point (Southwestern Ontario) 72
Vanessa (Southwestern Ontario) 70
Virgil (Festival Country) 145
Wallenstein (Festival Country) 117

Waupoos (Central Ontario) 244
Weather 18
Welland (Festival Country) 134
West Montrose (Festival Country) 115
Wiarton (Georgian Lakelands) 165
Winterbourne (Festival Country) 115
Woodstock (Southwestern Ontario) 66
Wyoming (Southwestern Ontario) 60

ORDER FORM

ULYSSES TRAVEL GUIDES

☐ Atlantic Canada	$24.95 CAN $17.95 US	☐ Lisbon	$18.95 CAN $13.95 US
☐ Bahamas	$24.95 CAN $17.95 US	☐ Louisiana	$29.95 CAN $21.95 US
☐ Beaches of Maine	$12.95 CAN $9.95 US	☐ Martinique	$24.95 CAN $17.95 US
☐ Bed & Breakfasts in Québec	$13.95 CAN $10.95 US	☐ Montréal	$19.95 CAN $14.95 US
☐ Belize	$16.95 CAN $12.95 US	☐ New Orleans	$17.95 CAN $12.95 US
☐ Calgary	$17.95 CAN $12.95 US	☐ New York City	$19.95 CAN $14.95 US
☐ Canada	$29.95 CAN $21.95 US	☐ Nicaragua	$24.95 CAN $16.95 US
☐ Chicago	$19.95 CAN $14.95 US	☐ Ontario	$27.95 CAN $19.95US
☐ Chile	$27.95 CAN $17.95 US	☐ Ottawa	$17.95 CAN $12.95 US
☐ Colombia	$29.95 CAN $21.95 US	☐ Panamá	$24.95 CAN $17.95 US
☐ Costa Rica	$27.95 CAN $19.95 US	☐ Peru	$27.95 CAN $19.95 US
☐ Cuba	$24.95 CAN $17.95 US	☐ Portugal	$24.95 CAN $16.95 US
☐ Dominican Republic	$24.95 CAN $17.95 US	☐ Provence - Côte d'Azur	$29.95 CAN $21.95US
☐ Ecuador and Galapagos Islands	$24.95 CAN $17.95 US	☐ Québec	$29.95 CAN $21.95 US
☐ El Salvador	$22.95 CAN $14.95 US	☐ Québec and Ontario with Via	$9.95 CAN $7.95 US
☐ Guadeloupe	$24.95 CAN $17.95 US	☐ Toronto	$18.95 CAN $13.95 US
☐ Guatemala	$24.95 CAN $17.95 US	☐ Vancouver	$17.95 CAN $12.95 US
☐ Honduras	$24.95 CAN $17.95 US	☐ Washington D.C.	$18.95 CAN $13.95 US
☐ Jamaica	$24.95 CAN $17.95 US	☐ Western Canada	$29.95 CAN $21.95 US

ULYSSES DUE SOUTH

☐ Acapulco	$14.95 CAN $9.95 US	☐ Cartagena (Colombia)	$12.95 CAN $9.95 US
☐ Belize	$16.95 CAN $12.95 US	☐ Cancun Cozumel	$17.95 CAN $12.95 US

ULYSSES DUE SOUTH

☐ Puerto Vallarta . $14.95 CAN | ☐ St. Martin and . $16.95 CAN
                    $9.95 US | St. Barts $12.95 US

ULYSSES TRAVEL JOURNAL

☐ Ulysses Travel Journal . . . . $9.95 CAN
(Blue, Red, Green, Yellow, Sextant) $7.95 US

ULYSSES GREEN ESCAPES

☐ Cycling in France $22.95 CAN | ☐ Hiking in the . . . $19.95 CAN
                $16.95 US | Northeastern U.S. $13.95 US
☐ Cycling in Ontario $22.95 CAN | ☐ Hiking in Québec $19.95 CAN
                $16.95 US | $13.95 US

TITLE	QUANTITY	PRICE	TOTAL

Name _____	Sub-total	
Address _____		
_____	Postage & Handling	$8.00*
_____	Sub-total	
Payment : ☐ Money Order ☐ Visa ☐ MasterCard		
Card Number _____	G.S.T. in Canada 7%	
Signature _____	TOTAL	

ULYSSES TRAVEL PUBLICATIONS
4176 St-Denis,
Montréal, Québec, H2W 2M5
(514) 843-9447 fax (514) 843-9448
www.ulysses.ca
*$15 for overseas orders

U.S. ORDERS: **GLOBE PEQUOT PRESS**
P.O. Box 833, 6 Business Park Road,
Old Saybrook, CT 06475-0833
1-800-243-0495 fax 1-800-820-2329
www.globe-pequot.com